VOLUME 469

SEPTEMBER 1983

T5-CWM-411

THE ANNALS

of The American Academy *of* Political
and Social Science

RICHARD D. LAMBERT, *Editor*
ALAN W. HESTON, *Associate Editor*
THOMAS FOGARTY *and* DAVID LUDDEN,
Acting Associate Editors

NUCLEAR ARMAMENT AND DISARMAMENT

Special Editors of this Volume

MARVIN E. WOLFGANG

President
American Academy of Political
and Social Science
Professor of Sociology
University of Pennsylvania
Philadelphia, Pennsylvania

ROBERT H. KUPPERMAN

Executive Director
Science and Technology Center for
Strategic and International Studies
Georgetown University
Washington, DC

SAGE PUBLICATIONS   *BEVERLY HILLS   LONDON   NEW DELHI*

THE ANNALS

© 1983 *by* The American Academy *of* Political *and* Social Science

MARY V. YATES, *Assistant Editor*

Editorial Office: 3937 Chestnut Street, Philadelphia, Pennsylvania 19104.

For information about membership* (individuals only) and subscriptions (institutions), address:

SAGE PUBLICATIONS, INC.
275 South Beverly Drive
Beverly Hills, Calif. 90212 USA

From India and South Asia, write to:
SAGE PUBLICATIONS INDIA Pvt. Ltd.
P.O. Box 3605
New Delhi 110 024
INDIA

From the UK, Europe, the Middle East and Africa, write to:
SAGE PUBLICATIONS LTD
28 Banner Street
London EC1Y 8QE
ENGLAND

*Please note that members of The Academy receive THE ANNALS with their membership.

Library of Congress Catalog Card Number 83-050420
International Standard Serial Number ISSN 0002-7162
International Standard Book Number ISBN 0-8039-2115-2 (Vol. 469, 1983, paper)
International Standard Book Number ISBN 0-8039-2114-4 (Vol. 469, 1983, cloth)
Manufactured in the United States of America. First printing, September 1983.

The articles appearing in THE ANNALS are indexed in *Book Review Index; Public Affairs Information Service Bulletin; Social Sciences Index; Monthly Periodical Index; Current Contents: Behavioral, Social, Management Sciences;* and *Combined Retrospective Index Sets.* They are also abstracted and indexed in *ABC Pol Sci, Historical Abstracts, Human Resources Abstracts, Social Sciences Citation Index, United States Political Science Documents, Social Work Research & Abstracts, Peace Research Reviews, Sage Urban Studies Abstracts, International Political Science Abstracts,* and/or *America: History and Life.*

Information about membership rates, institutional subscriptions, and back issue prices may be found on the facing page.

Advertising. Current rates and specifications may be obtained by writing to THE ANNALS Advertising and Promotion Manager at the Beverly Hills office (address above).

Claims. Claims for undelivered copies must be made no later than three months following month of publication. The publisher will supply missing copies when losses have been sustained in transit and when the reserve stock will permit.

Change of Address. Six weeks' advance notice must be given when notifying of change of address. Please send old address label along with the new address to insure proper identification. Please specify name of journal. Send change of address to: THE ANNALS, c/o Sage Publications, Inc., 275 South Beverly Drive, Beverly Hills, CA 90212.

The American Academy of Political and Social Science

3937 Chestnut Street   Philadelphia, Pennsylvania 19104

Origin and Purpose. The Academy was organized December 14, 1889, to promote the progress of political and social science, especially through publications and meetings. The Academy does not take sides in controverted questions, but seeks to gather and present reliable information to assist the public in forming an intelligent and accurate judgment.

Meetings. The Academy holds an annual meeting in the spring extending over two days.

Publications. THE ANNALS is the bimonthly publication of The Academy. Each issue contains articles on some prominent social or political problem, written at the invitation of the editors. Also, monographs are published from time to time, numbers of which are distributed to pertinent professional organizations. These volumes constitute important reference works on the topics with which they deal, and they are extensively cited by authorities through-out the United States and abroad. The papers presented at the meetings of The Academy are included in THE ANNALS.

Membership. Each member of The Academy receives THE ANNALS and may attend the meetings of The Academy. Membership is open only to individuals. Annual dues: $26.00 for the regular paperbound edition (clothbound, $39.00). Add $6.00 per year for membership outside the U.S.A. Members may also purchase single issues of THE ANNALS for $6.95 each (clothbound, $10.00).

Subscriptions. THE ANNALS is published six times annually—in January, March, May, July, September, and November. Institutions may subscribe to THE ANNALS at the annual rate: $45.00 (clothbound, $60.00). Add $6.00 per year for subscriptions outside the U.S.A. Institutional rates for single issues: $10.00 each (clothbound, $15.00).

Second class postage paid at Beverly Hills, California.

Single issues of THE ANNALS may be obtained by individuals who are not members of The Academy for $7.95 each (clothbound, $15.00). Single issues of THE ANNALS have proven to be excellent supplementary texts for classroom use. Direct inquiries regarding adoptions to THE ANNALS c/o Sage Publications (address below).

All correspondence concerning membership in The Academy, dues renewals, inquiries about membership status, and/or purchase of single issues of THE ANNALS should be sent to THE ANNALS c/o Sage Publications, Inc., 275 South Beverly Drive, Beverly Hills, CA 90212. *Please note that orders under $20 must be prepaid.* Sage affiliates in London and India will assist institutional subscribers abroad with regard to orders, claims, and inquiries for both subscriptions and single issues.

THE ANNALS

of The American Academy of Political and Social Science

RICHARD D. LAMBERT, *Editor*
ALAN W. HESTON, *Associate Editor*

─────────── FORTHCOMING ───────────

ROBOTICS:
Future Factories, Future Workers
Special Editor: Robert J. Miller
Volume 470   November 1983

PAYING FOR CULTURE
Special Editor: Patricia McFate
Volume 471   January 1984

POLLING AND THE DEMOCRATIC CONSENSUS
Special Editor: L. John Martin
Volume 472   March 1984

See page 3 for information on Academy membership and
purchase of single volumes of **The Annals**.

CONTENTS

BOOK DEPARTMENT CONTENTS

INTERNATIONAL RELATIONS AND POLITICS

AFRICA, ASIA, AND LATIN AMERICA

EUROPE

UNITED STATES

SOCIOLOGY

ECONOMICS

PREFACE

Humanity is on the edge of its existence.

Never before this half of our century have we been so close to our destruction, and the destruction of all life. We are in the Nuclear Age.

During the Commercial Age, or Revolution, of the seventeenth century, there was no turning back. Commerce moved ineluctably ahead. During the Industrial Revolution of the nineteenth century, industry not only forged steel but forged forcibly ahead as a predominance in our culture. Twentieth-century technology now touches us all. Cars, telephones, calculators, computers have become the developed countries' steadfast, stalwart symbols of successful enterprise. No one could have arrested the cumulativity of such knowledge of physical science.

And now we have nuclear power. It has positive functions for society if harnessed properly. It was initially hailed for efficiency and economy in serving humanity. But unlike commerce, industry, and computers, nuclear power has the capacity to destroy all of us and all of everything. When this power is mixed with politics and international conflict, it becomes a legal and social menace.

Nearly a year ago the Board of Directors of the American Academy of Political and Social Science suggested to us that the major social and political issue facing the world in mid-1983 would be nuclear armament-disarmament. That foresight has been validated by all current events since then. Never before have we witnessed so many conferences, workshops, meetings, seminars on this topic. How are we of the Academy different?

Most meetings on the nuclear arms issue have been advocates of nuclear freeze, of control, of conflict between the United States and the Union of Soviet Socialist Republics. They function as if the United States and the USSR are the enemies, and the only enemies, as if each country must arm itself against the other. Why? Because these are the two superpowers who possess the amazing mass of weapons. There is little discussion of cooperation, in the knowledge and accumulation of nuclear arms. Were there an extraterrestrial power threatening the Earth, we might readily collaborate. In the absence of external threat, we have created our own internal threats. The absurdity of nuclear build-up is recognized by all camps of opinion. Yet we continue to build arsenals of incredible destruction.

The American Academy of Political and Social Science takes no ideological stance on social-political issues. As the oldest social science organization in America, founded in 1889, we function to disseminate discussion of major social and political issues. Our bimonthly publication, *The Annals,* performs this function with printed perspicacity.

Our meeting this year is part of our history. We stand for wide, multilateral discussion of the issues. Papers during these two days have been presented by some who favor total disarmament, by representatives who express the views of the United States, by those who will dispassionately review the history of nuclear arms control, by those who will present the view of Western Europe and of the critical area of Germany, by one who gives the Russian perspective.

In short, we have had at our annual meeting of the Academy a broad spectrum of views on the general problems of nuclear arms control. We welcome any reactions or comments to this publication of papers.

MARVIN E. WOLFGANG
ROBERT H. KUPPERMAN

Opposition to Nuclear Armament

By ADMIRAL NOEL GAYLER (USN—Ret.)

ABSTRACT: In view of our security requirements, nuclear weapons are militarily useless; in view of the history of their development, they are militarily dangerous. The standard answers to the problem are not solutions: civil defense programs are inadequate, if not infeasible; sophisticated technological approaches to defense face unsurmountable technical and military difficulties; and our current deterrent policies—balance of forces, the use of deployments as signals—are delusions. Practical solutions depend on the avoidance of mutual enmity between the United States and the USSR, and the recognition of both our common interest in arms control and each other's legitimate security requirements. The renunciation of our doctrines of nuclear war fighting, counterforce, and limited war will change patterns of weapons development and deployment. Arms control agreement will still face significant problems of verification, classification, and equal capability. But certain practical proposals—50 percent across-the-board cuts, and the turning in of weapons by each side for conversion into nonweapons material, coupled with a halt in the production of weapons-grade fissionable material—are promising.

Noel Gayler, chairman, Deep Cuts Campaign, American Committee on East-West Accord, and former director, National Security Agency, served in the U.S. Navy, 1935-76, with experience as a fighter pilot and experimental pilot. As a four-star admiral he commanded U.S. forces in the Pacific, 1972-76, and received three Navy Crosses and the Distinguished Service Medal. He has been deputy director of the Joint Strategic Target Planning Staff, naval aide and military assistant to the secretary of the navy, and U.S. naval attaché in London. Responsible for research and development programs, he is a writer, speaker, analyst, and lifelong student of political and military affairs.

E veryone understands the extraordinary danger of the situation
that confronts us. Our political and
ideological dialogue, sometimes confrontation, with the Soviet Union has
the potential—still very small but
extraordinarily dangerous—of de-
generating into nuclear war; and the
prospect for the worldwide spread of
nuclear weapons has no apparent limit
at present.

We hear suggestions made at high
levels that nuclear threats, even nuclear
employments, are legitimate components of strategy. We entertain
delusions, apparently, that there can be
effective defenses against nuclear attack,
which will make nuclear war in some
way tolerable. We suffer the extraordinary confusion that nuclear devices
are usable military weapons. They are
not. We think in terms of nuclear
advantage, when that is a contradiction
in terms. And rather than trying to reach
agreement with the Soviet Union, we
seem to have the notion that somehow
nuclear weapons, or the threat of
building them, can force their
compliance.

In my judgment there are straightforward ways to improve the security of
the United States and her allies of the
free world, and at the same time to
reduce the peril of nuclear war. I believe
above all that the truth will set us free,
and I am going to suggest that all of us
have a responsibility to act.

MILITARY USELESSNESS

Let me first say what I mean by
security. It means that we and our allies
must have a decent respect for the
security of the Soviet Union, and must
be secure from the threat or use of

military attack or from blackmail under
that threat or use. Security has many
components; the principal ones are
political, economic, psychological, and
military. I am going to talk about the
military components, without at any
time losing sight of the great importance
of the others.

Our strategic needs have nothing to
do with weapons systems as such. They
are a function of geography. The Soviet
Union lies at the center of the Eurasian
landmass; within the land borders of the
Soviet Union and its contiguous allies
are all the sinews of war: men, energy,
materials. The United States, however,
is at the center of an oceanic alliance.
We and all of our allies are in some sense
deficient as individual countries. However, we have enormous strength operating together in a coherent alliance. In
order to sustain the oceanic alliance we
have to have certain military capabilities.
Among them are the capabilities to keep
open the sea and air links that tie
together our alliance, politically and
economically as well as militarily; to
hold ground at places of our choosing, of
our necessity; and to project power in
the interest of peace, in the interest of
stability, where it must be projected and
sustained.

The Soviet Union has its own military
imperatives. I am not going to speak
about those, but in my judgment, in a
rational world, they are not in conflict
with our own imperatives.

I see no military usefulness for nuclear
weapons. In the responsibilities I once
held as commander in chief of U.S.
forces in the Pacific, I was required to
look at the various potential theaters of
combat, and at the potential objectives
of the United States; it is a legitimate
and recognized practice to undertake

these military studies. I was never able to identify a campaign in the Pacific, however farfetched, in which the initial use of nuclear weapons would have been to the advantage of the United States. The same was true for the Middle East: think of the absurdity, for example, of protecting an oil field by nuking it.

There was a cult a while ago in the U.S. Navy that wanted to suggest that somehow nuclear war could be isolated, insulated into nuclear war at sea. It would not spill over into land—would not kill civilians, just sailors. That idea does not work either, because the U.S. Navy has the great preponderance of large ships. One nuclear weapon is one ship, so it does not really make sense even from the narrowest sort of military consideration.

And finally, Europe, where it is still official doctrine in the North Atlantic Treaty Organization (NATO) that an attack against NATO Europe would under some circumstances be repelled or stopped by initiating the use of nuclear weapons. To my mind there is no evidence that the USSR intends such an attack, or that there is any rational way Soviet planners could believe that such an attack were anything but fraught with extraordinary peril to the Soviet Union. But we seem to talk about such an attack all the time, I think as a consequence of the forward deployment of very strong Soviet conventional forces.

Should we start a nuclear war by the attempted limited use of nuclear weapons in the event of such an attack? What would happen? First, non-combatants would be killed by the millions. If you do the necessary strategic calculation, it turns out that to stop a reasonable number of tank break-throughs, you end up in the actual terrain, killing a million civilians. These would be mostly German, some American. It would fractionate NATO.

If that did not happen, the chance of keeping the war limited to an exchange on the battlefield would be practically zero. The Soviets do not recognize the possibility of limited nuclear war. The doctrine is clear. It does not make sense. It would be handy, perhaps, if tactical weapons went off with a green flash and strategic weapons went off with a red flash. That is not the case. I cannot imagine a commander getting reports of enormous nuclear explosions and being told not to be too unhappy about it, since these were only tactical explosions.

Even if the war did not escalate to the final all-out exchange, even if NATO did not fractionate, the outcome would still be adverse to the NATO alliance. We are the outfit that has the smaller number of absolutely vital targets, harbors, airfields, depots, and concentration points. We would be at a serious tactical disadvantage.

If we remove this security blanket that we ourselves offered the NATO alliance some 20 years ago, what is the consequence? The consequence is first to improve the unity of NATO, because there has been nothing in recent years quite so harmful to the unity of NATO as some of these nuclear proposals, which indeed started with NATO governments but are now being attributed entirely to the impetus of the United States.

There are many things that can improve the security of Europe. Many of them do not cost any money, and some can even save money. They are

— unity of purpose;

— a better decision-making process;

— sensible logistics, so that the armies are supported across the board by what is available, rather than each by its own national resources;

— order defenses, which do not now exist;

— antitank defenses, which may not stop tanks but will impede them, make them concentrate and slow down so that they can be effectively attacked;

— hitting weapons: we are in a new technological era when it is actually possible to make weapons that are intended to hit, rather than weapons that hit occasionally, accumulating statistically a lot of misses; and

— considerable military reforms: any doctrine that says we should risk nuclear war, or threaten nuclear war in the defense of that theater, is simply dangerous bluff; the perceived unity of NATO is real, and the recognition of that unity involves taking steps necessary for an effective conventional defense.

MILITARY DANGER

I think that I am justified in reaching the conclusion that the nuclear weapons have no military usefulness. They have in fact brought great military danger to the United States. Let me review the history briefly.

When we invented the atomic bomb, we invented the one thing that could place the United States at risk. Before that, we had the strongest naval power, the strongest air force in the world. We

were protected by broad oceans east and west, and by weak but friendly neighbors north and south. It was inconceivable that anybody should launch a military attack against us. We invented nuclear weapons and at once became vulnerable.

Not content with that, we raised the ante by a factor of about a thousand, by inventing the hydrogen weapon. Defense, which had merely been terribly difficult before, became impossible. Next we brought in intercontinental bombers, and after a competitive pause on both sides, we got back intercontinental ballistic missiles. The warning time, which had been hours, was now reduced to minutes. Then we invented submarine-launched ballistic missiles. Momentarily that reversed the trend toward instability, because submarines are extremely difficult to attack effectively, and so are relatively secure—invulnerable, as the jargon has it now.

We went ahead, and in a fit of almost absent-minded technical push, we invented multiple independently targetable reentry vehicles, and now we have created the vulnerability of the land-based ballistic missile forces, which is certainly destabilizing. We are proceeding hell-bent for cruise missiles, for mobile weapons systems, and those have one interesting characteristic: they are going to be very difficult, if not impossible, to verify. We talk—not with any reality, in my judgment, but talk counts sometimes—about weapons in space, whose adoption of course would abrogate the only really good nuclear arms limitation treaty we have, and in addition would tend to be perceived again as destabilizing.

People say to me, "Have you not heard, Admiral, that we have defenses against nuclear weapons? We have a magic shield and a silver bullet." Let me talk about that magic shield for a moment, civil defense.

CIVIL DEFENSE

Nobody now disputes that incredible damage would be done to cities, industries, agriculture, public works, and the military by multiple nuclear blasts. All buildings, all homes, all hospitals, all facilities are destroyed. The complex web of transportation and communication is totally disrupted. The life-giving land, the air, the water are poisoned. The livestock are killed, the crops destroyed. Perhaps no one can really know what even more far-reaching effects threaten the earth itself.

But the claim is made for civil defense: we can save the people, by moving everybody out of the cities before an attack, given a week's notice; by providing blast shelters for those essential people not evacuated; by suggesting plans for the expedient construction of fallout shelters for those who are evacuated; by protecting essential communications machinery and facilities for reconstruction after attack. The general idea is that with civil defense, nuclear war will not be so bad after all.

The trouble with all these ideas is that every one of them is nonsense. First, we are not going to have a week's notice. I do not believe for a moment that the Soviets are planning such an attack, but if they were, they would not give us a week's notice. Nor can we evacuate and sustain the population of great cities in the countryside. Even if we attempted to do so, the opponent could easily track the movement and retarget to the evacuation areas. The power and accuracy of nuclear weapons are sufficient to destroy any fixed target on earth.

Deep shelters would become deep tombs. Notice the U.S. plans to abandon deep shelters for senior officials in favor of mobile command posts. Now consider the notion that a family with shovels could improvise a fallout shelter and live in it for weeks. It is quite simply absurd. Food, water, disposal of waste, heat, all are required for survival. None would be reasonably available. As for digging in the ground, try that in Minneapolis in the winter, or Leningrad or Moscow or New York or Philadelphia. Collective shelters may be worse. They can be incubators of disease, are not conceivably adequate to cover the numbers involved, and are in any case themselves targetable.

We could expect too that because of the multiple effects of nuclear weapons, essentially all transportation would be destroyed—vehicles smashed, roads, bridges, and rail lines destroyed, ships sunk. No one has suggested even a remote possibility of preventing this destruction. Industrial capacity for repair or reconstruction would be nil.

All general purpose communications would be gone—telephone, telegraph, radio, television. With tremendous effort, we may or we may not be able to salvage specialized military networks connecting, for example, the assistant secretary of agriculture, who may be the only living constitutional successor, with the strategic air command (SAC) colonel, who is the surviving senior military officer. As a contribution to the military aspects of assured deterrence, such a surviving communications network, if attainable, makes sense. As a contribution to the survival of populations, it makes none.

So we have here a string of logical and practical absurdities. The claim that substantial additional numbers of the population may be saved by civil defense measures is quite simply wrong. Under certain circumstances—an attack during an attempted evacuation of cities, for example—it may even cost lives. None of this is to detract from the great potential usefulness of civil defense organizations in natural disasters—fire, flood, earthquake, industrial accidents— where help can be organized from the outside. That can be invaluable. But in a nuclear war, there is no outside that survives.

But what about the Russians? Do they not have a massive civil defense? Does it not give them a big strategic advantage? The short and accurate answer is no. The Soviets indeed have spent a lot of money. They have appointed General Altunin to direct their program. They have put out a lot of civil defense manuals, reminiscent of our own, in their innocent impracticality. They have built a lot of strong shelters for their leadership, but they now know, as we do, that there is no strong point that can sustain a direct nuclear hit. Evacuation of cities and expedient fallout shelters is even less practical in the Soviet Union than it is in the United States, and they do not even make much pretense of protecting their industry. The civil defense effort in the Soviet Union has lapsed into a characteristic show without substance. Soviet civil defense cannot have strategic value in the eyes of Soviet planners, because they know its emptiness even better than we do.

TECHNOLOGY

Let us now talk about the silver bullet, the idea that science will somehow protect us from the rain of nuclear ballistic missiles. This is an idea that the President has entertained, apparently, for some time. It had its principal public unveiling in a speech of 30 March 1983.

Unfortunately the President deserves more credit for the humanity of his vision than for the realism of his solutions. The specifics of the scheme— the basic ideas that ballistic missiles can be attacked during takeoff or in flight by energy beams generated in space or generated on earth and bounced off a mirror in space to the targets—are difficult to evaluate, for no details have been furnished. There is reason to believe that indeed no serious system design has taken place, probably because the technical difficulties have been overwhelming. The general argument seems to be that science will find a way, given enough time and money, but that argument does not give us much to analyze.

We can take a look at some publicly mentioned ideas.

1. Lasers. If they are based on earth, they have to penetrate clouds, but they cannot. There is unsurmountable energy absorption and defocusing. If they are based in space, lasers require many tons of fuel in orbit per shot, and the countermeasures are simple: make the missile reflective.

2. Particle beams. These can only propagate in space. If they are charged particle beams, they cannot hit anything because they pick up the magnetism of the earth's field and go in a corkscrew path. We do not know how to make neutral particle beams and accelerate them to the necessary massive total energy rates.

3. Space-based X-ray lasers pumped by nuclear explosives. This untried scheme involves hundreds of nuclear bombs orbiting in space, each to drive a

beam of hot X rays toward a target. Each shot of course destroys its own device. As in all these other schemes, countermeasures are obvious and simple.

4. Antiballistic missiles (ABMs). There is general agreement that while ABM systems can conceivably help the survival of some out of many hard targets, they cannot defend populations.

5. Nonnuclear space interceptors. These systems all run aground on the numbers problem. It is cheaper and easier to build additional warheads than effective interceptors.

The military problems are even more formidable than the technical problems. Tactical and physical countermeasures, even to single-shot engagements, are obvious and simple. The space platforms are more expensive and more easily attacked than the target missiles. The command, control, and accuracy problems—simultaneous engagement of hundreds of missiles, in the presence of deception and countermeasures, where none can be allowed to leak through—seem quite simply insuperable. In the end, even if by some miracle all ballistic missiles could be stopped, we still have the bombers and the cruise missiles to contend with, and they are perfectly capable of destroying either country by themselves.

When science is invoked as a god, it is difficult to make an absolute case that a desired objective is impossible. But we can say with some confidence that ballistic missile defense sufficient to safeguard populations will not be available in this century, and probably never.

Let us turn to the strategic implications of the value of passive and active defenses of populations. In order to entertain the idea of a preemptive or disarming nuclear strike, the attacker must be assured of one of two conditions. He has to be able to destroy substantially any retaliatory force, or he must be able to protect his control, protect his military's industry and his population against a counterstrike. Neither condition is attainable with the present force disposition of the United States and the USSR. In sum, there is no strategic usefulness to either superpower in having active or passive defense.

These defense ideas and programs, however, are much worse than useless. They divert resources from more useful tasks, both military and civilian. A nuclear-oriented civil defense program will cost many billions of dollars. Space-oriented active defense is literally a bottomless sink for money, billions and billions and billions without end. The diversion of resources and attention from real security and defense needs is serious. Most important, the impression conveyed that nuclear war can be defended against, can be mitigated, or is in some way tolerable is irresponsible and dangerous.

DETERRENCE

That leads us to deterrence. In deterrence, an opponent must be convinced that he has conceivably more to lose than to gain in initiating nuclear war. There must be no object of his policy that is worth it, no military objective for which it is a sensible solution. The loss must be certain and impossible to avert, either by defenses or by preemptive attack.

There are a lot of illusions floating around in this area. One is the illusion of nuclear balance, for it turns out that the consequences of a total nuclear exchange are quite insensitive to the actual force levels we now have on both sides. It makes quite a difference, however, whether cities are targeted or not. It makes quite a difference what the fusing policy is, whether the warheads are fused to blow on the ground and create the terrible, long-lasting fallout or not. It even makes a difference which way the wind is blowing on a given day, carrying the nuclear fallout over cities or not. But it makes very little difference whether one side or the other starts with an extra thousand missiles.

Technology too makes little difference. It makes little difference whether Philadelphia is destroyed by a maneuvering hypersonic reentry vehicle or by a tired old Bear bomber carrying a gravity bomb. The result is the same. Technology enters the equation only through the production of accuracy, and accuracy has a negative value because it is accuracy that makes the counterforce idea—if not actually, then at least theoretically—possible, and therefore creates the instability of an adversary with a weapon system that he must fire on warning, or maybe preemptively, or else lose.

The notion of counterforce raises that problem, but it is also unrealistic. There is absolutely no prospect that either adversary could turn off any retaliatory return by attack against missile silos, or against missile silos and bombers. Not all the bombers are going to be caught on the ground. Nor could all the missile silos be destroyed, but even if they could, the submarines would still remain.

The other major illusion is the notion that somehow nuclear weapons can be used on the battlefield in conjunction with conventional fighting. We even have special weapons, so-called neutron weapons, which allegedly only kill people and do not hurt anything else. They are not that different from other nuclear weapons, as a matter of fact. There is still an enormous explosion.

We choose to regard them as defensive. The Soviets do not regard them as such, but as a capitalist ploy to capture cities, killing the population without knocking down the buildings. The strategic usefulness of all of these weapons comes into play in chess-like scenarios with which the theorists like to play. But war is not like that. War is suffering, confusion, blood, agony, all of those things, but it is not chess.

It is suggested that these weapons can be useful signals. More than once in our fairly recent history, we have raised the nuclear forces of the United States to high levels of readiness in order to "send a signal to the adversary that we mean business." There has been some interesting experimentation done under controlled conditions on how effective deployments, states of readiness, are as signals. Without exception, they are misinterpreted. What you think is a sensible, preventive deployment appears to him as getting ready to jump off.

One of the major arguments of the Scowcroft Report for the MX and further nuclear weaponry is that we need it as a demonstration of national will, a signal, if you will. But how it is perceived is what counts, and it would be misperceived by the Soviets, just as these tactical gestures have been misperceived. The fact is that readiness conditions, military operations make lousy signals. Military programs make lousy signals because they are always misinterpreted, and by the way, if that is their purpose they also make lousy operations and lousy programs.

PRACTICAL SOLUTIONS

And now a little bit about problem solving: there are in fact straightforward ways to get out of a jam, to improve our security and to reduce the risk of nuclear war. It might come as a surprise to know that even at today's budget levels, there are serious shortcomings in useful military defenses, while we spend our time on this extraordinary preoccupation with nonuseful nuclear weapons.

We have to recognize that the game we are playing is at least two-handed. The USSR is a great country, enormous in size and population capability, the second largest industrial capacity in the world, enormous in its military capability. It is not going to go away. We have got to deal with the Soviet Union whether we wish to or not. We can deal by helping mutually to soak up mutual enmity, or we can deal with the rational containment of expansionism and a recognition of our common interests.

We have to recognize that our relationship with the USSR is not a zero-sum game. It is not true that what injures the USSR helps the United States, or that what injures the United States helps the Soviet Union. There are many things that are to the advantage of both; to get a handle on nuclear weapons is certainly the primary one.

There are others. This one costs no money: we could do away with the insulting and intemperate rhetoric with which the Soviet Union and the United States address each other. It is childish,

silly, pointless, and disturbing. It makes rational aggreement more difficult, and in my judgment the USSR and the United States have to have respect for each other's legitimate security requirements.

That requires, among other things, that we both renounce nuclear war-fighting doctrines, the doctrine of counterforce, and the doctrine of limited war. This renunciation would be a lot more than mere paper declaration. It would have its effect in the weapons that are provided, the deployments that are in existence, the military plans the commanders must generate on both sides, and we would see visible effects in development and deployment after a short period of time.

It would be handy to redeploy shorter-range nuclear weapons out of range of each other, specifically because of a deal on intermediate-range nuclear forces and the adoption of nuclear-free zones. It would be handy to put a mutual hold on the development, testing, and deployment of new nuclear weapons in the interest of stability. It would be particularly handy to make major reductions in nuclear stockpiles, which is in fact a formal objective both of the United States and the USSR.

The Scowcroft Report listed the objectives of arms control in a way which I think is extraordinarily correct. It suggests that

arms control can reduce the risk of war, limit the spread of nuclear weapons, reduce the risk of misunderstanding between the adversaries, turn off wasteful, dangerous, unhelpful developments, stabilize the path of development so that there will be no misunderstanding of our purpose, reduce the need to overinsure against worst-case contingencies, lead to arsenals that are less destructive and less costly, toward the objective of stability, as our primary objective.

I cannot fault those objectives at all. I have a little trouble both squaring it with the development and deployment of MX, and with the notion that the way to reduce weapons is to build up; but as objectives these are certainly good.

What is in fact our goal? If the goal is stability, then each side must end up with minimal invulnerable deterrents, and in the long history of negotiating with the Soviet Union, there have been three classic problems.

First is the problem of verification. What if they cheat?

Second is the problem of classification. What are these things we are talking about, anyway? What, for example, is a nuclear-capable airplane? After all, any airplane bigger than a Piper Cub can carry a nuclear bomb. There is no such class as a "nuclear-capable" airplane. Is the Backfire an intercontinental bomber or not? As a former experimental test pilot, I know that an airplane will go as far as its fuel supply, as long as its engines keep running.

These are the sorts of problems that have made it very difficult to get to an agreed framework for discussion, and they have to be addressed, I think, by doing away with these arbitrary frameworks, the arbitrary disctinction between strategic, theater, and tactical weapons, by treating them as a whole; and most especially by what the Scowcroft Commission recommended—treating the weapons themselves, not the delivery systems.

Finally, we have the problem of equality. The Soviet requirement is well documented, repeatedly stated. They want equal security, equal capability. We tend to define equality as equal capability to do damage, so that it is extraordinarily difficult to find some common measure for the systems.

Even the systems each side proposes to use as measures are different. This has bedeviled the Strategic Arms Limitation Talks (SALT) agreements; is bedeviling the Strategic Arms Reduction Talks (START); will bedevil, if we get serious with it, the idea of build-up and build-down, and almost all of the other weapons reduction programs that are seriously suggested.

ALTERNATIVES

We have an out, however. In a seminal speech, George Kennan suggested that we simply make 50 percent cuts across the board in every category, and do it without further wrangling among the experts. I have been privileged to work with Ambassador Kennan, and with a number of senior and respected nuclear scientists and arms control experts, in attempting to come up with a scheme that makes the Kennan vision practical.

We have done so, under the leadership of the American Committee on East-West Accord. The idea is that both sides turn in, to a central processing facility, very large and continuing numbers of nuclear weapons. There the explosive fission device is converted by dilution into material not suitable for bombs, but suitable for power plants; the rest of the weapons are ground up beyond recognition and destroyed.

Each side choses the weapons it wishes to turn in, which takes care of the problem of equity. The verification is absolute: a nuclear weapon is a nuclear weapon. The question of equality is addressed by a formula that counts both the number of weapons turned in and the mass of fissionable material. Accompanying that is a complete stop in the production of weapons-grade fissionable material, which in both countries is, most fortunately, produced in identifiable plants; and a complete stop is a highly verifiable thing.

Finally, appropriate safeguards must be adopted, probably International Atomic Energy Agency standards, on the diversion of nuclear material from power plants. I think that is a political necessity, although in the case of the United States and the USSR, with our many, many thousands of nuclear weapons, the diversion from power plants probably will not in fact be significant. It might be significant in the case of a nonnuclear power that wanted a dozen weapons, but not in our case.

There is good reason to believe that there can be agreement between us and the Soviet Union on these practical ideas. All of the political measures, all of the military measures, and all of the arms reduction measures taken together can drastically reduce the risk of nuclear war, while enhancing the security of the United States and our allies; and it does not bother me a bit that it will also enhance the security of the Soviet Union.

I think that we can afford to be optimistic about a conclusion like this because it is clear that we and the Soviet Union have at least two strong common interests: that we not get blown up, and that we not see nuclear weapons proliferating around the world, in the hands of people like Qaddafi and Khomeini.

CONCLUSION

We face extraordinary peril. The consequences are real and terrible beyond imagination. They cannot be defended against, but they can be prevented. To resort to more nuclear weapons is futile. Every time we ratchet up the nuclear arms race, or the Soviets do, each side finds itself in a worse position.

It is possible to have a sensible and stable balance—military, economic, and political. In this balance, nuclear weapons have no military value. Nuclear arms control and reduction is a necessity. It can be attained, and it is in our common interest. But it requires first and perhaps solely, the political will to attain it.

In this country, the ultimate political power and judgment lies in the hands of you and me. I profoundly believe that the United States should be number one in the world, because I think it is in the interest of freedom, peace, and the quality of life everywhere. The elements of our strength must, however, include some wisdom. We have a responsibility not to ignore the problem as too terrible to think about. We have a responsibility not to leave it to the experts, because this is primarily a place where common sense counts—it is a good idea not to get blown up; the way to get rid of nuclear weapons is to get rid of nuclear weapons, not to build them up. Common sense application will do the job.

To be against nuclear weapons is not anti-American, it is not antidefense, and it is not dangerous. In my judgment, under the present circumstances, it is profoundly patriotic.

*   *   *

QUESTIONS AND ANSWERS

Q (Julie Weber, East Stroudsburg, Pennsylvania): The military is an influential and powerful voice. Is there any hope that military people, in uniform, would be willing to speak out on the insanity of the nuclear arms race, since it is such a perilous issue? Did you, when you commanded forces in the Pacific, realize this and consider speaking out while in uniform?

A: Speaking out within the military is done in a way consistent with going along with discipline. You talk to your boss. You make the case. A decision is made, and you go with it. You do not appeal to the public. Nonetheless, I am content that my convictions on this issue have been properly and sometimes forcefully expressed in the right places over the years. Contrary to common belief, it is not very dangerous; I was promoted twice afterwards. To suggest, however, that people in uniform can unquestioningly support the nuclear freeze movement, I think, is asking that we discard in some respects our professional responsibilities and the long years of study some of us have put into these problems. I support the nuclear freeze. I

have done so publicly because I think it expresses an idea whose time has come, the idea that it does not make sense to build up while you are trying to reduce. Beyond that, when you get to specifics, one has to take the position that you can freeze some things, such as nuclear testing, but others simply are not practical and might be even destabilizing. So it is a qualified support. I expect my colleagues in uniform would make a similar analysis and probably do recommend in the chain of command what they think our reaction ought to be. When the SALT II Treaty was up before the Senate, and was clobbered on inconsequential grounds having nothing to do with the problem, the Joint Chiefs of Staff unanimously, publicly, and officially supported it. So did the commander in chief, Pacific, my successor; the commander in chief, Atlantic; and the commander of strategic air command—all serving officers with the responsibility. The suggestion that people in uniform cannot, do not, will not think or talk about these things is a mistake. I think our record is pretty good.

ANNALS, *AAPSS,* **469,** September 1983

The Nuclear Freeze
and the Politics of Illusion

By JOSEPH D. LEHMAN

ABSTRACT: The advent of the Reagan administration brought about a radically new approach to the issue of nuclear arms control. Some have said that this new approach is really going to destroy the process altogether, while others believe it to be a more realistic and thus more promising opportunity for real arms reduction. One of the negative reactions has been the rise of the nuclear freeze movement. The constituent groups of this movement are diverse but share a common trait: they depend on, or deal in, illusion. For that is what arms control was under SALT, and is under the freeze. These groups are a large number of more or less sophisticated but genuinely concerned and fearful citizens; a group of opportunistic politicians; and the arms control community-in-exile. Unless and until these groups recognize the failures of the past and the necessity of abandoning self-delusion, we will inevitably repeat our mistakes, and arms control will again put form before substance.

Joseph D. Lehman is the public affairs adviser of the Arms Control and Disarmament Agency. He received a B.A. in English from the University of Pennsylvania, and an M.A. in government and a certificate in national security studies from Georgetown. Active in the arms control field since the late 1960s, when he participated in the Philadelphia Collegiate Disarmament Conference series, he has been a vice-president of the Abington Corporation, a consulting firm specializing in defense analysis; an adviser to the Defense Sub-Committee of the Republican National Committee during the 1980 presidential campaign; and the principal U.S. spokesman at the opening of the intermediate-range nuclear force talks, Geneva, 1981, and of the Strategic Arms Reduction Talks, Geneva, 1982.

NOTE: Mr. Lehman's views as expressed here do not necessarily represent those of the U.S. government.

WHILE the depth of the nuclear freeze movement may be questionable, there is no doubt of its breadth. A combination of shrewd politics, compliant media, and, yes, even popular anxiety has produced a pervasive and curious hybrid. At times it appears ready to overwhelm what passes for intellectual analysis of the nuclear issue, not only on campus and in the streets but in the halls of Congress as well. The causes of this phenomenon bear study, not merely because of its evident sociological significance, but—much more important—because of its potential for the simultaneous, and perhaps long-term, polarization and trivialization of national security opinion.

Few will argue with the view that U.S. foreign and defense policies in the post-Vietnam era have suffered from a steady erosion of the consensus that had sustained this country theretofore. Many ascribe the election of Ronald Reagan to the presidency in 1980 as a reaction to this perceived drift in American policy. In any event, uncertainties in our relations with our allies, with the neutral and nonaligned, and with our potential adversaries exerted a slow and poisonous influence on our ability to make fundamental foreign and defense policy decisions in the 1970s. Angola and Iran, the B-1 and the neutron bomb—the list of miscalculation and inadvertence goes on.

And yet there was one area of security policy that had, at least outwardly, an air of quiet momentum: the Strategic Arms Limitation Talks (SALT). In the decade 1969-79 the United States and the Soviet Union, in most cases behind closed doors, discussed the development, testing, acquisition, and limitation of strategic nuclear weapons—and in the case of antiballistic missiles (ABM) the virtual elimination of defensive weapons. Through three administrations, Republican and Democrat, we negotiated and signed three major agreements that purported to reduce the threat of war and to codify a peaceful relaxation of tensions. Ironically this process crashed head-on into the frustration generated by the more chaotic general foreign policy trends.

THE END OF THE SALT ERA

One need not indulge in the who-struck-John of SALT II's failure. Regardless of SALT II's fatal flaws or alleged virtues, the Ronald Reagan who reestablished a pragmatic consistency in American security policy is the same man who, together with the Committee on the Present Danger and others, brought down the icons of the SALT era. With them he has brought down upon himself and his administration the wrath of the high priests of arms control. Their daily incantations against him have been accompanied by much smoke and not a little ritual dancing. And the drums have sent out an insistent message: nuclear freeze.

It is useful to examine the psychological dimensions of these events, and see what it is that could generate such vitriol and alarm on both sides of the issue. For rarely has the Left been so shameless in its peacemongering, nor the Right so blatant in its ultrapatriotism. That each should so readily bring to bear its own version of the superweapon strongly indicates the presence of big medicine.

Indeed such is the case. The public, to the extent that it paid direct attention, was mesmerized in the 1970s by the process of detente. Everywhere one looked—

Lincoln Center, Vienna, outer space, or, the ultimate proof, television—the signs and portents indicated that the millennium had, if not arrived, then been cleared for final approach. So the vision of Jimmy Carter and Leonid Brezhnev mugging for the cameras could become the perfect opportunity for the nation to indulge in what is called the willing suspension of disbelief. Alas, the morning after came for Carter with the Soviet invasion of Afghanistan, and for the rest of us with the parading of our blindfolded diplomats in downtown Teheran.

With this general reckoning came, of course, a change of venue for some of the revelers. They took the long walk from the Arms Control and Disarmament Agency and the State Department in Foggy Bottom, from the Old Executive Office Building and the Pentagon, to rather more plush if less influential quarters downtown. Some took their beacons, flasks, and wands to Cambridge, Massachusetts, where soon the cult of the nuclear freeze was born.

In fairness, administration figures invited such a development by a temporary disorientation. The terms in which one addresses a gathering of defense specialists do not always translate well to a world audience; as they became aware of the audibility of even their most casual remarks, these gentlemen began to shun terms like "limited nuclear war." But the nuclear freeze movement, invigorated by Robert Scheer's dark vision in *With Enough Shovels,* was not about to let loose talk go away as an issue, even if it did diminish as a commodity.

THE PERSISTENCE
OF ILLUSION

As is often the case in public policy, ironies abound in the confrontation between Reagan administration arms control policies and the analytical side of the freeze movement. While moving in decidedly different directions, each has proceeded from remarkably similar assumptions. Each asserts that the 1970s saw no diminution in the destructive power of U.S. and Soviet arsenals, but rather a continued growth in strategic capability on both sides. President Reagan holds the SALT process directly accountable for this—SALT constraints on launchers created an incentive for the construction of heavy, multiwarhead missiles, and produced the first-strike dilemma. The high priests, meanwhile, nervously shuffle and avert their eyes when asked to find a cause, finally settling for a whack at the old madness-of-the-arms-race answer. Each decries the complexity and ambiguity of the SALT treaties, President Reagan opting for the relative simplicity of his Strategic Arms Reduction Talks (START) proposal—primarily, a one-third reduction in missile warheads—and the high priests choosing the absolute simplicity of the freeze.

Let us examine the two approaches: President Reagan's most dramatic move is the change in the unit of account. Incredibly, both SALT I and SALT II limit launchers. That meant that, with the advent of the multiple independently targetable reentry vehicle (MIRV), neither treaty constrained or even defined the destructive potential of either side. One missile can, and now does, hold three, four, six, ten or more individually guided thermonuclear bombs. The START proposal would count the actual ballistic missile warheads—bombs—themselves, and would bring about a one-third reduction in their number.

The nuclear freeze would, of course, freeze the number of warheads at the present high level. But it would attempt also to freeze testing, development, production, and deployment of both warheads and delivery systems. There are of course complex questions as to whether some testing and development might be stabilizing. Perhaps more important, how could one possibly verify that in a country as large, compartmentalized, and secretive as the Soviet Union, such a ban were being honored? Two alternative, and equally unappetizing, scenarios might follow such a move.

1. It cannot be verified. Real or imagined Soviet violations certainly poison the atmosphere for arms control, by corroborating alarmist accounts, and perhaps gravely endanger U.S. national security.

2. It can be verified. Years of patient and detailed negotiation yield a codified and approved level of weaponry of mind-boggling extent, likely to be above present levels on both sides.

When seen in these terms, the nuclear freeze appears more to address the personal anxieties of its constituent groups than to deal with the real problem. A cry from desperate and fearful people, it is at the same time both a yearning by the high priests for the halcyon days of content-free arms control, and the opportunistic practice of politics by other means.

THE GRAND COALITION

It is worthwhile to examine the make-up of the freeze movement, for within its ranks one can find the best and worst of motives.

Certainly the largest component is composed of the anxious and perplexed many whose awareness of the nuclear dilemma, whether great or modest, gen-erates an almost primitive and, I might add, thoroughly wholesome fear of the menace and irrationality of nuclear weapons. Within this group, and politically active for perhaps the first time in their lives, are many conventional and conservative people. This of course is what has given the freeze a respectability, and an influence in Congress, that the remnants of the 1960s counterculture, who constitute the balance of this first group, could not perhaps elicit. This latter element does, however, provide valuable skills notably missing in the former: experience in political activism, grass-roots organizing, political theater, and—one of their favorite words—networking.

A second group is arguably less genuinely motivated—or, shall I say, has different motives. This is of course the pols.[1] Any movement of this nature is bound to draw, in the best traditions of democracy, its share of would-be leaders, but some senators and congressmen have particularly refined noses for issues such as this one, with its enormous opportunity for demagoguery and buncombe. The recently approved House resolution, which purports to support a nuclear freeze—though after 30 amendments it looks, as one wag put it, rather like a "slush resolution"—produced in floor debate an embarrassing welter of the purest drivel. Nearly all of it was designed to position freeze advocates, and those who know better than to stand on train tracks, for the election campaigns of 1984.

---

1. I would not include under this rubric a goodly number of members of Congress who are faithfully expressing personal and/or constituent concerns.

The third group is of course the high priests. There has grown up over the years a rather large cottage industry of academics, strategists, moralists, futurists, and just plain arms control groupies whose fascination with the idea and the process has rather dulled their appreciation of the pitfalls. So long as the jargon, the position, and the apparatus were theirs, shortfalls in actual arms reduction could be explained and excused by various sleights of hand designed to divert public attention— and perhaps their own—from the less than inspiring result of their art. In this specialized environment, commitment to the cult and to the ideal was sufficient. It is this group that has provided the spiritual leadership of the freeze movement, even if many of the high priests doubt its efficacy in doing anything but, perhaps, bringing about the demise of the Reagan administration.

It is in this sense a coalition of the worst sort: emotional, unaccountable, and unbound by the responsibilities of government. The dissolution of this coalition will likely come about in one of two ways: either by the achievement of a meaningful agreement by President Reagan, perhaps in the INF talks, or by a direct or indirect Soviet move that causes scales to fall from eyes. The former, while not necessarily the more likely, is certainly the event to be desired. Until such time, the pundits and pols will have much to occupy them.

CONCLUSION

How does one, as either policymaker or citizen, contribute to a reestablishment of consensus in security policy? For President Reagan, indeed for any president, the task must be to preserve and continue to earn the trust of the public, while at the same time availing himself of the broadest range of opinion on arms control topics. The Scowcroft Commission provides a promising vehicle for such a policy.

For the freeze movement, to the extent that it is reconcilable, the first order of business must be the shedding of illusions. The shattering of the SALT illusion by President Reagan has exposed the dependency in the arms control community on maintaining, if not that illusion, then some illusion. Call it what you will—humanity, idealism, a peculiarly Western hunger for intellectual symmetry—the willingness to embrace a position of dubious practicality but eminent purity is all but irrepressible. Those who were warmed all over by the glow of Vienna must recognize ashes when they see them. Otherwise we shall see the frightening spectacle of those once and —they hope—future practitioners of the mystic arts, like so many amnesiac sorcerer's apprentices, ready to utter the same incantations, and ever unmindful of the consequences.

America's Nuclear Ferment:
Opportunities for Change

By REAR ADMIRAL GENE R. La ROCQUE

ABSTRACT: Unprecedented public concern about nuclear weapons and nuclear war has been brought about by the bellicose rhetoric of the Reagan administration and preparations to fight and win a nuclear war. But Americans still for the most part share a profound fear and mistrust of the Soviet Union. Many of our more alarmist assumptions about Soviet aggressive intentions do not seem well founded. The vague concept of deterrence, used to justify everything we do in the nuclear area, has become a meaningless slogan. In our military planning we pay slight attention to how the Soviets may actually perceive our so-called deterrent actions. Ultimately nuclear weapons must be eliminated. For the forseeable future, a restrained nuclear weapons program limiting both the United States and the USSR to a retaliatory nuclear force posture is our best hope. The United States, Europe, and the Soviet Union must begin now to plan for vastly expanded cooperation and understanding if we are to prosper in the twenty-first century.

Rear Admiral Gene R. La Rocque is a veteran of 32 years of active duty in the U.S. Navy, cited during World War II for his participation in 13 major combat operations. Duty ashore included the faculty of the Naval War College; seven years in the Pentagon, during which he was awarded the Legion of Merit as a strategic planner; and the directorship of the Inter-American Defense College. He founded the Center for Defense Information and heads a staff of retired senior military and civilian analysts.

WE are witnessing in the United States today a period of unprecedented ferment on nuclear issues. The public is involved, the media are involved, Congress is involved, and even the Reagan administration has reluctantly responded. The movement for a bilateral U.S.-Soviet nuclear freeze arose unexpectedly and quickly gained mass support in all parts of the country. And during the last year over 100 books were published on nuclear weapons and nuclear war. As nuclear weapons become commonplace and as we and other nations plan, train, arm, and practice for nuclear war, public concern mounts. Why is this happening? After all, we have lived with the bomb for more than 35 years, and the basic parameters of U.S. nuclear policy were elaborated in the late 1950s and early 1960s.

The newfound American and worldwide interest must be credited to the jingoism of President Reagan and his close associates. In actuality he and his administration changed very little but were more explicit than previous administrations about our plans and preparations for nuclear war. Plans for a huge build-up of U.S. nuclear weapons and specific statements about fighting, winning, and prevailing in a nuclear war and firing so-called warning shots with nuclear weapons got people's attention. Polarization at home and abroad occurred immediately. Militarists rushed to embrace the president's program. Others became alarmed. When Ronald Reagan was elected in 1980 on a defiant cold war program, few guessed his actions would generate such strong public currents countering his fondest programs.

I have been concerned for many years that Americans do not appreciate the danger of nuclear war. For decades governments have cloaked the dreadful reality of nuclear war and nuclear weapons in reassuring and soothing language. Many, including political leaders and military men, have failed to understand the tremendously destructive nature of nuclear weapons and have approached the accumulation of military power in the nuclear age much as in earlier times—the more the better. Many have come to believe that a war with nuclear weapons could be controlled, won, and survived. It was Robert S. McNamara, early in his career as secretary of defense in 1962, who articulated the generally accepted view of nuclear war as an extension of previous wars:

The U.S. has come to the conclusion that to the extent feasible, basic military strategy in a possible general nuclear war should be approached in much the same way that more conventional military operations have been regarded in the past.[1]

Mr. McNamara evidently later came to understand that there was little "feasible" about this.

Failure to appreciate the revolution in warfare and international affairs brought about by nuclear weapons has been and still is a fundamental problem, although in recent years there has been a salutary increase in public education. More people are aware that a nuclear war would be unlike any other war in American history; we will not go to war next time—it will come to us. While the majority of Americans support the construction of thousands of new weapons each year, most know that a nuclear war

1. "Address at the Commencement Exercises, University of Michigan, Ann Arbor, 16 June 1962," *Department of State Bulletin,* 9 July 1962.

would be a war without winners. There is a growing demand among informed people to slow, stop, and reverse the nuclear arms race.

This demand is a positive and encouraging development. On the nuclear issue the public here and in Europe are ahead of their governments and many so-called experts. It has been our objective at the Center for Defense Information since it was founded in 1972 to educate the public and the media with the facts on nuclear war. This was the purpose of our nationally televised 1978 First Nuclear War Conference, and our 1981 Conference on Nuclear War in Europe held in the Netherlands.

But I fear that the shift in public attitudes has yet to make any substantial impact on the thinking of those in charge of the U.S. military establishment. Official policy continues to be enamored of nuclear weapons and to be based on attempts to pursue military advantage in the nuclear age. The fuzzy ideology of deterrence is proclaimed in public while strenuous efforts are made to prepare to fight and win a nuclear war. This is not new with the Reagan administration. It has been the dominant thrust of the U.S. military policy for decades.

From the beginning of the nuclear age there have been a small number of distinguished military men speaking out forcefully against nuclear weapons and the illusions that accompany them. Louis Mountbatten of Great Britain jolted many of his former military colleagues when he said,

As a military man who has given half a century to active service I say in all sincerity that the nuclear arms race has no military purpose. Wars cannot be fought with nuclear weapons. Their existence only adds to our

perils because of the illusions which they have generated.[2]

General Douglas MacArthur also turned against nuclear weapons:

Global war has become a Frankenstein to destroy both sides. No longer is it a weapon of adventure—the shortcut to international power. If you lose, you are annihilated. If you win, you stand only to lose. No longer does it possess even the chance of the winner of a duel. It contains now only the germs of double suicide.[3]

Many if not most military men are uncomfortable with nuclear weapons and frustrated by the inability to use them militarily. It is the job of the professional military in every country to prepare for war and to prepare to win. Nuclear weapons complicate the job tremendously. But despite these complications and uncertainties, the armed forces in both the United States and the Soviet Union have been almost totally nuclearized. We and they are constantly preparing for nuclear war. We have built our military power around nuclear weapons and depend upon their use to wage war against all prospective opponents.

Attempts are sometimes made to minimize the extent of our dependence on nuclear weapons by saying, as Secretary of Defense Weinberger did recently, that less than 15 percent of the annual

2. "On the Brink of the Final Abyss," *The Defense Monitor*, 9(4):4 (1980). Lord Mountbatten originally gave this speech on 11 May 1979 in Strasbourg, France, on the occasion of the award of the Louise Weiss Foundation Prize to the Stockholm International Peace Research Institute.
3. "Nuclear War: A Frankenstein," *The Defense Monitor*, 9(6):5 (1980). General MacArthur originally gave this speech before a Joint Session of the Congress of the Philippines on 5 July 1961.

military budget goes for nuclear weapons.[4] A more complete accounting of all funds, including all personnel and research and development costs, brings the total to nearly 25 percent.[5] But even that figure understates the degree to which preparations for nuclear war dominate U.S. and Soviet military planning. Almost every warship and submarine in the U.S. Navy carries nuclear weapons. Current planning makes nuclear weapons central to the conduct of combat operations in Europe by U.S. Army, Air Force, and Navy forces.

The U.S. has about 30,000 nuclear weapons. The Soviet Union has about 20,000. Any war between the two countries will be a nuclear war. Most military planners realize that and plan accordingly.

U.S. VIEWS OF THE SOVIET UNION

I believe we are at a point now where we should critically reassess some of the major assumptions for the use of nuclear weapons to achieve our national objectives. The acquisition of more nuclear weapons to deter Soviet actions can be valid only if we continue to be persuaded it is necessary and will be effective. Deterrence is totally dependent upon the attitude of Soviet government officials; hence we must clearly understand their motivations.

The major assumption underlying U.S. foreign policy since 1945 has been the devil image of the Soviet Union. We have assumed the Soviets to be diaboli-

cally aggressive and a malevolent force in the world. We have seen ourselves as the protectors of Western civilization from the communist menace. We have assumed that, but for our powerful military forces, the Soviet Union would take over the world through military conquest, and that Soviet officials understand only brute military force, ours or theirs. Our people and our government officials have shared a profound distrust and even hatred of the Soviets. The resulting fear has dominated our foreign policy. Any departure from this anti-Soviet stimulus has always been a brief aberration. President Reagan's rearticulation of the image of the Soviet Union as "the focus of evil in the modern world"[6] may strike some as crude, but I believe it accurately reflects both popular and official attitudes.

George F. Kennan[7] and a few others have attempted to make Americans reflect critically on these traditional attitudes. I believe many of our assumptions about the Russians are erroneous, and we need to reassess them quickly if we are to protect ourselves from their potentially disastrous consequences. War is inevitable sooner or later if we believe our contest with the Soviet Union is one of good versus evil. We will think the contest worth dying for in a nuclear war—and we will die—if such is our conception of our purpose. But in my view, there is no issue between the United States and the USSR that requires nuclear war.

4. Department of Defense transcript, "DOD Budget Briefing by the Honorable Caspar W. Weinberger, Secretary of Defense, at the Pentagon," for release 31 Jan. 1983, p. 3.

5. See "$400 Billion for Nuclear Weapons," *The Defense Monitor,* 12(4) (1983).

6. Quoted in Francis X. Clines, "Reagan Denounces Ideology of Soviet Union as 'Focus of Evil,'" *New York Times,* 9 Mar. 1983.

7. *The Nuclear Delusion: Soviet-American Relations in the Atomic Age* (New York: Pantheon Press, 1982).

I do not believe that there has ever been any evidence that the Soviets were planning to launch a military attack on the United States or Western Europe. At no time in their history would they have had anything to gain from such attacks, nor can I visualize any set of circumstances when it would be to their advantage. Soviet officials have never evidenced either any illusions about the mortally dangerous consequences of such action, nor any confidence that Soviet military power is such as even to raise the prospect of success.

More important than these negative factors, however, is the positive value of the West for the Soviets. The Soviets have consistently sought economic relations with the West, which would bring desperately needed goods and services to the Soviet Union: grain, technology, trade.

I must point out, of course, that rejection of the devil image of the Soviets does not convert them into angels or render them militarily harmless. Even though they have not had intentions of attacking the West, they have since the 1930s[8]—not just since the 1960s, it should be emphasized—sought to build a very large military establishment. They in fact are obsessed with national defense. But Soviet officials have not shaped their military effort around plans for highly risky, suicidal military attacks.

REASSESSING DETERRENCE

American military policy since World War II has been articulated chiefly in the concept of deterrence. Most recently, in March 1983, Defense Secretary Caspar

Weinberger stated, "We are simply maintaining the calculus of deterrence."[9] Deterrence has a reassuring sound to it. It is invoked on any and all occasions. But it is far from clear what we mean by "deterrence," or whether "deterrence" is an accurate description of our policy. It may not even be a good policy, particularly as we have been pursuing it.

Dictionary definitions may provide a starting point. To deter is "to discourage or restrain from acting, as through fear."[10] The *Dictionary of Military and Associated Terms* of the Joint Chiefs of Staff defines deterrence as "The prevention from action by fear of the consequences. Deterrence is a state of mind brought about by the existence of a credible threat of unacceptable counter action."[11]

The most striking aspect of deterrence is that even though everyone talks about it, nobody can say what it consists of. Who knows how much is enough to deter? No one knows, and in part for this reason, we—and the Soviets—have accumulated essentially unlimited nuclear arsenals and work constantly to acquire still more new weapons, new means of delivery, with new stratagems of use.

Deterrence is such a vague term that it can be and has been used to justify everything we do. It is now purely a slogan. It has no real value as a guide to either what we should do or what we actually do in our policy toward the Soviet Union.

9. Quoted in Terry Ganey, "Weinberger in Call for Arms Might," *St. Louis Post-Dispatch,* 13 Mar. 1983, p. B1.

10. *Random House Dictionary* (New York: Ballantine Books, 1978), p. 248.

11. Joint Chiefs of Staff, *Department of Defense Dictionary of Military and Associated Terms,* JCS Pub. 1 (Washington, DC: Government Printing Office, 1979), p. 108.

8. See David Holloway, *The Soviet Union and the Arms Race* (New Haven, CT: Yale University Press, 1983), p. 8.

Deterrence has been a useful concept for public relations purposes because it sounds good, just as the word "defense" sounds good, as in "Defense Department." Remember that we once had a "War Department." No one can oppose buying more weapons for the purpose of deterring war or to provide defense.

Deterrence has always been a small part of the U.S. military effort. Military men have always been unsatisfied with the limitations of a purely deterrent policy, as too passive, too inflexible, too limiting, too demoralizing, and even too immoral. Military men have wanted to make nuclear weapons manageable tools of warfare, weapons like any other that can be used to prevail in battle.

In part for these reasons, the U.S. version of deterrence has been remarkably elastic, all-encompassing, and ambitious. It has had almost unlimited goals of deterring any Soviet actions that we do not like. Inherent in our deterrent strategy is an overt willingness to use our nuclear weapons—that is, to attack and destroy the Soviet Union and kill its people. Of equal importance to our strategy of nuclear deterrence is relegating to ourselves the sole right to decide when deterrence has failed, requiring use of nuclear weapons. This understandably appears to the Soviets as one-sided, threatening, and coercive, and has resulted in stepped-up Soviet military response.

How would we Americans feel if the Soviets officially proclaimed a deterrent strategy to prevent the United States from taking military actions around the world? There need be no limit on the size of such a force because, like the U.S. deterrent force, it would be a matter for the Soviets to decide, on the basis of what they perceived to be necessary to deter us. Certainly there could no longer

be the criticism from the United States and other NATO countries that such a so-called deterrent force was larger than needed. I never have understood why the Soviets did not follow the open-ended U.S. policy of building deterrent forces, unless perhaps they really do see their military posture as defensive.

Of course nearly everything the Soviets do in the military arena is perceived by our side as threatening and never as deterrent. As early as 1950 in the National Security Council Report 68, American officials began proclaiming the discovery that "The Soviet Union actually possesses armed forces far in excess of those necessary to defend its territory."[12] As no American official has ever bothered to define what he thinks a Soviet military establishment that met the requirements of an adequate defense posture would be, I think we are forced to conclude that such official statements serve only propaganda purposes.

Because there never have been any reasons advanced for the USSR to invade Western Europe or launch a nuclear first strike on the United States, the constant U.S. invocations of these alleged Soviet intentions has been viewed by the Soviets as reflective of aggressive intentions. American fear and mistrust of the Soviet Union is exceeded only by Soviet fear and mistrust of the United States. They have attributed to us the same expansionist, aggressive intentions we have habitually pinned on them. It serves no useful purpose to dismiss Soviet concerns as "standard Soviet disinformation that's been poured out for years,"[13] as Mr. Weinberger recently said.

12. Rpt. in *Naval War College Review,* May-June 1975, p. 64.

13. Department of Defense transcript, "Secretary of Defense Casper W. Weinberger Inter-

If we were seriously attempting to implement a policy of deterrence, we would pay much more attention to Soviet attitudes than we do. American officials often describe deterrence as our ability to influence the Soviet mentality; the Joint Chiefs' definition refers to "a state of mind." But we have little competence to measure Soviet attitudes, and little interest in doing so. Mr. Weinberger recently said that "it's very hard to get inside the Soviet mind. I have not attempted to do that."[14] He does not seem conscious of how contradictory that is for a deterrent policy.

The sad state of Soviet studies in the United States reflects our basic indifference to learning what the Soviets are really thinking,[15] and the emptiness of our deterrent philosophy. Few diplomats bother to learn Russian. Fewer and fewer students are being taught Russian. Fewer and fewer graduate students are pursuing Soviet studies. There are not enough jobs for even the handful of Americans who have sought to prepare themselves for careers in Soviet affairs. Dr. Robert Legvold of the Council on Foreign Relations summed up the situation:

The gaps in our knowledge are enormous. And they are growing. . . . In the absence of serious, carefully researched studies, our view of the Soviet Union is shaped increasingly by popular impressions, a priori analyses, built from superficial reflections on the

Soviet actions that most catch the eye, and traditional habits of thought.[16]

If we are to improve the security of the United States, we should place first priority on improving our understanding of the Russians both in and out of government. Clearly there are various views of the Russians, there is no monolithic truth on the subject, and there is no panacea in simply learning more. But we start from a position of such abysmal ignorance that any improvement would be good. There needs to be intensive contact at all levels between Russians and Americans. Officials of both countries should be in constant communication. Few members of the U.S. Congress have visited the Soviet Union, although they vote every year for hundreds of billions of dollars for weapons to deter the Soviets.[17]

The Reagan administration recently put together an $85 million campaign to propagate anti-Soviet, pro-American attitudes around the world.[18] If only part of this money were spent to help improve American understanding of the Soviet Union, a real contribution would be made to U.S. security and a rational world order.

A RETALIATORY POLICY

Where should we go from here? The two major contending forces on the

viewed on NBC-TV 'Meet the Press' Sunday, March 27, 1983," p. 2.

14. Department of Defense transcript, "News Conference by Secretary of Defense Caspar W. Weinberger at the Pentagon Wednesday, March 9, 1983," p. 9.

15. See Senate Committee on Foreign Relations, *United States-Soviet Research Studies* (Washington, DC: Government Printing Office, 1982).

16. "The Study of Soviet Foreign Policy: The State of the Field and the Role of IREX," in International Research and Exchanges Board (IREX), *Foreign Area Research in the National Interest: American and Soviet Perspectives* (New York: IREX, 1982), p. 22.

17. See Jeremy J. Stone, "Let Our Senators Go! (To Russia)," *Washington Post,* 27 Mar. 1983, Outlook Section.

18. Don Oberdorfer, "Lawmakers Voice Skepticism on U.S. 'Project Democracy,'" *Washington Post,* 24 Feb. 1983.

American scene seem to be the Reagan administration's policies and those Americans who say we have enough weapons on both sides. Personally I believe the United States and the Soviets should reach agreement to stop the production, deployment, and testing of nuclear weapons in our mutual interests, as a first step in a more comprehensive effort for the Soviet Union and the United States to redirect their activities away from war and destruction.

But it is clear that the Reagan administration is bent on other priorities. Ronald Reagan and Caspar Weinberger seem genuinely to believe that the Soviet Union is following the path of Hitler Germany; that it is their mission to lead a Western crusade against the totalitarian menace; that their domestic critics are appeasers; that there is a good chance of war unless the United States engages in a huge military build-up and moves militarily around the world to snuff out Soviet subversion.

I do not take seriously President Reagan's recent speech announcing his plan to set a national goal of developing a perfect defense against Soviet nuclear weapons.[19] He is attempting to rescue his military budget and his nuclear build-up from mounting opposition. Advocates of a big U.S. military expansion such as Fred C. Iklé, now under secretary of defense,[20] have long attempted to use a moral attack on assured destruction as an expedient vehicle for justifying new weapons. It is essential to note that defense is not being substituted for offense: Reagan made no changes in the U.S. plans to build 17,000 new offensive nuclear weapons in the next 10 years.

I interpret Reagan's recent speeches as primarily political ploys, as attempts again to make the Russians look immoral, and to draw attention away from those who would slow, stop, and reverse the arms race. Once Defense Department officials realize that they are not going to get all the money they are hoping for in future years, the star wars fantasy will begin to lose its attraction. There is not enough money in the United States to build a perfect defense, just as there is not enough money to build an effective first-strike counterforce capability in either the United States or the USSR.

In our nuclear weapons policies I think we can do no better than maintaining a nuclear retaliatory force. A retaliatory force is a much more concrete and quantifiable thing than a deterrent force, which in fact has no measurable dimensions. No military man can tell you how many of what kinds of weapons are required for deterrence, but he can tell you how large our forces need to be to survive an opponent's first strike and to retaliate with devastating effect. That quantity is much less than we have today. In the 1960s McNamara attempted to quantify the approximate level of strategic forces required for retaliation and assured destruction. His calculations were in the range of 400 large nuclear weapons.[21] McGeorge Bundy has argued that even the prospect of a few nuclear weapons exploding on major cities would be enough.[22]

19. "President's Speech on Military Spending and a New Defense," *New York Times,* 24 Mar. 1983.

20. "Can Nuclear Deterrence Last Out the Century?" *Foreign Affairs,* Jan. 1973, pp. 267-85.

21. See Alain Enthoven and Wayne Smith, *How Much is Enough?* (New York: Harper and Row, 1974), pp. 207-10.

22. "To Cap the Volcano," *Foreign Affairs,* Oct. 1969, pp. 9-10.

When Jimmy Carter was first elected, it is reported, he briefly explored the possibility of a much lower level of U.S. strategic weapons but then abandoned this as too radical a break with established practice.[23] It would be a wrenching change, but I think that an American president could implement a drastic reduction in the deployment and obsessive building of nuclear weapons. Many military men would go along with this. Vice Admiral Gerald E. Miller, former deputy director of the Joint Strategic Target Planning Staff, observes,

The simple fact is that nuclear weapons are not very realistic tools for the military commander. Any commander basing the success of his campaign on the use (first use or last) of nuclear weapons has taken a major step toward defeat. . . . The Joint Chiefs of Staff, if left to themselves without all the political and diplomatic constraints, would probably give up plenty of the arsenal. And they could do so without reference to the Soviets. It is the harnessing of our actions to the Soviets that presents the complications, the restrictions on unilateral actions.[24]

We can deemphasize nuclear weapons and planning for nuclear war and improve our security, but aggressive presidential leadership will be required. A president can also inform the American people of the actual Soviet and American strengths and weaknesses. He can dampen the false alarms that have recently so distorted government decision making and public support.

23. Rowland Evans and Robert Novak, "Nuclear 'Blockbuster,'" *Washington Post,* 27 Jan. 1977; and Edward Walsh and George C. Wilson, "Carter to Get Study on A-Deterrence," *Washington Post,* 28 Jan. 1977.

24. "Beres and Others Have No Access to the 'True Strategy,'" *The Center Magazine* (Center for the Study of Democratic Institutions), Nov.-Dec. 1982, pp. 33-34.

NEW APPROACHES

In the current public and official ferment over nuclear issues, unexpected openings have been created—ironically, largely by the Reagan administration—for major departures from traditional approaches. At least for the next few years it should be possible to mobilize broad political support for containing, limiting, and nearly eliminating the nuclear arms race.

But at the same time as we move forward with arms negotiations, we need to start dealing with the basic issue of how to facilitate peaceful U.S.-Soviet coexistence. Fear and mistrust are at the heart of the nuclear arms race, and of our deterrence policy theories. We cannot slow the nuclear arms race if the current level of fear and tension continues. Even at greatly reduced numbers of nuclear weapons, the world will not really be much better off if we and the Soviets continue to engage in hostile confrontation.

A concerted effort is required to identify areas of possible U.S.-Soviet cooperation and understanding. Europe can serve as a bridge between the two superpowers, rather than as a battlefield again. In the early 1970s the United States and the USSR made initial steps toward setting up a comprehensive program of cooperation in many areas. The Apollo-Soyuz space linkup in 1975 was one result. But these initial efforts foundered on the U.S. defeat in Vietnam and American self-doubts.

We need to get back on the path originally devised by Eisenhower and Khrushchev and then followed by Nixon and Kissinger. Peaceful coexistence is possible, and is not a vacuous slogan but a necessity. We have many common interests with the Soviets. We can learn and benefit from them just as they can from us.

Looking ahead to the twenty-first century, if the Soviet Union, Europe, and the United States are to avert a nuclear war, we must embark on a dynamic program to enhance cooperation and understanding. If we nations understand each other, cooperate, and prosper, Latin America, Asia, and Africa will all benefit.

We at the Center for Defense Information have been developing a proposal that we call Project 2000. Our suggestion is that we spend the next three years drafting a series of blueprints for cooperative programs in science, education, trade, housing, and health, which could be developed by delegates in a series of conferences in different European countries. No mention of war or peace or weapons would be involved. The goal would be to improve the international climate, the infrastructure for easing international conflict and avoiding nuclear war. I have discussed the idea for Project 2000 with a number of leading Europeans, who have responded with surprising enthusiasm. I have also received initial positive reactions from Soviet officials.

Our Project 2000 is only one possible approach to exploiting the new opportunities created by our current nuclear ferment. I encourage you to contribute your creative energies to helping our country make the most of the new possibilities for change. Scholars, public officials, and citizens all can participate in the process of freeing ourselves from the self-destructive habits of the nuclear arms race.

* * *

QUESTIONS AND ANSWERS

Q (Jean Gelmer, American Association of Retired Persons): Is there a segment of individuals in the Pentagon and the Navy who can continue your policy of reaching communication between the American people and Russia?

A: I would not look to the Pentagon for any help in this area. Their job is to fight and win wars, and to get from you more and more money to build more and more weapons. They are frankly rather happy with the animosity between the United States and the Soviet Union. It is very convenient. It makes you much more willing to spend your money. We the people have to do it, and I think our Project 2000 Center for Defense Information will be very useful in that regard.

———

Q (J. Stikliorius, Wallingford, Pennsylvania): All historians are agreed that if the Western Allies, Great Britain, and France had spoken more strongly than they did in 1936-39, chances are good that Hitler would not have started World War II. He would have been deterred. What is your opinion?

A: We did not take a strong stand then, and should have. But it is very dangerous to try to make analogies with the prenuclear era. The time of flight now is 30 minutes from their missiles, 15 from the missiles of submarines. We are building weapons systems that can be activated by miscalculation, human error, or electronic malfunction. We are not just fighting a war in some particular geographic area, albeit as large as Europe; we are talking about the destruction of mankind on this planet in the matter of a few seconds. As Einstein said, since the advent of nuclear power, everything is changed except our way of thinking.

The Catholic Bishops'
Concern with Nuclear Armaments

By JOHN CARDINAL KROL

ABSTRACT: The bishops' concern with nuclear armaments is an exercise in religious leadership and responsible citizenship. As religious leaders they speak with the conviction that God is the creator of the universe, and of all in it; that God has given us a blueprint for the successful operation of the world; that human life is sacred; that human dignity and rights are inalienable gifts of God; and that the build-up of weapons of massive, indiscriminate destruction are not in accord with God's plan. The bishops are obliged to articulate the growing concern in the world that nuclear arms and their use exceed the limits of legitimate self-defense, and that any war in which innocent noncombatants are massively destroyed is a crime against God and man, and merits unequivocal condemnation. The bishops are bound to teach that love of God and neighbor are indispensable requisites for true peace. Peace in our time will find its realization as peace with God, peace in our heart, and peace among men.

Installed as archbishop of Philadelphia in 1961, John Cardinal Krol was elevated to the Sacred College of Cardinals by Pope Paul VI in 1967. He is a trustee of many schools and colleges, has held office in religious, civic, and cultural organizations, and is closely connected with Vatican affairs. The recipient of many honorary degrees and awards, including the Philadelphia Freedom Medal, 1978, he chaired and hosted the Forty-first International Eucharistic Congress, 1976, and broadcasts on Radio Free Europe and the Voice of America.

THE theme of this Eighty-sixth Annual Meeting of the American Academy of Political and Social Science is nuclear armament and disarmament. You have asked me to discuss the Catholic bishops' concern with nuclear armaments. To understand this concern it is necessary to appreciate the religious foundations of the role and mission of the bishops in the Church and in the world.

THE ROLE OF
THE BISHOPS

Jesus Christ told Pilate that he came into the world to bear witness to the truth. Christ commissioned his apostles and their successors, the bishops, to be witnesses and to proclaim his Gospel to all the world. The basis of Christ's teachings are the twin commandments of love—love of God and love of neighbor. The perfection of the Christian love for God is tested by his love for neighbor. The word "neighbor" applies to all members of the human family—friends, strangers, and even enemies.

The mission given by Christ to his apostles and to the bishops is not political, social, or economic. But the bishops must be concerned about human rights and freedoms, and economic justice. They must be creatively involved in the political process, criticizing it when necessary, and supporting it where possible. While the bishops should not align themselves with any political party or with any form of government, they must reject the false premise that religion has nothing to do with politics. Mohandas K. Gandhi said, "Anyone who says religion has nothing to do with politics, does not know what religion is." In 1960 Martin Luther King, Jr., said, "I am convinced that the Church cannot remain silent while mankind faces the threat of being plunged into the abyss of nuclear annihilation. If the Church is to remain true to its mission, it must call for an end to the arms race."

The concern of the bishops with nuclear armaments is an exercise in religious leadership and in responsible citizenship. As religious leaders the bishops speak with the conviction that God is the creator of the universe, and of all in the universe; that God has given us a blueprint for the orderly and successful operation of the world; that all human life is sacred; that human dignity and human rights are gifts of God and hence inalienable; and that the arms race and the build-up of weapons of massive and indiscriminate destruction are not in accord with God's plan for this world and for humankind.

As religious leaders the bishops are obliged to articulate the growing concern of an increasing number of people in this country and in the world that nuclear arms and their use exceed the limits of legitimate self-defense, and that any war in which innocent noncombatants are massively destroyed is a crime against God and man, and merits unequivocal condemnation.

As religious leaders the bishops are bound to teach that love of God and neighbor are indispensable requisites for true peace in our heart, in the family, in the nation, and among nations. According to the Christian philosophy of love, peace in our time will find its realization as peace with God, peace in our own heart, and peace among men.

As responsible citizens, enjoying the rights of freedom of speech and of religion, the bishops are bound to influence public opinion by articulating the principles of religion and morality that are the indispensable supports of our form of government. Ours is a government of the people, by the people, and for the people. The bishops strive to teach Gospel truths to the people with a view to informing and molding public opinion. It is public opinion that ultimately influences public policy. It is quite evident that the bishops have contributed in no small measure to alerting the people to the risk and dangers of the arms race and of nuclear war. In turn the people express their concern to their legislative representatives. The bishops exercise their role as witnesses to Christ and to truth. They articulate the Gospel of love, without directly intruding into the area or competence of the civil government.

THE CATHOLIC POSITION

The concern of the bishops about questions of peace and war is not new in the history of the Church. Such a concern has been evident from the earliest days of Christianity. During the first three centuries, the practice of the Christian faith was generally outlawed. After the Edict of Constantine in the early fourth century, Christians who had shown passive resistance to their persecutors became concerned about the raids and invasions of the barbarians. Augustine (354-430), the bishop of Hippo, developed a set of just-war principles. While he advocated, "Destroy war by words and negotiations, but do not destroy men by the sword," he also acknowledged that a just war is permissible but necessary to safeguard and promote peace.

The most influential compendium of medieval teaching on peace and war is found in the Decretals of Gratian (1139-42). The theologian Thomas of Aquinas (1225-74) developed the teaching of Augustine and of the decretals into a system. The just-war principles are based on the premise that war is an evil, but sometimes an unavoidable one. The decision to wage war must be morally justified. Thus the war must be declared by legitimate public authority, provided that every means of a peaceful settlement has been exhausted, and there must be a sufficiently just cause for the declaration and continuance of the war. Moreover those prosecuting the war must have morally good intentions, use only legitimate and moral means in prosecuting the war, and proportionately the damage caused must be less than the evil to be corrected.

In the history of the Church there has been and still is a strain of pacifism; however, the just-war principles are dominant in the teachings of the Church. In his speech to the United Nations on 4 October 1965, the late Pope Paul VI pleaded, "No more war—War never again." He added, "If you want to be brothers, let the weapons fall from your hands. One cannot love with offensive weapons in his hands. . . . As long as man remains that weak, changeable and even wicked being he often shows himself to be, defensive armaments will, alas be necessary."

In the Pastoral Constitution on the Church in the Modern World, the Fathers of the Second Vatican Council discussing the need for curbing the savagery of war declared,

Certainly, war has not been rooted out of human affairs. As long as the danger of war remains . . . governments cannot be denied the right of legitimate self-defense once every means of peaceful settlement has been exhausted. Therefore, [those] who share public responsibility have the duty to protect the welfare of the people entrusted to their care. . . . Those who are pledged to the service of their country as members of the armed forces should regard themselves as agents of security and freedom on behalf of their people. . . . they are making a genuine contribution to the establishment of peace (CMW 77).

In their 15 November 1968 pastoral letter, "Human Life in Our Day," the Bishops of the United States condemned wars of aggression, recognized the right of legitimate self-defense and the need for recourse to armed defense; and condemned the use—not the possession—of weapons of mass destruction to deter possible enemy attack; but they questioned the policy of maintaining nuclear superiority.

In his message of 11 June 1982 to the United Nations Special Session on Disarmament, Pope John Paul II said,

The teachings of the Catholic Church in this area have been clear and consistent. It has deplored the arms race, called nonetheless for mutual progressive and verifiable reduction of armaments, as well as greater safeguards against the possible misuse of these weapons. It has done so while urging that the independence, freedom, and legitimate security of each and every nation be respected.

In that same message, the Holy Father said that he neither wished nor was able to enter into the technical and political aspects of the problem of disarmament. He limited his remarks "to some ethical principles which are at the heart of every discussion and decision that might be looked for in this field." On the subject of deterrence he said,

In current conditions "deterrence" based on balance, certainly not as an end in itself, but as a step on the way toward a progressive disarmament, may still be judged to be morally acceptable. Nonetheless, in order to ensure peace, it is indispensable not to be satisfied with this minimum, which is always susceptible to the real danger of explosion.

APPLICATION OF CATHOLIC PRINCIPLES

The Catholic principles on peace and war have been clear and consistent. However, the application of these principles to current concrete facts requires a knowledge of all the facts as well as a discerning judgment. The bishops pastoral letter is an effort to apply such principles to concrete facts for the sake of providing Catholics and others with a knowledge of the truth, and a guidance for their own actions. Through such a pastoral letter, the bishops strive to fulfill their role as religious leaders, and as responsible citizens.

The yearning for peace characterizes the whole history of humanity. Yet from the earliest recorded times, people knew that the fury of war—defying all desire for peace—ever and again prevailed. As Shakespeare observed, "War and stupidity are always in style."

Today we live in a paradoxical situation. On the one hand the longing for peace spreads increasingly throughout humanity. On the other hand, the stockpiling of conventional and nuclear weapons continues, even though these weapons today have the destructive force of some three tons of TNT for every human being on this earth. This stockpiling arouses in many people a paralyzing fear of war, and elicits unconditional emotional pacifism. Yet a sober evaluation of the situation provides grounds for anxiety that humanity may move from the grave crisis of today, "To that dismal hour, when the only peace it will experience, will be the dread peace of death" (CMW 82).

In modern times, the idea of peace has regrettably been divorced by some from its religious foundations. During the nineteenth and twentieth centuries, the idea of a so-called secular salvation and worldly redemption, a final state of peace and happiness for human society, began to fascinate the masses as never before in history. The expectation of a secular eternal peace was to be effected by a world revolution, which would magically abolish all evil, misery, class conflicts, and wars. Karl Marx enshrined the working man as the redeemer who would open the gates of a worldly paradise for all men.

In reality Marxism is a philosophy of life that amounts to a false religion—an anti-Gospel contradiction of God's message. Marx said, "The religion of the workers has no God, because it seeks to restore the divinity of man." Lenin was blunt in saying,

Every religious idea, every idea of God, even flirting with the idea of God, is unutterable vileness of the most dangerous kind, contagion of the most abominable kind. Millions of sins, filthy deeds, acts of violence, and physical contagions are far less dangerous than the subtle spiritual idea of a God.

Lenin also said, "We must hate, hatred is the basis of communism." He also enunciated a new ethic: "Everything is moral which is necessary for the annihilation of the old exploiting order."

The communists talk a great deal about peace, but it is important to understand their concept of peace. Lenin gives us an idea of that concept in these words: "After we have totally defeated and expropriated the bourgeoisie through-

out the entire world, wars will no longer be possible. The victory of socialism in a country will by no means exclude or eliminate all wars. On the contrary, this victory makes wars inevitable." This is another way of saying that there will be no peace until communism subjugates the entire world, and that detente and coexistence are only periods of rest and regrouping of the forces that must conquer the whole world.

In 1961 Krushchev predicted, "By 1981 the Communist society with its basic characteristics of an ever increasing of surplus goods" would be firmly established. However, this prediction, as well as the promise of a final state of everlasting peace, is like a horizon, which recedes as one approaches it. Marx's enshrinement of the workers in order to restore to them the divinity of man apparently was not operative to the workers of the Solidarity Union in Poland. The communist regime in Poland did not hesitate to crush the workers whom Marx divinized.

These observations about communism have to be mentioned to make it clear that bishops are not a group of starry-eyed dreamers whose pursuit of a just and lasting peace are utopian, or who have been duped by the communists. The bishops have issued pastoral letters exposing the errors and dangers of communism. In fact in 1981 a pastoral letter was issued giving a philosophical treatment of the theory of communism. The Judeo-Christian tradition is eloquent about the vision of peace, but it is also realistic about the fact of war. The Catholic Church has felt the crushing burden of communist oppression and persecution in many parts of the world. The bishops are not blind to the harsh realities of the never rescinded communist objective of rooting out every trace of belief in God and of religious practice. Coexistence of religion and atheistic communism is as impossible as the coexistence of fire and water.

THE PASTORAL LETTER

It may be of interest to know the procedure used by the committee preparing the pastoral letter. After being charged with the preparation of the letter, the committee for about 18 months sought input from a broad spectrum of witnesses: government officials, military experts, theologians, scripture scholars, physicists and medical experts, persons involved in negotiating treaties on the limitation and reduction of arms, and so on. Following a discussion of the information gathered and submitted, the committee prepared the first draft. This was submitted to the bishops in this and other countries, to the Vatican, and also to the various governmental officials and various experts. All were invited to submit their comments. Taking careful note of all the comments and suggestions, a second draft was prepared. This was also submitted to the bishops and to others, and it was discussed in a special meeting in the Vatican, which was attended by some bishops from European countries. Again taking careful note of all the comments, a third draft was prepared, which is being submitted to the bishops of this country at a special meeting to take place in Chicago on 2 and 3 May 1983.

The process is important because the bishops do not presume to be experts in the technology of weapons of war, or in the field of politics. Their competence is in the field of the moral and ethical principles. They must rely on experts in the various other fields to learn the concrete facts and issues to which the ethical principles must be applied.

The third draft will be discussed, debated, and amended at the May meetings. As yet it is not in its final and approved form. However, I feel safe in sharing with you some of the main thrusts of the pastoral.

The pastoral is directed primarily to the Catholic community, but with the intention of making a contribution to the wider public debate in our country on the dangers and dilemmas of the nuclear age.

The pastoral is not primarily technical or political, but is issued with the conviction that there is no satisfactory answer to the human problems of the nuclear age that fails to consider the moral and religious dimensions of the questions faced.

The pastoral declares that keeping peace in the nuclear age is a moral and political imperative; peace is not just the absence of war; peace is the fruit of order, and order in human society must be shaped on the basis of respect for the transcendence of God and the unique dignity of each person, understood in terms of freedom, justice, truth, and love.

The pastoral declares that war is no longer an acceptable means of settling disputes among nations. However, every nation has the right and duty to defend itself against unjust aggression. The intentional killing of innocent civilians and noncombatants is always wrong, and it is never permitted to direct conventional or nuclear weapons to "the indiscriminate destruction of whole cities or vast areas with their population." Even defensive response to unjust attack can cause destruction that violates the principle of proportionality, going far beyond the limits of legitimate defense.

In current conditions deterrence based on balance, certainly not as an end in itself, but as a step on the way toward progressive disarmament, may still be judged morally acceptable. Any use of nuclear weapons that would violate the principles of noncombatant immunity or proportionality may not be intended in a strategy of deterrence.

The arms race is one of the greatest curses of the human race. Negotiations must be pursued to stop the arms race, and to reduce arsenals equally and simultaneously with effective methods of control. Nuclear weapons should ultimately be banned.

The deliberate initiation of nuclear war is an unjustifiable risk, and defensive strategies must be developed to preclude any justification for using nuclear weapons in response to non-nuclear attacks.

The pastoral supports immediate, bilateral, verifiable agreements to curb the testing, production, and deployment of new nuclear weapons. It also supports, in an increasingly interdependent world, political and economic policies designed to protect human dignity and to promote the human rights of every person.

Such is the gist of the Pastoral Letter of the Catholic Bishops on War and Peace. It does not use the word "freeze". It does not advocate unilateral disarmament nor universal pacifism. It acknowledges the right of legitimate self-defense. It does acknowledge a conditional acceptance of the deterrence policy. It does label the deliberate initiation of nuclear war as an unjustifiable moral risk. It calls for increased and intensive negotiations to achieve simultaneous and progressive disarmament with effective and verifiable safeguards and controls.

CONCLUSION

For nearly 15 years I have been articulate in calling for an end to the arms race. I have spoken often in Philadelphia, and in the Vatican at the Synod of Bishops. I have spoken at a symposium in Washington and I have testified before the Senate Foreign Relations Committee.

At this point I venture to say that disarmament is an urgently valuable measure, but I consider it at most a temporary measure. We must acknowledge that a permanent defense against communism must be based on a two-pronged program of education of people in our country, in the world, and especially in the Soviet Union. We must educate the people in what is false and harmful about communism, and we must also educate them in what is true and beneficial to man in the Christian and other religions.

The real enemy is the false religion that has sworn and dedicated itself to conquer and dominate the world. The one weapon that will ultimately defeat communism is truth. Our Lord came to bear witness to the truth. We must bear witness to him and to the truths of the Gospel. We must be zealous in proclaiming truth through all available channels of communications, including the Voice of America, Radio Free Europe, and Radio Liberty. It was the power of Karl Marx's word—*Das Kapital*—that started the mischief of constant wars and of hate. We must with confidence proclaim the teachings of the Prince of Peace, and his Gospel of love. The task is certainly a difficult one, but it is a possible one, and with God's help, we can be assured of eventual victory.

* * *

QUESTIONS AND ANSWERS

Q (Theresa C. Smith, Rutgers University, New Jersey): From a reading of early Soviet literature His Eminence suggested that the Soviet Union feels there will be no world peace until the communists have subjugated the entire world. How does he reconcile that view with more recent trends in the literature, especially documents from the Twenty-first and Twenty-fourth Party Congresses, which emphasize the role of world peace and say things like, "Wars must not and cannot serve as an instrument for the resolution of international disputes."

A: I do not know that anybody uses the term "peace" more than the communists do, but we have to understand the frame of reference. We must consider their actions, their constant objective: when they talked about detente Brezhnev said, "That does not limit our program of expansion." Yes, they talk about peace and they want peace, but by their understanding of the term: "you agree and submit to us." There is a fierce, zealous missionary concept among the communists. My point was not that we should reach some agreement on ideology. But we must counter and get information and expose the terms they use and the meanings they attach to them. The reports, for example, they sent back to their own people after going into Afghanistan are not exactly solid. There must be a long process of education for the good Russian people, the Soviet communists, and I personally am for opening every possible avenue of discussion, negotiation, and dialogue to get our ideas across, because if you reach an agreement and shake hands with someone who says, "We only stay by an agreement if it is to our advantage," then you do not have any sure guarantee of an enduring and everlasting peace.

ANNALS, *AAPSS,* **469,** September 1983

Nuclear Arms as a
Philosophical and Moral Issue

By ROBERT P. CHURCHILL

ABSTRACT: Philosophical concern over nuclear armaments raises questions about the logical and conceptual basis for deterrence theory as well as the effects of threats of nuclear annihilation on our common humanity. However, most philosophical concern centers around the morality of nuclear deterrence. It is sometimes thought that the doctrine of just war can provide a moral justification for nuclear deterrence based on threats of massive retaliation. Yet attempts to apply the doctrine of just war lead to a moral dilemma: although nuclear deterrence seems justified as self-defense, there are compelling reasons for concluding that threats of retaliation are immoral. Alternative deterrence policies might be thought to overcome the moral dilemma. However, counterforce strategy and antimissile defense, as recently proposed by President Reagan, must still depend upon immoral threats of retaliation. Proposals for a nonviolent national defense offer a possible solution, and serious attention should be given to claims that nonviolent defense would deter aggression.

Robert P. Churchill received his Ph. D. from Johns Hopkins in 1975, with a dissertation on civil disobedience. Associate professor of philosophy at George Washington University, he teaches philosophy of law, logic, history of philosophy, and philosophy and nonviolence. He has published articles on the philosophy of nonviolence and of law, and a forthcoming textbook in logic. He is also on the Board of Advisers of the Institute for Advanced Philosophic Research.

PHILOSOPHICAL reflection about the problems of nuclear armament and deterrence give rise to three kinds of questions: (1) logical and conceptual questions about nuclear strategy; (2) questions about the effects of nuclear technology on the meaning of humanity and our visions of life and death; and (3) moral or ethical questions about justifications for the use or threatened use of nuclear weapons.

An important role for philosophical analysis lies in scrutiny and criticism of the main concepts involved in deterrence and the assumptions underlying the arms race. What is the logic of the classical *para bellum* doctrine, which offers the paradox that the best way to ensure peace is to prepare for war? What is the meaning of "defense" and "security" in the nuclear age? What does "strategy" really mean when any use of nuclear power renders one liable to a massive counterattack? There is presently much disagreement among strategists preparing war scenarios over the proper criteria for rational decision making under uncertainty. Some defense analysts employ models of rationality imported from economics and game theory to describe the risks and options facing world leaders. A crucial task for the logician is to examine the wisdom of extending game theoretical criteria of rationality, such as the concept of utility maximization, to the situations of deterrence strategy.[1]

A second and different category of questions concerns the meaning of human life under the cloud of nuclearism. Secretary of War Henry Stimson declared, at the dawn of the nuclear era on 31 May 1945, that the making of the atomic bomb "should not be considered simply in terms of military weapons, but as a new relationship of man to the universe."[2] What is this relationship? And what is man's responsibility to the biosphere that sustains him and without which future generations will be impossible?[3] What is the phenomenon of psychic numbing that makes so many of us unable to contemplate sudden annihilation, and this strange double life that comes with the realization that all we have ever known or loved could be extinguished in a moment?[4] How has it come about that homicide has been bureaucratized and terror so easily domesticated in our lives?[5] These are among the philosophical questions to be asked about a world suddenly threatened with nuclear holocaust.

However, the issues that continue to receive most philosophical attention concern the morality or immorality of deterrence policies and the question whether the just-war doctrine can justify a national defense based on threats of massive retaliation. John Bennett forcefully stated the problem when he called on us to explain how we can live with our consciences knowing that our leaders are prepared to kill millions of

---

1. See Philip Green, *Deadly Logic* (Columbus: Ohio University Press, 1966); and Robert P. Wolff, "Maximization of Expected Utility as a Criterion of Rationality in Military Strategy and Foreign Policy," *Social Theory and Practice,* 1:99-111 (Spring 1970).

2. Quoted by Robert Jay Lifton and Richard Falk, *Indefensible Weapons* (New York: Basic Books, 1983), p. 66.

3. See Jonathan Schell, *The Fate of the Earth* (New York: Avon Books, 1982), pp. 99-178.

4. Lifton and Falk, *Indefensible Weapons,* pp. 3-127.

5. Henry T. Nash, "The Bureaucratization of Homicide," in *Protest and Survive,* ed. E. P. Thompson and Dan Smith (New York: Monthly Review Press, 1981), pp. 149-60.

children in another nation if worse comes to worse.[6]

MORAL QUESTIONS

If we maintain deterrence, must we live with a troubled conscience? This article will attempt an answer, and will discuss the moral case for and against nuclear deterrence—in particular, the morality of the deterrence proposals that presently guide our defense strategies, and the justifiability of these policies given reasonable beliefs that because of the uncertainties and dangers of the world, it is necessary to prepare a defense against aggression. Thus for the purposes of this discussion I presume that (1) some form of deterrence is necessary as a national defense, and (2) however we solve our defense problems, we must do so unilaterally, without expecting cooperation from the USSR, or any other adversary, on a nuclear freeze or multilateral disarmament. Of course these assumptions may be false; in fact I hope they will soon prove to be so. But it is certainly not now known that they are false, and starting with a worst-case analysis allows me to frame the issue as sharply as possible. Given quite reasonable beliefs in the need for self-defense against an adversary with nuclear arms, what is the moral justification for threatening to use our nuclear weapons to deter him from aggression?[7]

In evaluating answers to this question, I presuppose familiarity with the basics of deterrence theory. In addition the inquiry will be limited to cases in which the problem of aggression is most extreme, and therefore justifications most plausible. Thus while American strategists have often contemplated possible uses for nuclear arms in a "diplomacy of violence,"[8] I am concerned only with nuclear weapons as deterrents to direct attack upon the United States or its allies. For this purpose, strategic nuclear weapons exist as a second-strike capability that ensures U.S. ability to inflict unacceptable suffering upon the USSR even after sustaining an all-out nuclear attack. It is the threat of this retaliatory second strike, combined with the adversary's perceptions of the credibility of threats to use it, that produces the deterrent effect. As the political scientist Michael Walzer has said, "deterrence works by calling up dramatic images of human pain."[9] The object of the offense is not the adversary's armed forces so much as his mind.

DOCTRINE OF JUST WAR

What moral justification, if any, can there be for a policy of deterrence that rests the risk of mutual annihilation upon each superpower's perception of the other's intentions? Some theologians and ethicists do believe that such second-strike deterrence policies are not only

6. "Moral Urgencies in the Nuclear Context," in *Nuclear Weapons and the Conflict of Conscience,* ed. John C. Bennett (New York: Charles Scribner's Sons, 1962), p. 109.

7. This discussion also presupposes that moral principles are relevant to issues of war and national defense. Anyone who doubts this should see Richard A. Wasserstrom, "On the Morality of

War: A Preliminary Inquiry," in *War and Morality,* ed. R. A. Wasserstrom (Belmont, CA: Wadsworth Pub., 1970), pp. 78-101; and Michael Walzer, *Just and Unjust Wars* (New York: Basic Books, 1977), pp. 3-20.

8. Thomas C. Schelling, "The Diplomacy of Violence," in *Peace and War,* ed. Charles Beitz and Theodore Herman (San Francisco: W. H. Freeman and Co., 1973), pp. 74-90.

9. See *Just and Unjust Wars,* p. 269.

morally permissible but morally obligatory. Their arguments are drawn from a venerable tradition of reflection and moral suasion. The doctrine of just war concerns warranted uses of force or violence as a necessary means to secure a just cause: if it is necessary for a nation's leaders to threaten annihilation in order to protect innocent civilians from unjust attack, then it is morally obligatory that this threat be made.

Many contributions have been made to the doctrine of just war, but its classic formulation is generally attributed to St. Augustine.[10] St. Augustine reasoned that war is always an evil in the sense of being a human calamity, and violence in its nature is always evil. However, war viewed as a necessary measure, undertaken as the only means of defending the innocent from unjust attack, is not sinful. Under severe necessity, the lesser evil of violent resistance to injustice is the morally preferable act, tragic but not wicked.

How much does the doctrine of just war justify? It starts with the assumption that the rightness of the resistance depends upon the cause for which the war is fought. It also presupposes that the violence threatened or employed is required as the only recourse. The doctrine will therefore justify only wars waged in self-defense or for the protection of the innocent. Moreover, the cause must be backward looking, war waged only because of something intolerably unjust done by the adversary. This means that the doctrine will not justify war waged on the basis of forward-looking consequential or utilitarian grounds, even if this were a preventive or preemptive strike on a belligerent planning an attack. Thus the doctrine justifies nuclear deterrence only insofar as threats to retaliate are necessary to prevent unjust assault.[11]

Is the threat to retaliate really necessary? The familiar but dreadful truth is that we cannot be guaranteed that a nation capable of making a nuclear threat will not use it to its—perceived—advantage. In fact the effects of an adversary's use of a nuclear advantage would be so devastating that it is an intolerable risk, however small the probability of actual use. Consequently any nation confronted by a nuclear adversary, whatever the ideologies or adversary relationship involved, and capable of developing its own nuclear armaments, will find the reasons for seeking—relative—safety in a balance of terror compelling. Against an enemy willing to use the bomb, or perceived to be willing, self-defense is impossible by any means short of threatened retaliation. It therefore makes sense to say that the only compensating step is the awful threat to respond in kind.[12]

10. See selections from his *The City of God,* in *War and Christian Ethics,* ed. Arthur F. Holmes (Grand Rapids: Baker Book House, 1975), pp. 61-87; and Ralph Potter, "The Moral Logic of War," in *Peace and War,* ed. Beitz and Herman, pp. 7-16. Modern versions of the doctrine have a variety of theoretical bases. Barrie Paskins and Michael Dockrill, *The Ethics of War* (Minneapolis: University of Minnesota Press, 1979), pp. 191-245, derive the doctrine from Kantian ethical principles, although they deny its justification of nuclear deterrence. In *Just and Unjust Wars,* Walzer develops a version of the doctrine that is independent of any particular theological or ethical position.

11. See David Wells, "How Much Can the 'Just War' Justify?" *Journal of Philosophy,* 66:819-29 (Dec. 1969).

12. Walzer, *Just and Unjust Wars,* pp. 272-73.

Thus despite the monstrosity of the threat, deterrence averts a graver danger and thereby meets the test of necessity for just war. Much evidence also shows that despite the danger of instability, deterrence works. The Soviets believe in deterrence, and as David Holloway's research shows,[13] there is no evidence to suggest the Soviets believe either that they can win a nuclear war, or that victory in a global war would be anything other than catastrophic.

JUS AD BELLUM AND JUS IN BELLO

Despite the air of morality given to nuclear deterrence by the doctrine of just war, there are strong reasons for believing that retaliatory threats may not be justified after all. Even if war or preparations for war are justified as measures of restraint, the instruments of enforcement are so faulty that further constraints upon the waging of war must be imposed. The most important of these are restraints on the means of pursuing the just cause. In effect the doctrine insists upon the distinction between *jus ad bellum,* the morality of going to war, and *jus in bello,* moral choice in the selection of the tactics and instruments of warfare. Among the principles of *jus in bello*, three are directly relevant to nuclear deterrence: (1) the immunity of noncombatants from direct attack; (2) the use of the least amount of force necessary to restrain or neutralize the aggressor effectively; and (3) the rule of proportionality, which asserts that there must be due propor-

tionality between the end to be accomplished by a military action and the unavoidable harm inflicted in its pursuit.

It is in connection with the principles of *jus in bello* that charges of the immorality of nuclear deterrence arise. Threatening civilian populations completely disregards the distinction between combatants and noncombatants. Deterrence requires that millions be threatened as a means to influence the decisions of a few leaders. Thus deterrence requires that we treat human life as a mere object of policy and a means rather than an end. The theologian Paul Ramsey draws the analogy of deterring reckless automobile drivers by tying babies to the front bumpers of their cars. He points out that this would be no way to regulate traffic even if it succeeds in regulating it perfectly, for "such a system makes innocent human lives the *direct object* of attack and uses them as a mere means for restraining the drivers of automobiles."[14]

In response to Ramsey's argument by analogy, Michael Walzer maintains that the moral wrong of actions that harm the innocent is not a reason also to condemn actions that only threaten to risk harming.[15] Ramsey's innocent babies are not only exposed to terrible risks but also forced to endure a terrifying experience that is an actual harm. But nuclear deterrence, according to Walzer, imposes threats that do not restrain us or deprive us of our rights:

We are hostages who lead normal lives. It is in the nature of the new technology that we

13. *The Soviet Union and the Arms Race* (New Haven, CT: Yale University Press, 1983).

14. *The Just War* (New York: Charles Scribner's Sons, 1968), p. 171.
15. *Just and Unjust Wars,* pp. 270-71.

can be threatened without being held captive. This is why deterrence, while in principle so frightening, is so easy to live with. It cannot be condemned for anything it does to its hostages . . . it involves no direct or physical violation of their rights.[16]

Yet even if nuclear deterrence does not violate the rights of its hostages, it is nevertheless immoral. It commits a nation to a course of retaliation, since if a nation bluffs its adversary may learn this through espionage. But if deterrence does fail, and the opponent launches an attack, there would be no rational or moral reason to carry out the threatened retaliation. Indeed the leaders of the stricken nation would have conclusive moral reasons not to retaliate. Retaliation would punish the leaders who committed this unprecedented crime and would prevent them from dominating the postwar world; but it would accomplish no deterrent effect while massacring millions of innocent civilians in the attacking nation, and in other nations, would set back postwar recovery for the world immeasurably, and might even render the earth unfit for human survival.

IMMORAL THREATS

The immorality of nuclear deterrence lies in the threat itself, not in its present or even likely consequences. Paul Ramsey also recognizes this point: "Whatever is wrong to do is wrong to threaten, if the latter means 'means to do'. . . . If counter-population warfare is murder, then counter-population deterrence threats are murderous."[17]

Since it would be wrong to retaliate, and through moral intuition we know it to be wrong, then it cannot be right for us to intend to do it. Indeed moral systems depend upon some version of the so-called wrongful intentions principle: to intend to do what one knows to be wrong is itself wrong.[18] The necessity of this principle is obvious from reflection about our moral experience and is not denied by any major system of morality.[19]

Yet it might be objected that U.S. leaders intend not to annihilate Soviet citizens but to preserve peace. Thus by threatening to kill, they intend not to kill. This objection contains elements both of error and of truth. When these are sorted out, the intention to retaliate is still immoral, although certainly not as wicked as a direct and unconditional intention to kill.

In objecting that it is not immoral to intend retaliation, one may be confusing "intending an action" with "desiring the outcome of that action." Ordinarily an agent will form the intention to do something because he desires doing it either as an end in itself, or as a means to other ends.[20] In the case of nuclear deterrence, however, the intention to retaliate is entirely distinct from any

---

16. Ibid. But perhaps nuclear weapons can be condemned for their psychological effects on hostages. For a discussion of the psychological evidence, see Lifton and Falk, *Indefensible Weapons*, pp. 48-52, 54, 68, 77.

17. "A Political Ethics Context for Strategic Thinking," in *Strategic Thinking and Its Moral Implications,* ed. Morton A. Kaplan (Chicago: University of Chicago Center for Policy Studies, 1973), pp. 134-35.

18. Gregory S. Kavka, "Some Paradoxes of Deterrence," *Journal of Philosophy,* 75:285, 289 (June 1978).

19. Ibid.

20. Kavka, "Paradoxes of Deterrence," p. 291.

desire to carry it out. In fact the intention to retaliate is entirely consistent with a strong desire not to apply the sanction. Thus while the object of our leaders' deterrence intention is an evil act, it does not follow that in adopting that intention, or even desiring to adopt it, they desire to do evil, either as an end or as a means.

While the absence of a desire to kill is important, it is not sufficient to exculpate our national leaders for the intention to retaliate. What counts in establishing the immorality of their intentions are the preparations they make to retaliate, the signals they send to the adversary, and courses of action that may leave their hands tied and make retaliation almost automatic. These plans and actions underscore their willingness, in order to deter aggression, to accept the risk that in the end they will apply the sanctions and allow the world to be consumed.

The objection that it is not immoral to intend massive retaliation may also be based on the claim that the U.S. intention is entirely conditional upon the behavior of the adversary. We are intending not to attack, but to launch a strike only if the opponent attacks. Such conditional intentions seem strange because they are by nature self-extinguishing: the purpose of forming the intention to retaliate is to prevent the very circumstances in which the intended act would be performed.[21] Nevertheless the wrong intentions principle applies to conditional just as to unconditional intentions. When a terrorist hijacks an airplane at gunpoint and threatens the lives of his hostages, the immorality of his threat is not canceled by its being conditional upon the behavior of the officials he seeks to coerce. The same is true of nuclear deterrence. In addition to the leaders who decide to launch a first strike, millions who have no part in the decision will die or suffer. Thus one does not significantly change the immorality of the threat to kill innocent persons by making it conditional upon the actions of national leaders.[22]

A MORAL DILEMMA

Where we have persuasive moral reasons both for and against the same action, we have a moral dilemma. We must either accept our obligations to defend the innocent, in which case we threaten retaliation, or we do not threaten retaliation, in which case we abandon hope of effectively protecting the innocent. Thus it is both morally wrong for our government to commit us to a policy of massive retaliation involving immoral threats, and at the same time morally wrong not to do so. Walzer seems entirely correct when he says that "nuclear weapons explode the theory of just war."[23]

This moral dilemma surrounding nuclear deterrence policy is intolerable. But by what means can we escape from it? We could show that the dilemma does not really exist by denying one of its horns. We might marshal new arguments to show that there are moral reasons we had overlooked but which justify threats of nuclear retaliation. A second possibility is to show that there is

---

21. Kavka, "Paradoxes of Deterrence," p. 290.

22. But see Kavka's objection to this argument, ibid., p. 289.

23. *Just and Unjust Wars,* p. 282.

a nuclear deterrence strategy that evades moral censure. Ramsey has asserted that just war can support a counterforce deterrence strategy.[24] His argument is especially important because since 1973 counterforce strategy has become the officially preferred nuclear strategy in the United States.[25]

COUNTERFORCE DETERRENCE

Ramsey argues that it is possible to prevent nuclear attack without threatening to strike population centers in response. Strategic nuclear weapons can be targeted against nuclear installations, conventional military bases, and isolated economic objectives. This strategy could have the same deterrent effect as the conventional countervalue strategy, because although only military objectives would be targeted, a consequence of retaliation would inevitably be the unacceptable loss of millions of collateral civilian deaths.

However, the civilians likely to die would be the incidental victims of legitimate military counterstrikes. Herein lies the alleged moral superiority of counterforce strategy. These civilians are not hostages whom we have formed the—conditional—intention to kill. These collateral damages would be justified as an unavoidable consequence of a justifiable response; hence it is also justifiable to intend—conditionally— such a response.

Nevertheless there are serious difficulties with Ramsey's argument. First, could a retaliatory counterforce strategy really deter a first strike? Deterrence works only if the defender threatens

unacceptable harm, and in recent years there has been much speculation that with evacuation, hardened industrial sites, and civil defense, the Soviets might escape with as little as 10 million casualties—judged to be an "acceptable loss" by some defense consultants.[26] Thus the danger of collateral damage is likely to deter only if the threatened damage would be very great indeed, disproportionate to the value of the military site targeted. The proportionality rule bars use of the doctrine of just war to justify any number of civilian casualties on the grounds that although these casualties were unavoidable, we did not intend to kill them since we did not really aim at them.

Ramsey's response is to maintain that in nuclear deterrence, proportionality is to be measured against the value not of a particular military target, but of world peace itself.[27] But how are we to reckon proportionality between the—certain— loss of human life and any—uncertain— increase in world peace? World peace is obviously an end we value very highly, but does this mean that, according to Ramsey's logic, the more highly we value peace, the more lives we may threaten so long as any actual deaths would be only collateral? If this is what Ramsey means, then the word "collateral" has lost most of its meaning and "proportionality" has been defined so broadly as to void the rules of just war.[28]

In any event, Ramsey' proposal does not overcome the problem of immoral

24. *The Just War*, pp. 285-366.

25. James Fallows, *National Defense* (New York: Vintage Books, 1981), pp. 141-45.

26. See the testimony before the Senate Foreign Relations Committee of Retired General Daniel O. Graham, former director of the Defense Intelligence Agency, as quoted in Fallows, *National Defense*, pp. 145-46.

27. *The Just War*, p. 303.

28. Walzer, *Just and Unjust Wars*, p. 280.

threats. Since we know that counter-force strategy will deter aggression only if the threat to the civilian population is very great, and since we intend these threats to deter, it follows that we have formed the conditional intention to bring about their deaths after all. Like other deterrent theorists, Ramsey wants to prevent nuclear attack by threatening to kill very large numbers of innocent people, but unlike other deterrent theorists, he expects to kill these people without aiming at them. However, we might as well aim at them, if we know that a direct and necessary consequence of our attacking military targets would be their death.[29]

RENOUNCING RETALIATION

Counterforce deterrence provides no real solution to our moral dilemma, but there may be a second means of escape. This would involve denying the alternatives presumed in formulating the dilemma. It had been assumed, not without reason, that we must either accept our obligations to defend the innocent, in which case we threaten retaliation, or we do not threaten retaliation, in which case we abandon hope of effectively defending the innocent. But is it not possible to meet our obligations of self-defense and protection of the innocent without threatening nuclear retaliation? An affirmative answer has been offered: we develop a technological capacity for self-defense

that does not require threats of massive retaliation against the adversary.

On the evening of 23 March 1983 this proposal was dramatically presented to the American people by President Reagan. The president asked, "What if free people could live secure in the knowledge that their security did not rest upon the threat of instant U.S. retaliation to deter a Soviet attack, that we could intercept and destroy strategic ballistic missiles before they reached our own soil or that of our allies?"[30] The inference he knew we would draw is that such a system of self-defense would remove the moral opprobrium surrounding present deterrence policies. Such a system, if it could work, might also inaugurate a new era in strategic nuclear deterrence, a technological solution to the problem of vulnerability created by nuclear technology in the first place.

Could such a purely defensive strategy work, and would it really eliminate the need to make immoral threats? The development of new antimissile weapons would be destabilizing and might dangerously increase the risk of a preemptive Soviet strike. In the game of deterrence, the adversary's perceptions of our intentions are what ultimately count. And the Soviets are not likely to trust our claims that the new devices are purely defensive. Soviet leaders would correctly reason that since such weapons could knock out Soviet missiles sent in a second strike, it might increase U.S. capacity to prevail in a nuclear war. At present, the Soviet deterrent to a U.S. first strike is massive retaliation, and Reagan's proposed antimissile defense would effectively eliminate that deterrent threat. Consequently the Soviet's increased vulnerability would cause them to fear the possible sense of

29. I certainly agree that threatening to kill 10-20 million civilians by counterforce retaliation is not as immoral as threatening to kill 60-100 million by countervalue retaliation, other things being equal. But this reduction in the immorality of the threat can be achieved in a more straightforward way simply by cutting back on our overkill capacity, so that retaliation would be less massive.

30. *Washington Post,* 24 Mar. 1983, p. A12.

adventurism that knowledge of this edge might give our leaders.

An antimissile defense system would also consign the United States to the spiraling costs of a runaway anti-arms arms race. The history of the arms race since 1945 suggests that the new defensive systems would be quickly matched by technological break-throughs designed to overwhelm or outmanuever them.[31]

More important still is the following consideration. Suppose the Soviets continue to arm; then in the event of an attack, we could never be sure our antimissile system would completely neutralize their offensive weapons. Even a very low rate of failure during an all-out attack would result in horrendous losses, perhaps even annihilation. Thus it is clear that the threat of a retaliatory second strike must remain as the unexpressed but final recourse if the United States is to deter aggression with nuclear arms. The point is that Reagan and our national security managers know we would need to hold onto our second-strike forces as an insurance policy, and that is why the president's proposal seems so deceitful. By attempting to push the immoral threat of retaliation away from the light of debate and analysis, our leaders hope we will overlook its hideous reality. The Soviets also know we would keep a second-strike insurance, and that is why these so-called defensive antiballistic weapons would be perceived by them as offensive.

MORAL FAILURE OF NUCLEAR DETERRENCE

Nuclear deterrence as practiced by the superpowers fails the test of morality; its appearance of moral respectability arises from close association with perceptions of dire emergency. A stop-gap effort at conflict containment or postponement, it does not resolve international conflicts by removing their cause, nor does it bring about changes that lessen the danger of clashes. By exchanging immoral threats, the superpower players merely push the real problems into the background, taking the position that no solution at all is preferable to the risk of escalating a conflict that could lead to a nuclear exchange. In fact nuclear deterrence may well be self-defeating over the long run. Although real security no longer exists, our national security managers relentlessly seek to instill a sense of security in us by pursuing actions that objectively increase the danger: they build more and deadlier weapons.[32]

Furthermore, since nuclear deterrence requires credible threats that weapons may be used, its success diminishes its own credibility, and efforts to reassert its credibility threaten to bring about its failure. The runaway arms race is due only in part to worst-case analyses on both sides and current methods of weapons procurement;[33] it is also a product of the constant need to underwrite deterrence with the image of Armageddon. Since perceptions of our preparation for self-protection and of

31. For a discussion of the arms race and the futuristic weapons defenses envisioned by some analysts, see Ground Zero, *Nuclear War: What's In It for You?* (New York: Pocket Books, 1982), pp. 72-82, 199-211.

32. Lifton and Falk, *Indefensible Weapons,* p. 25.

33. Mary Kaldor, "Disarmament: The Armament Process in Reverse," in *Protest and Survive,* ed. Thompson and Smith, pp. 134-82.

our willingness to retaliate are directly correlated, nuclear deterrence will require greater efforts to ensure the survivability of our nuclear forces. What better way to communicate the seriousness of our intent than to commit a staggering proportion of the federal budget to the development of new weapons? President Reagan argued that defense budget cuts "will send a signal of decline, of lessened will, to friends and adversaries alike."[34]

Both President Reagan's proposal and Paul Ramsey's approach attempt to overcome the immorality of nuclear deterrence by making changes in strategic uses of nuclear weapons. Is there a common error in the assumption that deterrence is equivalent to military, and especially nuclear, defense capability? Neither deterrence nor self-defense is necessarily equivalent to threatening military might, and it may be this fact that a solution to the problem of self-defense must recognize.

NONVIOLENT NATIONAL DEFENSE

Deterrence connotes retaliation but this association is not logically part of the concept. As Thomas Schelling has indicated, deterrence occurs whenever a potential enemy is persuaded to abandon a certain course of activity because he sees that it is in his own self-interest to do so.[35] Thus deterrence is essentially a process of persuasion, and the method that persuades most clearly deters most effectively.

Nobody understands this fact more emphatically than the advocates of

nonviolent national defense or civilian resistance. Here is offered an approach to defense that escapes the moral dilemma. It takes seriously the obligation to defend the innocent, and its advocates claim that it would deter aggression; moreover it would overcome occupation and oppression if deterrence were to fail.[36]

Civilian resistance focuses upon the defense of a nation's basic social institutions, culture, and ideological beliefs by training the civilian population in organized nonviolent resistance and noncompliance. In addition to protecting human lives, a national defense must successfully protect a way of life: the institutions, rights, and principles that form the stable framework for life and provide a group with an organized expression of conscious preferences and commitments.[37] Civilian resistance therefore seeks to deter aggression by making it clear to any potential invader that he could not control and dominate the political and social life of the nation he seeks to invade. He would see that military occupation would not by itself give him political control and would not be experienced by the population as defeat; rather it would mean an extension of the contest of will and ideology.

36. Anders Boserup and Andrew Mack, *War without Weapons* (New York: Schocken Books, 1975); B.H. Liddell Hart, *Defence of the West* (New York: Morrow, 1950); idem, *Deterrent or Defence* (New York: Praeger, 1960); H.J.N. Horsburgh, *Non-Violence and Aggression* (London: Oxford University Press, 1968); Adam Roberts, ed., *Civilian Resistance as a National Defence* (Baltimore: Penguin Books, 1969); and Gene Sharp, *The Politics of Non-Violent Action* (Boston: Porter-Sargent, 1973).

37. Horsburgh, *Non-Violence and Aggression,* p. 106.

34. *Washington Post,* 24 Mar. 1983, p. A1.

35. *The Strategy of Conflict* (Cambridge, MA: Harvard University Press, 1960) pp. 6 ff.

Gene Sharp, a leading advocate of civilian resistance, asks us to reflect about the conditions that are most likely to create a nuclear attack.[38] Who fears and expects a nuclear attack the most today, and who expects one the least? It is precisely the nuclear powers who fear a nuclear attack the most, and this fear of attack, or of defeat in a major conventional war, may itself be the overriding temptation for a superpower to launch a first strike. Civilian resistance, which unlike nuclear forces can be used only for defensive purposes, would remove that danger and thereby reduce the chances of annihilation. In addition, while there remain some circumstances under which a nuclear attack might seem rational, given present deterrence policies, there appear to be no circumstances under which a nuclear attack on an unarmed nation would appear rational. It will surely be objected that civilian resistance could not save a nation from a maniacal opponent. However, since no one can predict what a maniac would do, there is no more reason to suppose that he would respond rationally to nuclear threats than that he would pointlessly devastate an unarmed and unthreatening country.

Walzer has objected that while nuclear deterrence depends upon inspiring fear in the adversary, in nonviolent defense the adversary would experience no fear, but at best only guilt, shame, and remorse. "The success of the defense [would be] entirely dependent upon the moral convictions and sensibilities of the enemy soldiers."[39] But this presumption appears mistaken. First, it has frequently been noted that inhibi-

tions of a political, social, and cultural nature are normally more decisive than fear in holding back the hand on the trigger.[40] Second, there is no reason to suppose that nonviolent deterrence must depend more than nuclear deterrence upon the moral sensibilities of the adversary. All deterrence policies must depend upon the adversary's calculations that the costs of aggression would outweigh the benefits, and this would be true no less for nonviolent defense than for nuclear deterrence.

The case for nonviolent defense has not been completed, but serious and intelligent criticism has also hardly begun. Civilian resistance has not received the attention it deserves. It may turn out that a nonviolent national defense would be impossible, or if possible, less acceptable morally than nuclear deterrence. But nonviolent defense is not foolish on its face, nor is it merely pacifism or unilateral disarmament under a different guise.[41] Its apparent moral superiority to nuclear deterrence obligates us to give it our careful attention. Indeed if threats of nuclear retaliation are morally permissible, then they are permissible only because deterrence is absolutely necessary, and nuclear threats are the only means of effecting this deterrence. Thus even those who argue for the moral superiority of nuclear deterrence, if they are earnest and sincere, must attempt to demonstrate the moral inadequacy of civilian resistance.

38. "National Defense without Armaments," in *Peace and War,* ed. Beitz and Herman, p. 360.

39. *Just and Unjust Wars,* p. 334.

40. Boserup and Mack, *War without Weapons,* p. 176; Green, *Deadly Logic,* p. 201.

41. Unlike many proposals for unilateral disarmament, nonviolent defense responds to the need for deterrence; and unlike traditional versions of pacifism or passive resistance, it advocates nonviolent force and coercion. On the concept of nonviolent coercion, see Judith Stiehm, *Nonviolent Power* (Lexington, MA: D. C. Heath, 1972).

Ballistic Missile Defense:
Reflections on Current Issues

By DAVID N. SCHWARTZ

ABSTRACT: Renewed interest in ballistic missile defense (BMD) must be seen against the background of technical, strategic, and political uncertainties. Technically a shift in emphasis from traditional to exotic technologies involves many uncertainties. While these may be resolved in the future, any such system will have to be extremely leakproof to offer an attractive defense of cities. Strategically BMD can have destabilizing consequences if not coupled with severe constraints on offensive forces; in particular, unbridled BMD competition could provide incentives for either super-power to strike the other first in a crisis. Politically the most salient consideration is the ABM Treaty of 1972; any move by the United States that seems to call its commitment to the treaty into question will raise political opposition domestically and among U.S. allies, and suspicions in the USSR. Future prospects may be enhanced if the United States makes clear that it has no intention of revising the treaty; moves ahead with offensive arms limitations; and reorients its BMD focus to the marginal role of defending retaliatory forces that remain after a period of offensive arms limitations.

David N. Schwartz received his B.A. in political science from Stanford and his Ph.D. in political science from MIT. A research associate in the Brookings Foreign Policy Program, he has just completed two years on the staff of the State Department Bureau of Politico-Military Affairs, with responsibility for policies relating to intermediate-range nuclear forces (INF). In this capacity he served on the U.S. delegation to the INF arms control negotiations in Geneva, May-July 1982. He is currently codirector of the Brookings-MIT ballistic missile defense project.

NOTE: The author wishes to thank his colleagues on the Brookings-MIT ballistic missile defense project for the sound education they provided on this issue; he would also like to thank Leon Sigal and Paul Stares for their helpful comments on an earlier draft. The views expressed herein, however, are solely those of the author, and should not be attributed to other members of the project, or to the Brookings Institution, its staff, or its trustees.

THE issue of ballistic missile defense (BMD) would probably have emerged on the political agenda even if President Reagan had not made his 23 March 1983 speech. BMD research had been moving forward at a reasonable pace, stimulated by the intensive efforts of the Carter and Reagan administrations to find some way of enhancing the survivability of U.S. land-based intercontinental ballistic missiles (ICBMs) against a Soviet first strike. Indeed BMD systems and configurations had been conceived as part of the MX/MPS system, and the more recently moribund MX/CSB—dense pack—system. No doubt the issue of how to protect our land-based strategic forces from preemption will remain with us for years to come. For this reason alone, observers of the BMD issue were predicting long-term interest in maintaining a vigorous BMD research program.

So the president's speech has not created an issue that otherwise never would have reared its ugly head. What the speech has done, however, is to raise the issue in the most dramatic way to the center of the national political agenda. It has also redirected the focus of attention on BMD, from the mission of ICBM defense accomplished via traditional technologies, to the mission of complete defense via exotic technologies. In the process, the president has created a national debate on the issue far earlier than it would naturally have occurred. He has placed considerable hope on breakthroughs in technologies that are highly uncertain.

Let me first review some of the basics of BMD technology, clarifying the distinction between traditional and exotic technologies. I shall then summarize some of the technical uncertainties involved with particular missions. Finally I shall turn to some of the strategic and political implications of the program the president has initiated.

TECHNOLOGY: DEMANDING CRITERIA

BMD systems are designed to destroy attacking nuclear weapons before they can hit their targets. The vast majority of these systems—traditional and exotic alike—must perform the same tasks in order to function effectively:

1. Acquisition. The BMD system must be able to determine, via remote sensing devices such as radars or infrared sensors, that an enemy missile has been launched, and locate it.

2. Tracking. The BMD system must be able to determine the speed and direction of enemy missiles and reentry vehicles (RVs) with enough precision to enable the system to predict its trajectory throughout its flight. Remote sensors such as radar, married to high-speed data processors, serve this function.

3. Discrimination. The BMD system must sort out signals to distinguish the incoming nuclear warhead from various decoys and radar chaff that the enemy will use to fool the BMD system into attacking the wrong target.

4. Interceptor control. The BMD system must direct the interceptor—be it a nuclear missile or a directed energy beam—onto the target, guiding the interceptor on the basis of the acquisition, tracking, and discrimination information derived from the first three steps.

5. Target kill. The BMD system must allow the interceptor to kill the incoming target. For a nuclear-tipped interceptor missile, this means that the interceptor must explode its nuclear charge close enough to the incoming

target to destroy it either by heat or by radiation, or else to knock it off target by blast. For a directed energy weapon, this means directing the beam onto the target, and assuring that the beam rests on the target long enough to destroy it.

It is not my intention to engage here in a detailed technical discussion. But this simple breakdown of the tasks for a BMD system permits some relatively straightforward technical observations.

First, the major technical controversy today is over different mechanisms for target kill. The traditional, well-understood kill mechanism is a ground-based interceptor missile, armed with a nuclear weapon, which can be guided close to an incoming warhead and then detonated to destroy it. Exotic technologies provide new kill mechanisms, some of which include X rays, chemical lasers, optical lasers, charged-particle beams, and nonnuclear munitions. Proponents foresee these systems deployed in space, to destroy enemy ICBMs soon after they are launched, or before the warhead separates from the booster rocket. Some of these technologies can also be deployed on the ground, to destroy warheads as they reenter the atmosphere, as ground-based interceptor missiles are designed to do.

The uncertainties over exotic technologies are considerable. Can they be packaged into an integrated system capable of performing the tasks described previously? Can the interceptor control and target kill tasks be done with enough speed and accuracy to handle the many thousands of enemy warheads against which it would be required to defend? Can development

and testing of these systems be accomplished without violating U.S. treaty commitments, not only with respect to the Anti-Ballistic Missile (ABM) Treaty of 1972, but the Outer Space Treaty of 1967 and the Limited Test Ban Treaty of 1963?

These questions are best left to the technical community, though even within this community there is disagreement regarding the feasibility of exotic systems. We can, however, set a standard against which the feasibility should be measured. Each of the tasks described can be associated with a probability of successfully completing the task. Assuming the probability of performing each task successfully to be independent from that of successfully performing each other task, we can multiply probabilities to get an overall probability of system success.

Let us assume, therefore, that a hypothetical system has a very high probability—99 percent—of successfully performing each individual task. This would translate to an overall system success probability of somewhere around 85 percent. This amounts to 15 percent leakage. A system with such a leakage may be quite acceptable for defending U.S. missile silos. At a minimum, it would force the enemy to allocate two warheads to every defended silo; if the enemy could be kept ignorant of which silos were being defended, the same effect could be had, with a smaller number of BMD systems than defended systems.

This assessment changes, however, if BMD is evaluated as a defender of cities or large populated areas. A BMD system with 85 percent overall reliability would be cold comfort to the citizens of, say, Philadelphia, who would have to cope with the damage done by the fifteen percent of the attacking weapons that leaked through the system. This is not to say that population defense is not feasible, though there is substantial reason to doubt the feasibility of total population defense. Rather the point is that 99 percent of reliability in performing each of the BMD tasks is not sufficiently leakproof to be interesting for a city defense.

STRATEGY: THE ROLE OF STRATEGIC DEFENSE

Questions of technical feasibility aside, BMD raises profound questions to which engineers and physicists can give no more confident answers than the layman relying on common sense. Is BMD a good thing? Does it promote stability and reduce the likelihood of war? Does it promote instability, and create new pressures for war? How does BMD interact with offensive strategic forces?

One way to approach these questions is to ask whether there are circumstances in which defensive measures can be viewed as provocative. At first blush this may seem to be an absurd proposition. Defensive measures by their very nature are not provocative; they cannot be used against an enemy, only against an attack. Indeed defensive weapons without offensive weapons are quite unprovocative.

But when the superpowers have a vast panoply of systems, most of which are offensive, there is a synergism between offensive and defensive systems that can produce an unstable result. Let us first examine the problem in the abstract, using argumentation familiar in general strategic deterrence theory.

If one superpower has substantial offensive capabilities to destroy a major portion of the other's offensive retaliatory forces, a BMD system could be viewed as an important part of that superpower's first-strike posture. The undefended superpower could fear that, after absorbing a first strike, its crippled retaliatory forces would be too small, and too uncoordinated, to breach the attacker's BMD system in order to mount a successful retaliation against the attacker. In this situation, an undefended nuclear power would have strong incentives to preempt, since this would be the only way to assure that its attack would have the desired effect. Even if the superpowers had roughly comparable BMD protection, this instability would persist in the presence of offensive forces capable of mounting a relatively successful first strike against enemy retaliatory forces.

It would be unlikely for a superpower to view the development of a serious BMD capability by the other side with equanimity. While preemptive posture has certain attractions, it also carries grave risks, and any country can reasonably be expected to attempt to avoid being confined to such a risky choice if an alternative is available at an acceptable cost.

With respect to BMD, such an alternative usually exists; every BMD system tested or deployed to date, and by far the majority of those being considered for future development, can be overwhelmed by an increase in offensive capability. Saturating a BMD system with a high number of RVs and with penetration aids of various sorts, including decoys, radar chaff, and so on, is always an option for a superpower determined to have an offensive retaliatory force that could ride out an enemy attack, and fearful of the impact of BMD on its own capacity to retaliate. This fact does not by itself render BMD meaningless; the defending country indeed may seek only to force the enemy to pay a higher attack price for destroying a particular set of targets. The issue rather is how easy it is to do this, and how determined an opponent is to overwhelm the BMD system. The destabilizing result of this may be that an extensive BMD deployment by one side may result in an offsetting offensive deployment by the other side; in addition, the other side may well seek BMD development of its own, which may create pressures for the side that initially deployed BMD to increase its offensive forces to offset the defensive reaction its BMD deployment has stimulated.

As articulated thus far, this strategic analysis is completely abstract and, while troubling, must be applied to a concrete strategic reality before any judgments about the stabilizing or destabilizing nature of BMD can be made. Several noteworthy points describe the present reality:

1. Both superpowers have enormous arsenals of strategic offensive weapons.

2. Even operating against the constraints imposed by the Strategic Arms Limitation Treaty (SALT) II regime, both sides have been able, through a combination of improved accuracy, reliability, and the multiplication of RVs with multiple independently targetable reentry vehicle (MIRV) technology, to develop the capability, in theory at least, to destroy a substantial portion of the other side's land-based strategic retaliatory forces in a first strike. While both sides have such a capability, some have

argued that the Soviets have the advantage in this regard; much of the strategic debate in the United States over the past five years has been directed at whether this asymmetry means anything. But this debate should not be allowed to obscure the point that both sides have this capability.

3. Neither the United States nor the Soviet Union is likely to develop, in the foreseeable future, BMD systems that offer a total defense, that is, one capable of providing either U.S. society or U.S. military assets with 100 percent protection. The most fruitful avenues for BMD research and development are likely to be in the direction of marginally increasing the survivability of strategic retaliatory assets.

The theoretical arguments about strategic stability, therefore, apply to the current U.S.-Soviet relationship only insofar as one can assess whether the U.S.-Soviet strategic offensive competition can be moderated through bilateral arms control. In an environment with no constraints on the offensive forces of the superpowers, the arms race phenomenon postulated in the theoretical construct could take on the aspect of a troubling reality.

THE POLITICS OF BMD:
THE PERILS OF PREMATURITY

Unfortunately the president's speech has placed the BMD issue—politically controversial for at least 15 years—at the front of the national agenda a bit prematurely. It came too soon in two respects: technically the direction he has charted has many uncertainties, and it probably would have been wiser to spend several years in quiet but intensive

R & D before raising the hope, or specter, of a total defense based on new technologies; politically he spent no time doing the careful preparation required to provide reassurance to those for whom BMD remains a highly controversial issue.

These problems will merge to present some serious risks to the administration as it moves ahead on this course. Perhaps the most important political factor here is the ABM Treaty of 1972 and its protocol of 1974, whose combined effect is to limit each superpower to no more than 100 BMD interceptors and associated launchers and radars, deployed either around the national capital or around an ICBM site. The treaty also forbids the deployment of mobile BMD, space-based, air-based, or sea-based BMDs, and places heavy constraints on R & D on BMD concepts based on new physical principles.

The treaty's strategic significance can be understood by elaborating some of the ideas of the previous section. Principally it has placed a cap, at a very low level, on systems that if left unconstrained could generate powerful arms race dynamics and pressures for preemption in a crisis. Its political significance lies in part in this achievement; indeed, for precisely this reason, there are many who view the 1972 treaty as the single most significant arms control agreement the United States has entered into. However, its political significance goes well beyond its strategic ramifications. It is seen by a large segment of the U.S. public, and by most Allied governments, as the cornerstone of the strategic arms limitation process. Indeed it is the only SALT agreement constraining weapons that is fully ratified and in force; SALT I has long expired, and SALT II, though signed, has never been ratified by the U.S. Senate—and probably never will be.

As such an important piece of the SALT edifice, the ABM Treaty is seen as a touchstone of East-West relations. The portion of the domestic public concerned with promoting strong, stable East-West relations will view any U.S. initiative that threatens to call into question U.S. commitment to the treaty with the deepest of suspicions. This is the principal reason for the controversy already aroused by the president's speech; the direction charted by the president, his protestations to the contrary notwithstanding, implies a willingness to take steps at variance with the treaty as it now stands, either through negotiating a revision to the treaty to permit testing and deployment of systems based on new physical principles, or through abrogation of the current treaty. This domestic political constraint on the president, imposed by the treaty, will require him to make a truly compelling case for such actions—a stronger case in fact than the Johnson or Nixon administrations were forced to make in the pre-ABM Treaty world when justifying Sentinel and Safeguard. In principle at least such a case could be made, but it is difficult to see the outlines of the argument in the absence of specific workable technology and a system concept that specifies most of the relevant parameters, including cost.

Thus the president is likely to find that he has stepped on a domestic hornet's nest, without insect repellent readily at hand. But this is not the end of his problems. The North Atlantic Treaty Organization (NATO) Allies will have distinct concerns over the course the president has chosen. These concerns will be of three sorts. Will a new U.S. BMD deployment protect them as well from attack? Will a U.S.-Soviet BMD race jeopardize the independent retaliatory forces of Britain and France? Will such a deployment irreparably damage the fabric of East-West relations?

The first concern derives its importance from the current, long-standing NATO policy of relying on the U.S. strategic retaliatory forces as the ultimate guarantor of alliance security. The U.S. extends its deterrent umbrella over its allies. Any move that tends to deemphasize the importance of strategic nuclear offensive arsenal of the United States will set them to worrying about what is to replace this guarantee.

In reality such fears are likely to be blown out of proportion, as they usually are when controversies arise over the credibility and reliability of the U.S. security guarantee to its allies. It would be wise for all parties concerned, primarily Allied governments, to await the outcome of the U.S. R & D effort before getting thoroughly worked up over the prospects of extended deterrence being undermined.

The second question, while of great consequence to Britain and France, is impossible to answer in the abstract. The viability of these countries' deterrents will depend not only on the scope and magnitude of Soviet BMD, but also on the objectives and missions set for these forces. What can be stated with confidence, however, is that Britain and France will share some basic apprehensions as a result of any renewed U.S.-Soviet BMD efforts.

On the third level, however, Allied fears will be easier to articulate. The NATO Allies have long viewed U.S.-Soviet relations as a bellwether of East-West relations. Firmly committed to East-West detente, they are likely to view with alarm any move that holds the potential of driving an even greater wedge between the superpowers than already exists. They are likely to fight hard for continued U.S. commitment to the ABM Treaty, and to view with greatest suspicion any U.S. initiative that implies modification or abrogation of the treaty. Importantly, this perspective is likely to be held not only by antinuclear demonstrators in Europe, but by the governments of each of our allies. So the president will have to make a compelling case not only to a domestic audience, but to a foreign audience as well.

The United States should not expect the Soviet Union to make this task of persuasion any easier. The Soviets know that the United States would pay a tremendous political price by unilaterally abrogating the ABM Treaty. For this reason alone, they are unlikely to be moved by an American initiative to negotiate modifications to the treaty. They could well take the attitude that unilateral U.S. abrogation of the treaty, which forces the United States to pay this price but leaves the Soviets free to respond, is preferable to a negotiated revision that lets the United States off the political hook but constrains Soviet options. They would perhaps feel differently if they actually wished to pursue an initiative of their own in the BMD area, and felt constrained by current treaty obligations from doing so.

Uppermost in the considerations of the Kremlin, however, is likely to be an assessment of whether the United States could gain a decisive strategic advantage, through technological breakthroughs that may not be available to the Soviet Union. On this subject we can only speculate, but it does seem clear that Soviet scientists are aware of the technical complexities involved in exotic technologies, and that they appreciate the difficulties the United States, or any country, will face in transforming these technologies into practical systems.

PROSPECTS FOR THE FUTURE

In addressing future prospects, a few caveats are in order, for the administration and for those to whom the administration must appeal for support for whatever initiative the United States pursues in this area.

To address the latter group first, it should be stressed that virtually no one can or does object to BMD in principle. Put another way, most people would find a BMD initiative, properly defined and structured, to be an acceptable proposition. To take an example, how many arms control advocates would oppose a limited new deployment of ground-based BMD interceptors to enhance marginally the survivability of ICBMs if the Soviets agreed to revise the ABM Treaty as appropriate, if offensive forces were slashed to very low levels, if the BMD could not be misconstrued as an effort to achieve a major population defense, and if the associated financial costs were relatively low? Very few, I would guess. The reaction to this proposition might be that the conditions postulated are implausible and irrelevant; but this only highlights the point that for most people, whether they realize it or not, the assessment of BMD is not a matter of abstract principle, but rather a matter of the circumstances in which it is pursued.

With this in mind, those who would tend toward a critical stance on BMD should clarify for themselves what types of systems, and what types of applications, are most troubling; what types of associated efforts the United States must pursue—for example, negotiations to gain Soviet agreement; and what financial costs would be acceptable. They may discover what they have believed all along, that BMD initiatives are not a particularly good idea. But in the process they will have gained a better understanding of why they feel the way they do, and will have developed a responsible and informed position that any administration will have to take seriously.

For its part, the administration faces the difficult task of pursuing a renewed effort to research the BMD problem without unleashing a domestic political backlash that will prevent it from doing so, and without placing relations with the Allies, and with the Soviet Union, in a state of total disarray. The task is difficult, but it is feasible. Certainly required is a concerted attempt to cool the rhetoric that has characterized its approach to Moscow over the past few months. Any initiative it chooses to pursue will be facilitated if it can avoid appearing to court confrontation with the Soviet Union, and if it can make a plausible case that it is attempting to achieve a stable *modus vivendi* with the other superpower.

Second, because of the highly controversial nature of BMD, and the value that many segments of society and Allied governments place on the 1972 treaty, it will be advisable for the administration to stress that it has no intention of pressing for a revision of the treaty. Technological breakthroughs, or other unpredictable factors, may make revision of the treaty at some distant time an attractive option. But there is no reason to raise the issue at this time, when the promise of such breakthroughs is clearly beyond the horizon.

A third approach, which will be useful in supporting the first two, would be for the administration to continue to press for serious strategic arms limitation on offensive weaponry. Leaving aside the issue of this administration's particular approach to START, it is clear that constraints on offensive force competition have merit on their own; they can promote stability, create the basis for a more stable political relationship, and bound the uncertainties facing U.S. strategic planners in the years to come. More to the point, a sustained, successful record of offensive constraints can work to reduce, in marginal but useful ways, the potential arms race instabilities that could result from a BMD initiative.

Looking into the future, one can imagine, far down the road, a world in which BMD plays a new, useful, but somewhat narrower role in the strategic equation than that envisioned by the president. If the START process can be made to succeed over the long term, and offensive forces—in particular MIRVed warheads—can be brought under control to the point where the capability of each side to destroy the other's retaliatory forces is materially reduced, BMD systems could be incorporated into an arms control approach that would allow them to perform the task of adding a margin of additional survivability to the remaining retaliatory forces.

There can be no expectation that such an approach can be adopted next year or even over the next decade. Many years of difficult negotiation on offensive forces would be required to pave the way for such an approach. Fortuitously, just such a period of time may be needed to understand fully the technical problems associated with new BMD concepts.

This may seem to some a radical approach, but it is not. After all, the president has called for an effort to provide a "total defense," and this alternative assigns BMD a far more limited task. However, given what we know about current technologies, and what we have committed ourselves to in ABM Treaty obligations, it is perhaps the only approach that would be sensitive to the many pitfalls of an intensified BMD effort, and yet permit such an effort to move forward.

*   *   *

QUESTIONS AND ANSWERS

Q (Paul Scheiter, La Salle College, Pennsylvania): How is it that President Reagan made his star wars speech? Is there something defective in the administration's policy planning system? Are some of the people ignorant of the technical aspects of these weapons systems, or is there incomplete communication between the administration and the CIA or other information or security groups, as to the true estimate of Russian power?

I read in *Science* magazine a week ago that Pentagon and State Department policymakers had very little input into that speech. It seems to have been almost all the work of President Reagan and Dr. Teller.

A: I think the story you read is basically true. In the drafts of the speech that were circulating around various agencies, the star wars paragraphs were deleted, and it was kept as a surprise to virtually all the bureaucracy involved. The morning of the speech, Pentagon officials testified before a Senate committee on strategic technology that the kind of exotic technology the president seemed so taken with was way down the road and held very little promise. They were administration officials from the Pentagon; there was obviously a disconnection. As to the reasons for the speech and why the president chose this particular thing to grab on to, we can only speculate. According to one school of thought, about this time in their terms, presidents become very frustrated with the problems of nuclear war and their inability to do anything except build, build, and build; this was one president's response to that very personal, agonizing insight. On the other side, there are some who would say that the president was trying to distract attention from the critical issue of the day: the budget, the hundreds of billions of dollars in deficit, the fact that Congress wants to cut his defense budget increase by half. I think he sincerely believes it. He was persuaded by some very persuasive scientists, but the fact is that there is a lot of disagreement about it; he listened to one side before he made the decision.

COMMENT (La Rocque): I agree. But the Pentagon did look at this, and testified in Congress several months before that they did not hold out much hope for it. It would cost not $100 billion but $200-300 billion. We are already spending $1 billion a year on antiballistic missiles, and simply by changing the name, as Dr. Schwartz properly pointed out, to ballistic missile defense—God knows, we are all for defense—they have made it much more palatable to the public. But I think the president painted a very cruel illusion. I do not care whether he believes it or not. It was fraudulent because it gave the people the impression that if we just keep spending money, if we just go the way we are, we can somehow defend ourselves. Even if we can defend ourselves against Soviet ballistic missiles and it worked 100 percent, it still would not deal with Soviet bombers, or the weapons and systems they would put in the air, as decoys or as actual weapons, to counter what we were putting up. The president has created an illusion, and a dangerous one.

COMMENT (Hirschfeld): The very day the president made his speech, the space systems program manager appeared before the House Armed Services Committee and was asked, "Do you need any more money for this stuff?" He said, "Gee, no, we have quite enough." He added that under the right circumstances, we could probably get 50, maybe 60 percent effectiveness out of existing systems, projecting them forward about 12 years.

COMMENT (Ralph Clark, Arlington, Virginia): The star wars business is based on a project called High Frontier in Washington. They are well organized. They have an office there. It is headed by retired General Daniel Graham, and Ed Teller is involved in it. They told me that this sort of thing is feasible when we can put one pound in low earth orbit for $100. I asked the director of research at NASA, "How much does it cost to put a pound in orbit now?" He thought a minute and said, "Well, right around $10,000." I asked, "How low do you think you can get it by the end of the century?" He said, "We might be down to $1000"—a tenfold increase right there.

Here Today, Gone Tomorrow—Nuclear Deterrence in the 1990s?

By ROBERT H. KUPPERMAN with Debra van Opstal

ABSTRACT: The United States faces a curious yet profound dilemma: we want to reduce the world's nuclear weapons but do not know how to do so without increasing rather than decreasing the threat that these weapons will be used. More and better of everything is clearly no answer; but it is not axiomatic that less is always more secure. Indeed the danger with small nuclear forces is that even marginal alteration in agreed-upon numbers can create a possibly decisive difference in the real balance of power. Nor does a defensive strategy—specifically the use of antiballistic missile systems— offer the technological panacea to render nuclear weapons obsolete. All systems leak; the question is, How badly? Anything much less than a perfect defense would more likely fuel an arms race—resulting in escalation on both the offense and the defense—than end it. In the end, what we need are analytically derived combinations of offense and defense by which we can realistically achieve dramatic weapons reductions without commensurate reductions in national security.

Robert H. Kupperman has been executive director for science and technology, Georgetown University Center for Strategic and International Studies, since 1979. He was chief scientist and deputy assistant director for military and economic affairs, Arms Control and Disarmament Agency, 1973-79, and assistant director for government preparedness in the President's Office of Emergency Preparedness, 1967-73. A member of the American Association for the Advancement of Science, and a fellow of the New York Academy of Sciences, the Operations Research Society of America, and the Los Alamos National Laboratory, he has published extensively on operations research, terrorism, crisis management, and strategic policy and arms control.

Debra van Opstal is a research associate with the Center for Strategic and International Studies, Georgetown University.

AS Edward Teller succinctly commented, "Mutual assured destruction is not an idea anyone can be happy with . . . and no one is."[1] Indeed we stumble mentally over the contraintuitive concept that the basis of peace is a solid deterrent, which really says that sheer, mutual terror is all that separates us from nuclear oblivion. That leap of faith has grown too large for many to bridge. The big-stick mentality appears naive in a vastly armed world.

In fact the nuclear perils that lie ahead are no longer limited just to the actions of the superpowers. Nuclear war can spread catalytically as the result of a detonation occurring at any trouble spot in the world; it can result from the efforts of a rogue state intent on promoting global carnage; it can occur by accident or as the result of miscalculation at a time of crisis.

We today face this grim reality of a world with many power centers, a world in which the United States and the Soviet Union can neither dictate the course of events with any certainty nor control them at times of crisis. The entire international system is marked by growing uncertainty simply because of the proliferation of independent actors and advanced weapons systems on the world stage. The mysteries of the atom are neither as difficult to master nor as secret as we had once hoped. There appear to be few barriers, and indeed a great many incentives, to the acquisition of nuclear weapons know-how and sophisticated delivery systems. Given the likely spread of weapons of great de-

1. Speech on Offense/Defense Mixtures, Science and Technology Seminar Series, Center for Strategic and International Studies, Georgetown University, Washington, DC, 18 Jan. 1983.

structive capabilities, superpower promises of world peace through a balance of terror appear singularly unconvincing.

In such an environment, the United States faces a curious yet profoud dilemma: we want to reduce the world's nuclear weapons, but we do not know how to do so without increasing rather than decreasing the threat that these weapons will be used. The menu of arms control proposals before the nation virtually blankets the spectrum between unilateral disarmament and continued nuclear arms competition.

Some, like George Kennan, flatly suggest that the United States could cut its nuclear arsenal in half without any profound effect on national security. The House of the United States is in the process of deliberating a resolution to freeze any further deployment of nuclear weaponry, thereby in some respects stabilizing the arms race. The president proposes to provide the country, at some point in the future, with a nuclear defense umbrella to end the arms race and virtually rid the world of offensive nuclear weapons; in the interim, however, modernization of our strategic and theater forces will continue.

A workable arms control process must certainly be consistent with perceived notions of national security; the problem is that there are very few notions about what national security really is or how best to achieve it. At one end of the security spectrum, more and better of everything seems to be the prevailing logic—a disputed position, which has fueled a worldwide antinuclear movement of potentially revolutionary proportions. At the other end of the spectrum are those who support, at a minimum, a nuclear freeze—a concept dismissed out of hand by force designers, most security analysts, and some arms control practitioners.

What has become perfectly clear is that we share no grand vision of a better world, a vision that recognizes where we are, where we want to be, and how we can get there. As long as the scriptures of hawk and dove remain holier than the quest for sanity and security, one fact remains: we shall never get there from here. Without a new willingness to re-think publicly the options for stable and substantial arms reductions, we are heading not for arms control but for Armageddon.

A STRATEGY FOR ARMS CONTROL

It is, regrettably, true that nuclear weapons cannot be uninvented; we cannot go backward in time to reconstruct a happier present. No magic wand can return us to a prenuclear era or even to a time of unquestioned military supremacy. In a very fundamental sense, we have little choice but to move forward with a responsible, wide-ranging arms control agenda.

The question of how much is enough to deter the Soviets from attacking us is always difficult. "More" is clearly not the answer. The proposed deployment of new systems like the MX—as a viable weapons system or as the bargaining chip President Reagan claims he needs —does not begin to address the real issue. It is not enough to cover ourselves in the now threadbare cloak of national security when we do not even know what patchwork will be needed to close yet another future window of vulnerability. On the other hand, it is not axiomatic that less is always better. In fact we must recognize quite specifically that under certain circumstances, there can

be greater risks in maintaining small atomic arsenals than large ones.[2]

The key to this convoluted logic is the requirement for verification. With the overwhelmingly large and seemingly absurd numbers of nuclear weapons and delivery systems that currently abound, we have little reason to worry about minor imbalances in opposing force structures. Another hundred warheads, slipped in among the thousands that already exist, would hardly upset the balance of power.

The danger with small nuclear forces is that even marginal alteration in agreed-upon numbers can create a decisive difference in the real balance of power at a time of crisis. Say, for extreme simplicity, that the United States and the Soviet Union mutually agree to reduce their intercontinental ballistic missile (ICBM) arsenals to 100 missiles apiece; at this level each believes that it could absorb a first strike and still inflict unacceptable damage on the other side. Now assume that the Soviets secretly add only 40 missiles to their arsenal, a level of treaty infringement that would be virtually impossible to detect. With 10 warheads on each of these missiles, the Soviets would then possess the potential capability of eliminating our entire missile force with a first strike.

With small nuclear forces, therefore, undetected treaty violations or even minor errors in verification can propagate overwhelming strategic advantages for the attacker. The incentives to cheat and the pressures for hair-trigger defensive launches increase even as the ability to deter war through the threat of retaliation decreases. One may suspect but

2. See Robert H. Kupperman, "Arms Control: The Impossible Dream," *Washington Quarterly* (Fall 1983), in press.

cannot be sure that the other side is cheating; the costs of being wrong are so high that both sides may very well adopt an offensive launch-on-warning strategy. The smaller each side's forces are, the more the verification of treaty provisions becomes essential—but in reality unachievable. Casting aside the usual political rhetoric, the instabilities arising from the wrong kind of agreed-upon arms reduction measures may turn out to entrench already profound fears, the kind that may make arms reductions impossible or worse yet lead to thermonuclear war.

This is not to imply that nuclear arms reductions are not possible; rather it is to insist that the process of mutual disarmament not be permitted to become a source of additional instabilities. One way to achieve sensible arms reduction is to design a core force structure that is relatively insensitive to Soviet folly and would be stable under a variety of arms control arrangements. The Achilles heel of all Strategic Arms Limitation Treaty (SALT) negotiations—namely verification—does not have to be as binding a constraint on strategic arms reductions. A core force could be designed in such a way that we need not worry if the Soviets wish to waste their money by marginal cheating.[3]

There are a number of opportunities for immediate arms reductions. One approach would be to withdraw the battlefield nuclear weapons now deployed in Europe. It is hard to conceive why the North Atlantic Treaty Organization should have anywhere near the 5000 nuclear weapons it now possesses. These

3. For more information, see Robert H. Kupperman and Donald M. Kerr, "A New Nuclear Force Architecture," *Washington Quarterly,* 5(1):119-30 (Winter 1982).

systems are in many cases approaching 20 years old. They were built without modern insensitive high explosives or secure fusing systems and are in fact insecure and unsafe. They are vulnerable to terrorist seizure or theft and are hardly credible to shore up a losing conventional war. Indeed these short-range systems are held at risk by conventional armaments fielded by the Warsaw Pact.

Another means of reducing the level of nuclear weaponry is to make our forces more efficient by exploiting the complementarity among the various systems. It is easy to create an illusion of vast force requirements by insisting that each element of the triad forces— ICBMs, bombers, and submarines— stand alone as an adequate deterrent, or that each element of our theater and strategic forces be a mirror image of its Soviet counterpart. But effective deterrence is based on the integrated capabilities of our theater and strategic land-, sea-, and air-based systems.

There is, for example, considerable overlap among the components of our traditional strategic deterrents; ballistic missiles, bombers, and submarines serve both assured destruction and counterforce roles. By dwelling incessantly on the vulnerability of any one element in our strategic arsenal, such as the land-based ICBM, we lose sight of the horrifying effectiveness of the entire force and assign wrong values to our judgments.

By the same token, there could be a great deal of complementarity between our strategic and theater forces. Under conventional planning, our strategic and intermediate-range nuclear weapons may be independently pretargeted without adequately exploiting their cross-targeting potential. Strategic weapons could be programmed to attack theater targets, while long-range theater systems could attack strategic targets as well.

If we were to reorganize the decision-making chain of command in a way that permits rapid and flexible retargeting, we could in effect multiply the utility of our existing forces; this in turn may permit substantial numerical reductions without diminishing the overall defense of the West. Equally important, cross-targeting of strategic and theater weapons may make the penalties of limited nuclear warfare unlimited.

THE STAR WARS DEFENSE

A wholly different approach to arms control, recently advocated by the president, postulates that the deployment of defensive systems—the so-called star war defense—can make possible dramatic arms reductions. This school of thought optimistically projects that new technologies, specifically antimissile systems, will make ballistic nuclear weapons obsolete. Reversing Clausewitz's dictum, President Reagan has taken a first step in advancing the notion that our best defense might be a good defense, seemingly a sound proposition in the nuclear age. Obviously if we could develop a perfect defense, there would be no need for ballistic nuclear weapons.

The catch-22 in this logic is that there are no technological panaceas; all systems leak. The question is, How badly? The inability of an antinuclear system to negate a few incoming missiles targeted against our forces would create merely a statistical problem: calculating how much we have left with which to counterattack. The failure to destroy only one incoming warhead aimed at a city could mean the death of hundreds of thousands of people, a risk we ought not to be willing to take.

Anything much less than a perfect defense, particularly if there are significant asymmetries between each side's defense systems, would more likely fuel an arms race than end it. With less than perfect defenses, we face two equally unpalatable options. If we continue to contemplate mutual substantial arms reductions—beyond removing antiquated systems or exploiting the synergies among our existing forces—we run the risk of having neither the defensive capability to negate an attack nor the certain retaliatory capability to deter one, the worst of all possible worlds.[4]

The combination of mutually reduced forces and imperfect defenses may actually create political incentives for a first strike. With a mutual assured destruction (MAD) strategy, unsatisfactory as it may seem, there can be no winners or losers; neither side can sanely claim a victory after a nuclear exchange. In a world of asymmetrically imperfect defenses, one party might perceive itself as a possible winner, a view that could upset the already fragile balance of forces. With imperfect defenses, the side that strikes first could use a large portion of its warheads and still reserve enough for a second strike against its opponent's cities or nuclear forces. The

4. A key issue here is the important distinction between point defense—defense of our ballistic missile systems—and area defense—defense of our cities. Point defense should not prove destabilizing, because it only diminishes the other side's ability to launch a successful first strike. By contrast, a substantial but imperfect city defense would undermine the other side's ability to retaliate punitively and thus destabilize the balance of power.

defender, who has already lost at least some portion of his potential retaliatory forces, must retaliate in sufficient numbers to penetrate the attacker's defense system, which is completely intact; he may not be able to reserve an adequate second-strike capability. The relative damage to be inflicted, as well as the forces to remain, may be perceived as favoring the side that attacks first.[5]

On the other hand, if neither side can afford to relinquish an unquestioned retaliatory capability—that is, if there is no concomitant force reduction—we face the prospect of parallel escalation of both the offense and the defense, at an appalling cost.

Ironically the greatest danger with this option is that the Soviets will refuse to compete. Despite a massive Soviet investment in military hardware, theirs is an inefficient economic system. An arms race expanded to both the offense and defense could severely strain our resources, but would likely bankrupt the Soviet Union. On resource and economic grounds alone, they may not be able to keep pace with this new level of threat. Hence the Soviets might be forced to look for new war-fighting outlets; indeed we may push them into the position of using unreliable proxies armed with chemical, biological, or radiological weapons to bolster a sagging deterrent.

THE POLITICAL DIMENSION

If we postulate the disruption of the bipolar balance, under a defense-dominant nuclear strategy, we cannot ignore the ripple effect around the globe. The diffusion of power, influence, and weaponry, and the proliferation of potential actors are trends already under way. The international system itself is becoming increasingly unstable simply because the traditional mechanisms of restraint have become decreasingly effective; it will be far less clear who can do what to whom and with what effect.[6]

It is ironic that we may one day look back upon the cold war era as a time of relative stability, an era in which the one major threat to the world was that its two largest powers would annihilate each other. For better or worse, that simpler age of bipolar confrontation is gradually evolving into an ambiguous and multiactor world. The question is, Can we afford to hasten its end by putting at risk the nuclear deterrent on which the current world order is based?

We may not know with any precision the extent to which developing nations have refrained from acquiring sophisticated and destructive weaponry because of superpower guarantees of peace. We do know, however, that there are few permanent barriers to the acquisition of such weapons. While the development of an atomic bomb is a dangerous and

5. Because the Soviets at present cannot launch a simultaneous attack of all their weapons against all U.S. force targets, there is no window of vulnerability inhibiting our capability to retaliate against their cities. Bombers and cruise missiles are inherently weapons of retaliation, whereas ICBMs and the next generation of submarine-launched ballistic missiles (SLBMs) can be used in either a city-busting or silo-busting mode. As long as we presume that our submarine force at sea is immune to surprise attack, this tends to reduce first-strike incentives even in the face of an effective ICBM/SLBM active defense.

6. For more information, see Robert H. Kupperman, Debra van Opstal, and David Williamson, Jr., "Terror, the Strategic Tool: Response and Control," *The Annals* of the American Academy of Political and Social Science, 463:24-38 (Sept. 1982).

difficult engineering job, the capacity to produce biological agents of mass destruction is all too realizable, the requisite technical talent and the laboratory facilities being virtually ubiquitous.

It is clear from the Sverdlovsk incident that the Soviets are already producing large quantities of anthrax, an ultra-lethal bacterial agent. It is equally clear that biological weapons can be no less lethal, and certainly no less capable of mass destruction, than nuclear armaments. An efficient aerosol anthrax attack delivered by Third World clients of the Soviets could be just as lethal as limited atomic warfare at the hands of the Soviet Union.

It is entirely conceivable that any rapid disintegration of the bipolar order would produce a scramble for just this kind of mini-deterrent. In such an environment, the dangers posed by well-armed rogue states like Libya or Iran— states that refuse to adhere to the most basic covenants of international relations —abound. But the danger that the Soviets will be forced to increase their reliance on these and other proxy states —in effect to substitute unconventional mechanisms for a strong nuclear deterrent—is even greater.

On stability grounds alone, the development of a defense-dominant strategy, which might force the Soviets along this path, must be approached with caution; the longer-term strategic implications of excessive dependence on area—city— defense systems could prove costly and potentially destabilizing.

A STRATEGY FOR DEFENSE

Were it feasible, a near perfect or perfect defense on both sides would likely be the *deus ex machina* to put an end to the arms race madness. Unfortunately technology cannot perform the impossible, and anything less than a very nearly perfect defense would be a disaster. This does not automatically imply, however, that there is no role for the defense in arms control. To the contrary, without some form of defense, there may be no credible arms control arrangement that would result in mutual deep cuts.

The problem is that we would like to achieve perfection but cannot and must not settle for its distant cousin; an imperfect defense is not just a minor step down from a perfect one. If we look to the other end of the spectrum, however— very limited, highly saturable defenses— we may derive cost-effective combinations of offense and defense that would permit secure, sensible, and substantial reductions in the number of nuclear weapons in our arsenal.

One critical stumbling block of all arms control processes has always been that of mutual trust; neither side can be expected to act in a manner apparently inimical to its own interests unless it is certain that the other side will act correspondingly. This reflects one of the classic problems in logic, the prisoner's dilemma. In its simplest version, this is the dilemma of two partners in crime who, after arrest, are each offered liberty if one will confess and implicate the other. If both confess, both will serve time; if neither confesses, they both will go free. Each criminal has two choices that give him freedom: confess and go free because the partner is silent, or remain silent in the hope that the partner will not confess. But who dares trust the partner to be silent? Without trust, both confess, both implicate the other, and both serve time—the least acceptable result for both. The analogy to the arms control process is clear, and the proxy for mutual trust is verification. Since verification is inherently imperfect, this proxy for trust needs to be bolstered, especially if very large reductions in arms are being sought.

One such proxy for trust might be a limited, indeed readily saturable, ballistic missile defense (BMD) designed to cope only with accidental launches or with just the first few warheads of an attack against our missile sites. In a world of very few weapons, very small numerical violations or even very small errors in verification can have a disproportionate effect on the balance between the two sides. It is here that some limited form of BMD, which by its very nature poses no threat unless the other side acts first, can eliminate the prisoner's dilemma by making small differences in parity immaterial, essentially replacing the need for blind trust with a defensive capability and thereby minimizing the effects of cheating.

Assume, for example, that the Soviets do violate an arms control agreement by adding 40 missiles, each armed with 10 warheads, to their arsenal. The level of treaty violation is small, virtually undetectable, but the effect on the strategic balance would be enormous, particularly after reaching a stage of having negotiated small nuclear forces. If we then assume, for simplicity, that anything over that 40-missile level of cheating is probably detectable by the United States, we can define the parameters of limited BMD: a buffering mechanism with a built-in upper limit designed to handle only that margin of undetectable violations that could upset the balance of power.

Such a precisely tuned system would allow us to deal with error or with miscalculation defensively without attracting war to our population centers. At the same time, it would deny an attacker any advantages gained from cheating. With limited BMD, it becomes irrelevant whether one regards Soviet intentions as benign or demonic; the system itself provides protection in the event that our faith in bilateral agreements proves misplaced, as well as a cooling-off period at a time of accidental crisis.

It is clear that there are no quick fixes, either technological or political, that will result in substantial mutual arms reductions. Bilateral political agreements, by themselves, offer few guarantees of a better world. The agreements, for example, to ban testing of nuclear weapons—while a useful area of cooperation—do not halt the development of more reliable or more accurate nuclear weapons; we must never delude ourselves by thinking that they might. Nor are treaties, once signed, necessarily inviolate or irreversible. The end goal of arms control is stability, not stasis. While BMD is not the easy answer we might wish for, it does provide a pathway to achieve dramatic weapons reductions without commensurate reductions in national security.

BEYOND DETERRENCE

At any level of weaponry, offensive or defensive, we must recognize that we pay an exorbitant price to achieve what amounts to a negative gain. More or fewer weapons is not the underlying problem; the end result of any strategy of deterrence can never be true peace but merely the absence of war through bilateral terror. Is it not time we begin to think beyond mutual assured destruction? Should not the mission of arms control be extended to developing the techniques and apparatus to disentangle the superpowers at a time of crisis?

Were the unthinkable to occur—and there is every reason to be concerned, as nuclear weapons proliferate, that it will—we must have foolproof ways of saying "stop" to the parties involved. Parallel saturable defense systems to provide a technical, albeit small, firebreak in the escalation process are only one initial avenue of approach. Beyond that, we should be looking for long-term, cooperative efforts that go beyond mutual recrimination.

Currently one of the prized showpiece accomplishments of the arms control process is the Standing Consultative Commission, a permanent body of military and intelligence professionals from both sides, which takes up alleged treaty infringements. Would it not be as reasonable to establish a new body, or expand the jurisdiction of the Standing Consultative Commission, in order to construct joint crisis management mechanisms that could terminate the threat of unwanted war in its earliest phases?

Such a body could examine new methods of crisis communications, procedures, and information sharing—possibly sharing analytic models of warfare to avoid miscalculation at a time of crisis. Even in peacetime, the risks of accidental launches and human or mechanical failure of command and control systems cannot be dismissed. The concept of a peacetime hot line is a good one, but it is at best a rudimentary and uncertain tool once tensions begin to rise. What is required is a guaranteed real time connection between the national command authorities on both sides to permit at least a temporary halt in hostilities. Conceivably such a body could jointly design a limited BMD capability to assure each side not only that the system itself was not invulnerable but also what levels of attack it could withstand.

We need to consider the kinds of joint efforts that may result in mutual advantages rather than stalemates; we need to find the physical, analytical, and diplomatic tools to achieve an understanding that represents more than merely the absence of war. Such cooperation between the superpowers does not obviate the need for distrust, but it can provide each side a better understanding of the other's intentions and capabilities at a time of stress. It may one day prevent us from blundering into nuclear holocaust.

Reducing Short-Range Nuclear Systems in Europe: An Opportunity for Stability in the Eighties

By THOMAS J. HIRSCHFELD

ABSTRACT: Assumptions about European security that have sustained the North Atlantic Treaty Organization (NATO) alliance since the 1950s are coming apart. Although steady Soviet force improvements continue, many European observers no longer see the Warsaw Pact as an overwhelming conventional force. Some think new conventional weapons technologies could hold the line; others just worry less about the danger of invasion. Strategic parity among superpowers has called NATO's flexible-response strategy into question, just as growing minorities have begun to ask whether nuclear weapons have become more menace than deterrent, thereby inhibiting nuclear weapon modernization plans. Arms control has lost credibility as a solution because there has been so little in contrast to the pace of weapons development and deployment. Some new, orderly pattern that restores support for NATO defense and credibility to the arms control process is badly needed. One way to begin is to draw down tactical nuclear arsenals on both sides, which could reduce the risk of nuclear war in Europe, enhance conventional strength, and support the Strategic Arms Reduction Talks and intermediate-range nuclear forces negotiations.

Thomas J. Hirschfeld is a retired State Department official and arms control negotiator. He was the deputy U.S. representative to the negotiations on Mutual and Balanced Force Reductions in Vienna (1979-82), deputy assistant director of the Arms Control and Disarmament Agency (1977-79), and a member of the Department of State Policy Planning Staff (1976-77). In addition he has served at U.S. embassies in Stockholm, Phnom Penh, and Bonn. A Marine Corps officer during the Korean War, he has degrees from the University of Pennsylvania and Columbia University.

N OW, as in the past, the precise military balance in Europe seems impossible to calculate to everyone's satisfaction. What is new is that for many Europeans who should be directly concerned, the Warsaw Pact seems less worrisome, or at least secondary, now that prospects of a Soviet invasion of Poland have receded. North Atlantic Treaty Organization (NATO) threat analyses pointing to steady and continuing Soviet force improvements no longer draw respectful and anxious audiences. Many have heard it all before, and either half-disbelieve the message or do not care much.

After all, despite warnings spanning more than a generation, the Russians have not come, at least not to Western Europe. That they have used their forces repeatedly in Eastern Europe does not necessarily increase the Warsaw Pact threat; Afghanistan is far away, and as long as the Russians are busy there, they will presumably leave Europe alone. People who would rather not spend money on defense in hard times find the alleged political consequences of force disparities unconvincing. They need more than doctrinal evidence of alleged intent to invade, or charts and graphs depicting continuous Soviet force modernization to become frightened and act, even in their own defense, without some immediate danger.

For a large and growing minority of Europeans it is nuclear war that seems the most frightening prospect, thanks in part to the failure of arms control negotiations and because of public statements by U.S. administration officials suggesting that nuclear war, even in Europe, and extended nuclear war in general is conceivable.

Thus rather than increased concern about Soviet force improvements, a peace issue has emerged to bedevil European elections, complicate NATO decision making, and interfere with Western force improvement plans, at least for nuclear forces. The peace issue takes the now familiar form of asking whether or not negotiations in Geneva on intermediate-range nuclear forces (INF) are sufficiently sincere, and whether the superpowers are serious about the Strategic Arms Reduction Talks (START). If the United States is not believed to be negotiating in good faith, then paradoxically the NATO bargain to deploy medium-range missiles to offset Soviet deployments of SS-20 missiles erodes. The United States is the unfortunate primary target of European pressures even from well-disposed politicians, not only because an ally is a more amenable target than an adversary, but also because much of the intelligentsia and almost all of the Left now have doubts about U.S. arms control intentions, fueled by Soviet propaganda and, among other things, by U.S. failure to ratify the Strategic Arms Limitation Treaty, abandonment of the Comprehensive Test Ban negotiations, and continued development of the neutron bomb. Arms control, the presumed ultimate alternative to nuclear confrontation, is now in doubt.

In short, while European security arrangements of yesterday like NATO are alive and functioning, divisions between Europeans and Americans on security issues are deeper today than they have been for a long time. Today Allied force improvements are harder to organize, and nuclear substitutes for perceived conventional NATO weaknesses are far more difficult to impose or agree on. Nuclear weapons themselves are no longer a mystery or an American monopoly, but a subject of increasing public debate, U.S.-style.

THE RUSSIANS ARE COMING?

Politics and peace issues notwithstanding, military problems do not go away. The best available unclassified source, the *Military Balance* for 1982-83 published by the London-based International Institute for Strategic Studies, describes the NATO-Warsaw Pact balance this way:

The numerical balance over the last twenty years has slowly but steadily moved in favor of the East. At the same time, the West has largely lost the technology edge which allowed NATO to believe that quality would substitute for numbers. One cannot necessarily conclude from this that NATO would suffer defeat in war, but one can conclude that there has been sufficient danger in the trend to require remedies. . . . The overall balance continues to be such as to make military aggression a highly risky undertaking. Though tactical redeployments could provide a local advantage in numbers sufficient to allow an attacker to believe that he might achieve tactical success, there would still appear to be insufficient overall strength on either side to guarantee victory. The consequences for an attacker would be unpredictable, and the risks, particularly of nuclear escalation, incalculable.[1]

In attempting to refine these judgments, analysts interested in suggesting either balance or superiority tend to pick those static indicators that appear to demonstrate their case. For example, the overwhelming military superiority

1. *The Military Balance, 1982-1983* (London: International Institute for Strategic Studies, 1982), p. 123.

of the Warsaw Pact is normally shown by counting the number of men and divisions each side could bring to bear on the center region over a 30-day period. Also pessimists normally compare the 17,000-odd Warsaw Pact tanks in Central Europe to the 7000 or so NATO tanks, without any reference to NATO's anti-tank weapons.

Those who would prefer to worry less about the military balance in Central Europe point to virtually equal overall figures for NATO and Warsaw Pact forces in numbers of men and aircraft and some equipment holdings, without reference to whether these forces are properly located to defend. Optimists also point to the reinforcement capability of the Federal Republic of Germany. The latter has claimed publicly to be able to put more than one million additional men into uniform and on line in three or four days.

Also ignored are political factors. For planning purposes the presence of France on the NATO side fairly early in a conflict is usually assumed by optimists and avoided by skeptics. One also could speculate about the reliability of the USSR's Warsaw Pact allies. The Czechs, for instance, have declined two opportunities to defend their soil against foreign invasion in this century. A scenario in which the Czech army invades Bavaria is therefore hard to imagine. Poland's interest in attacking the West is similarly open to question, at least for now. Indeed, the 19 Soviet divisions that now threaten the Federal Republic from the German Democratic Republic seem more likely to be employed in an easterly than a westerly direction in the near future.

Virtually everyone agrees that NATO force improvements must continue. The arguments, as always, focus around how much more to spend; money here and in Europe is harder to find in times of recession. More profoundly, however, a debate is emerging within the NATO alliance on what to spend it on, a debate that turns on the issue of further nuclear enhancement or pursuing an alternative conventional option.

NO FIRST USE?

NATO's nuclear doctrine, long a sacred cow, is now a matter of public debate. Four elder statesmen, McGeorge Bundy, George Kennan, Robert Mc-Namara, and Gerard Smith, have suggested that NATO reexamine its flex-ible-response nuclear strategy and substitute a policy of no first use.[2] These men represent responsible political voices from both major U.S. parties. Indeed Robert McNamara is one of the fathers of flexible response.

There also can be little doubt that all four are well aware of how difficult, divisive, and therefore dangerous a NATO debate about nuclear strategy can be. Yet they obviously believe that their recommended shift to a non-first-use strategy is timely, necessary, and worth the long, internal, alliance-bruis-ing process that would accompany a major policy change of this kind. Of all people, these four must remember that the current Allied agreement on a strategy of flexible response was reached in 1966 only after years of contentious debate on the possibility of providing NATO with a multilateral nuclear force involving a German finger on the nuclear trigger. It is therefore easy to understand

2. "Nuclear Weapons and the Atlantic Alliance," *Foreign Affairs,* 60:754-68 (Spring 1982).

former Secretary of State Haig's swift negative reaction and his estimate that very large conventional forces would be needed for deterrence were NATO to adopt a non-first-use strategy. As a former Supreme Allied Commander, he knew the players, the arguments, and the difficulties he and other officials would face in any NATO debate on changing the strategy head on, arguments he clearly hoped to avoid.

"Nuclear strategy" and "nuclear doctrine" are contradictions in terms because they imply that strategies for actual use exist, and that there are actually plausible ways to fight with nuclear weapons. Yet the 1981 public debate in the United States about whether NATO plans for demonstrative nuclear use at sea actually existed suggests that there is no clear idea of how a nuclear war would actually be fought in Europe, were one to start.

In fact, flexible response, the existing strategy for NATO deterrence, is a tacit compromise between two fundamentally different sets of hopes and expectations: on the one hand there was a European hope that, should nuclear war begin at some low tactical level in Europe, it would accelerate promptly to a strategic exchange in which the Americans and Soviets would incinerate each other over the heads of an only slightly damaged Continent. The American inventors of theater nuclear strategies, on the other hand, obviously hoped that conflict could somehow be limited and contained at the lowest possible level, presumably in Europe.

The existing NATO doctrine of flexible response clearly implies escalation to an intercontinental U.S.-Soviet nuclear exchange, without requiring it. Indeed it requires no nuclear use at all, but only warns that the alliance is willing to defend Allied territory with nuclear weapons, should the need arise. It specifies moreover that use of nuclear weapons will be appropriate to the need, without identifying further what that need might be. When the strategy was established, the expectation was that with a clear, uninterrupted link to American central strategic forces with various possible levels of escalation in between, the Soviets would pause lest they be smashed. This is less credible, now that the United States and the USSR have comparable nuclear arsenals.

In the past five years, the United States has attempted to improve deterrence at the European end by enhancing and modernizing the nuclear capabilities of NATO forces. This process, formerly an orderly and largely secret military matter, became a subject of public concern in 1978 with a U.S. proposal to deploy an enhanced radiation round—neutron bomb—on three short-range systems: 155 millimeter and 203 millimeter artillery, and the Lance surface-to-surface missile (SSM). Proponents pointed out that this largely incremental force improvement involved deployment of a weapon that had a safer—that is, easier to handle—round, was a better tank killer, and although more dependent on radiation than previous generations of weapons, was still primarily dependent on blast for its destructive effects.

The public uproar, however—begun in Europe by the Swedish press, which charged that the United States was about to deploy an antisocialist weapon that destroyed people rather than property—soon became a more sophisticated if shrill debate that fostered widespread public interest in nuclear weapon numbers, their location, characteristics, and modes of employment. Since that time, nuclear weapons deployments and nuclear strategy have become political issues and subjects of public debate in Europe in a way that has made further deployments difficult. The NATO strategy, although less credible than before, seems unlikely to change by fiat. It will have to shift slowly.

Almost concurrently, NATO commanders, most recently General Bernard Rogers, have begun to stress conventional alternatives to nuclear weapons, at least to short- and medium-range systems. Although no individual new weapons seem likely to revolutionize conventional warfare, several new kinds bid fair, if deployed, to assure a more confident conventional defense for the NATO alliance. These systems include precision guided munitions or smart bombs and missiles with their own sensors or guidance systems that can independently home all the way to the target; antitank guided missiles; laser-guided artillery shells; unmanned aircraft, or drones to spoof antiaircraft defenses; fuel-air explosives, many times more powerful than conventional explosives; and new electronic methods to identify targets and guide weapons to them. In combination, these new capabilities are designed to complicate the attacker's task and to make him less confident of a breakthrough, let alone a victory.

In Europe the presumed attacker has a difficult enough problem to begin with. The North German Plain, one area where Soviet tanks are supposed to execute their breakthrough, no longer exists as such; cities, towns, and shopping centers break up the terrain. To assure an initial breakthrough, the attacker must mass his tanks. Massing invites retaliation, or at least provides warning. Massing is also dangerous because it creates the most inviting kind of nuclear target. Declared strategies notwithstanding, no attacking Soviet general can expect to mass unseen and make his breakthrough. For the Soviet Union to win a war in Europe,

the USSR would have to conduct a general offensive without provoking an all-out war. Yet, while Soviet military literature emphasizes the offensive, and suggests that the USSR expects a nuclear exchange, nothing in Soviet writings discusses how to decouple a European nuclear war from a general one.[3]

Indeed the Soviets argue that it cannot be done.

What seems to emerge from all these factors is a situation in which NATO, as presently configured, continues to deter a Soviet attack by a combination of nuclear and conventional capabilities. Planned U.S. nuclear improvements at the strategic, intercontinental level seem unlikely to shift the balance in favor of the West in any profound way. Furthermore, any projected nuclear improvements at the theater or tactical level are today subjected to the kind of political scrutiny and resistance that suggests that further nuclear enhancements are difficult. Meanwhile the credibility of the NATO flexible-response nuclear strategy gradually erodes, not fully compensated for by improved conventional defense because new generations of weapons are expensive, and experience shows that most

systems do not work as well as advertised, once deployed.

Nevertheless, the potential aggressor, the USSR, has an attack problem as confusing, difficult, and fraught with lethal choices as ever. He cannot, in all likelihood, expect to mass sufficient force to mount a decisive attack without discovery and without risking nuclear retaliation, which by Soviet admission still implies the sort of strategic nuclear exchange that would devastate the USSR too.

THE OTHER FACTOR:
ARMS CONTROL

Today's conventional wisdom, here and in Europe, tends to favor arms control in general, if not in particular. The general arguments that disarmament is a snare, a delusion, and historically a failure are now heard largely on the extremes of the political spectrum—those conservatives not in office, and those on the Left and in the Third World who have heard a great deal of rhetoric about the need for arms control but have not seen as much as they profess to want.

Most observers agree, however, that arms control has not fulfilled the hopes of its earlier proponents, and that in the race between arms control and weapon development and deployment, the weapons seem to be winning. Yet something is being done—START in the strategic realm, INF negotiations for the intermediate-range or theater systems, the Mutual and Balanced Force Reductions (MBFR) in Central Europe, which today deals with conventional forces only. At issue in the European political debate is whether these three enterprises are serious, whether progress is possible, and, if so, whether any progress portends

3. Christopher Jones, "The Soviet View of INF," *Arms Control Today*, 12:3 (Mar. 1982).

a more stable, safer, and lower balance of confrontation or not.

There are serious doubts on all these points. Without resolving these arguments, it is worth looking at what systems these negotiations cover, and how the negotiations are linked, at least conceptually. What one discovers from this examination is the existence of an entire class of short-range nuclear systems deployed in the NATO and Warsaw Pact forward area apparently not limited by any existing or prospective arms control negotiations. Yet it is these very short-range systems that are the most likely to be used initially in the event of war. A case can be made that their gradual thin-out on both sides of the demarcation line, when coupled with conventional improvements, could sustain security and make the outbreak of war less dangerous by lowering the chance of early nuclear use and subsequent escalation.

ONGOING ARMS CONTROL TALKS

START is the substitute for what was called Strategic Arms Limitation Talks (SALT) by preceding U.S. administrations. Nevertheless, the limitations on strategic weapons established by the unratified SALT II agreements, SALT I, and the Anti-Ballistic Missile (ABM) Treaty, are being honored by the START participants, the United States and USSR.

Indeed START would have to have a different shape if these limitations did not exist. In START the United States proposes that both sides accept a ceiling of 5000 nuclear warheads, a one-third reduction for each side, and a limit of 850 missiles. Further, equalizing cuts on each side in total missile destructive power are to follow. The Soviets have counterproposed a freeze on the production and deployment of long-range systems and a ceiling of 1800 missiles and bombers in each nation's arsenal, in effect a 25 percent cut. However, the Soviet proposal is conditional; the reductions are tied to U.S. agreement not to deploy two new theater systems in Europe: the Pershing II and the ground-launched cruise missile (GLCM).

The Soviet nondeployment condition makes a mockery of the parallel U.S.-Soviet negotiations on intermediate-range nuclear systems, the so-called INF talks, by requiring the United States to give up its only leverage for elimination of the medium-range systems facing Europe as a concession in talks about long-range systems. This Soviet condition brings back a long-standing feature of Soviet SALT positions, insistence that all weapons that can strike Soviet territory, called forward-based systems, regardless of how they are characterized by the West, be included in the negotiations. It is interesting to see that this latter point is repeated, in other forms, in the Soviet INF positions, as will appear later.

The INF talks, sometimes called Euromissile talks, were initiated by NATO in 1979 to forestall further growth in the Soviet intermediate-range missile force. NATO was specifically concerned by the growing numbers of mobile SS-20 missiles. These consist of a mobile launcher with three independently targetable nuclear warheads and a range of 2300-2700 nautical miles. NATO countries agreed among themselves that unless agreements were reached between the United States and the USSR on reducing these systems, deployment in Europe of 572 American

Pershing II ballistic missiles and U.S. GLCMs could begin by the end of 1983. Whether to begin U.S. missile deployments on schedule, or delay deployments pending arms control progress, is presently the number one security issue in public debate in Europe. Preventing U.S. deployments seems to be the USSR's primary strategic concern for 1983, or at least the most immediate one.

Both parties differ on what is to be negotiated away, and therefore on what the balance is. The United States says that the Soviets lead six to one—that is, 3825 to 560—in intermediate-range launchers. By adding systems of Allies to the U.S. count and dropping certain systems from their own side, the Soviets try to show balance—986 U.S. versus 975 Soviet. Depending on what weapons are counted, and whose, one perceives superiority, or rough balance. These are of course essentially political calculations.

As in START, the actual positions of the two sides are still far apart. The United States calls for the dismantlement, rather than just removal eastward, of all Soviet intermediate-range missiles, not only those currently deployed in the western USSR, in exchange for NATO scrapping its Pershing II and cruise missile deployment plans. The United States offers to follow agreement on the land-based systems with limits on other intermediate-range systems, without specifying what these would be. The USSR has proposed to reduce, by moving the mobile launchers eastward, the number of intermediate-range missiles based in the western USSR to the level currently deployed by France and Britain—a total of 162 missiles maintained by both countries outside the NATO framework. In exchange, Moscow wants no deployment of U.S. Pershing II and cruise missiles in Europe, and agreement with NATO to reduce to equal levels Europe-based nuclear capable aircraft.

Finally, the MBFR negotiations in Vienna are now concerned exclusively with the reduction of conventional forces in Central Europe. They remain stymied on issues like the Warsaw Pact personnel count, and what on-site inspection, if any, is tolerable. There is agreement in principle on other points, like a ceiling of 700,000 ground force personnel in Central Europe on each side, as the outcome of the negotiations. Between December of 1975 and December of 1979, NATO offered to trade U.S. Pershing I launchers, F-4 nuclear capable aircraft, and warheads against Soviet tanks. Warsaw Pact failure to take up this offer resulted in its withdrawal after four years on the table. There is no longer any nuclear equipment in MBFR.

Thus ongoing arms control negotiations, as they affect European security, presently cover nuclear weapons as follows: the unambiguously long-range or strategic systems—intercontinental ballistic missiles and bombers, and submarine-launched ballistic missiles— of the United States and the USSR, in START; and the intermediate-range, land-based ballistic and cruise missiles belonging to the United States and the USSR, in the INF negotiations. British and French systems are still excluded because the British and French accept neither coverage of their nuclear weapons as bargaining chips, nor any compensation for the continuing deployment of their systems by trading U.S. systems.

NUCLEAR SYSTEMS NOT COVERED BY NEGOTIATIONS

Not limited by any ongoing negotiations are the short-range or tactical nuclear systems, which exist in large and growing numbers. These are listed in Table 1.

As discussed earlier, the shorter-range systems are normally justified by their ability to complicate the attacker's problems. Their deployment makes the organization of an offensive build-up and a massed armored attack difficult, because of the attacker's calculations that they may be used early by the defender. Put differently, a potential attacker's assumption that the artillery tubes facing him could fire nuclear rounds suggests, for instance, a need to eliminate the forward-deployed artillery before massing armor. Massing armor, a clear signal of intention to attack, on the other hand, invites strikes by nuclear artillery. Short-range systems are dangerous because their forward position risks their early use and the subsequent escalation of nuclear conflict; moreover many short-range systems like artillery could be overcome early on.

No one has come up with a plausible scenario in which a significant forward area has been overrun and sizable Western forces endangered, without requiring use of some small nuclear weapon. Reliance on the cool heads of U.S. presidents and local politicians seems somewhat quixotic under those circumstances; preventing more nuclear use after the initial shot or shots is a hope and a prayer rather than an expectation. Although this combination of imponderables is supposed to deter Soviet attack in the first place, it is less comforting to contemplate what happens if an attack actually takes place.

Deployment of short-range systems, which has been going on since the late 1950s, has also been justified by a perceived conventional inferiority. This perception reflects more than simply counting the Warsaw Pact forces potentially arrayed against NATO. In Central Europe, at least, it reflected the need to defend as far forward as possible for political reasons, that is, it is unreasonable to expect the Germans to sit in the front lines and provide half the troops for the common defense without assuring them that every inch of their narrow territory will be defended. Yet planning to meet this political requirement denies the defender the normal advantages of maneuver and the organization of defense in depth. Calculations of inferiority also reflect U.S. warfighting practice, which requires destruction of identified targets. This in turn depends critically on the relative number of weapons and firepower that each side brings to bear on each target. In the 1950s nuclear weapons with their awesome firepower seemed like a good way and a cheaper one than deploying additional conventional forces to compensate for these perceived shortcomings.

Yet the escalatory dangers of short-range systems were recognized early. Still in Germany and undeployed for 25 years are hundreds of nuclear land mines. Were they deployed, and were one set off by an invading tank, World War III's first nuclear explosion could

TABLE 1
TACTICAL NUCLEAR DELIVERY VEHICLES IN EUROPE*

	Number	Range (kilometers)		Number	Range (kilometers)
U.S. systems in Europe			Soviet systems in Europe		
Pershing 1A short-range ballistic missile (SRBM)	108	720	Scaleboard SRBM/12/SS-22	70	490-1000
Lance SRBM	36	110	Scud SRBM/SS-1/SS-23	460	150-350
203 millimeter artillery	56	16	FROG (Free rocket over ground) SRBM/SS-21	482	70-120
			S-23 artillery	168	30
155 millimeter artillery	252	18			
U.S. systems under double key with European forces			Launchers of other Warsaw Pact states		
			Scud SRBM	143	150
Pershing 1A SRBM	62	720	FROG 3-7	205	70-120
Honest John SRBM	90	40			
Lance SRBM	61	110			
203 millimeter artillery	231	16			
155 millimeter artillery	1454	18			
French systems					
Pluton SRBM	42	120			

SOURCE: John Grimwade, "Nuclear Weapons in Europe" (Chart), *Times* (London), 16 Nov. 1981, p. 6; *The Military Balance, 1982-1983* (London: International Institute for Strategic Studies, 1982), pp. 112-13, 115-18; Jane M.O. Sharpe, "Four Approaches to an INF Agreement," *Arms Control Today,* 12(4):7 (Mar. 1982).

*Nuclear capable aircraft are sometimes included as tactical nuclear systems. Including aircraft, however, raises almost intolerable complexities, including issues of where they are based, what their range is, what their flight profiles might be—what range and what load at what altitude—and whether the aircraft's primary mission is nuclear or not. The systems listed here are unambiguously tactical, systems with a range of 1000 kilometers or less. "In Europe" includes systems in the European territory of the USSR. In fact, most of the Soviet systems are on Soviet territory: some 40 SS-12/SS-22, some 270 Scud/SS-23, and some 320 FROG/SS-21 launchers. Soviet launchers and Eastern European launchers with warheads in Soviet custody are located in the German Democratic Republic, Poland, Czechoslovakia, and Hungary, in addition to the USSR. On the Western side, one or more of the tactical systems listed are located in Belgium, the Netherlands, the Federal Republic of Germany, Italy, Greece, and Turkey, not to mention Pluton in France. Figures are illustrative of relative magnitudes, rather than precise.

punctuate the first day of conflict. Escalation to artillery, other launchers, and air-dropped nuclear weapons, and for that matter progress toward strategic exchange, would presumably be accelerated. So they remain undeployed.

ALTERNATIVE PROPOSALS

It would seem best to scale down those systems that are most likely to be used early. Former Secretary of Defense James R. Schlesinger said it best:

Several hundred U.S. tactical nuclear weapons carefully selected and tied to a coherent nuclear doctrine would make far more sense than the current potpourri of thousands. . . . Forward deployment of U.S. tactical nuclear weapons also invites early Soviet and Warsaw Pact nuclear preemption in any conflict. Forward deployment for both reasons thus would shorten the time of a purely conventional attack. A first line conventional defense backed by a second line theatre (i.e., longer range) nuclear weapon defensive force makes more sense.[4]

Yet as shown in Table 1, since Schlesinger's 1975 statement the USSR and its allies have deployed large numbers of tactical launchers themselves. Although NATO deploys more— 2402 NATO to 1528 Warsaw Pact—this numerical advantage disappears when one removes the shortest-range systems, the artillery tubes. If one removes artillery tubes, or rather confines artillery to conventional loads, and compares the remaining NATO nuclear launchers with Warsaw Pact nuclear launchers outside the USSR, the

4. *The Theatre Nuclear Force Posture in Europe: A Report to the U.S. Congress in Compliance with PL 93-365* (Washington, DC: Department of Defense, 1975), pp. 25-30.

launcher balance is some 409 to some 630, a significant numerical advantage for the Warsaw Pact.

The International Commission on Disarmament and Security Issues, a high-level study group with NATO and Warsaw Pact membership, led by Swedish Prime Minister Olof Palme, recommended in 1981 the negotiated withdrawal of all nuclear weapons in Europe to a distance of 150 kilometers from the line of demarcation in each direction. When this suggestion was more formally broached to the USSR the following year by the Swedes, the Soviets agreed in principle but suggested instead a band of 600 kilometers in either direction. Aside from making them look even more peaceful than Palme, the Soviets' modification would have had the self-serving effect of moving the forward area out of range of all deployed Western short-range systems except Pershings, and aircraft, and of largely denuclearizing both parts of Germany. For its part, NATO objected on the grounds that this suggestion called the established flexible-response strategy into question, and presumably because even a 300-kilometer-wide denuclearized zone removed large numbers of those systems, which complicated the attacker's tactical choices by making it more difficult to mass armor.

Here an arms control scheme designed to prevent the outbreak of nuclear war collided with what the strategists in place regard as their defense requirements. Thus for practical reasons other ways to reduce nuclear risks should be considered. Four more or less simultaneous efforts seem worth trying.

1. NATO should plan to reduce the shortest-range systems—nuclear artil-

lery, Honest John SSMs—and ultimately eliminate them. Initially these could be partially replaced by some smaller number of longer-range systems, such as an improved, longer-range Lance launcher. Denuclearizing perhaps half of the nuclear artillery and deploying a smaller number of longer-range SSMs would continue to complicate the attacker's job, improve control over nuclear release, and enhance conventional defense by freeing artillery for conventional fire missions. Some appropriate version of the newly planned mix of shorter-range systems should be subjected to negotiated East-West limitations through arms control (see number 4, following).

2. NATO needs a simultaneous modern conventional system acquisition program, focused on complicating the potential adversary's armored attack problem. Western force modernization that concentrates on making life difficult for an adversary armored assault commander can be perceived as defensive, and in any event provides a militarily rational substitute for short-range nuclear systems.

3. Useless, undeployable, unsafe, or antiquated systems—e.g., nuclear land mines and older warheads—should be withdrawn promptly, for those very reasons, and as a painless way to acknowledge Allied concerns about the risks of nuclear war. These weapons are dangerous, and except for beefing up the Western count in numerical force comparisons, their retention makes little sense. Guarding and maintaining them takes manpower, consumables, equipment, and money away from conventional defense. Retaining these systems in Europe as arms control bargaining

chips is probably useless. It is hard to see what the Soviets would pay for undeployable nuclear land mines, for example.

4. We should engage the Soviets in talks on limiting and then reducing short-range systems and the nuclear storage sites that serve them. Since virtually all governments concerned claim they want fewer nuclear weapons in Europe, some scheme for East and West to thin them out, in common, should not be impossible to devise with a little patience and a great deal of ingenuity. Once we decide on ways to thin out the shortest-range systems, and deploy fewer, longer-range ones, we should engage the Soviets in a dialogue on how to cap and reduce theirs, in parallel. Here the MBFR negotiations would seem the likeliest forum. Adding back a nuclear element would give these talks a degree of military relevance they no longer enjoy, and the kind of political attention that makes arms control progress possible. It is also true that all the countries where nuclear weapons are deployed in Europe, except France, are participants in the MBFR negotiations. Thus organizing multilateral discussions, a difficult and time-consuming diplomatic problem in itself, is largely done.

What the actual tradeoffs might be on each side is too complicated to deal with here. As to verifying such arrangements, systems that potentially carry other kinds of warheads, like chemical or conventional explosives, are particularly difficult to verify by space-based sensors, the so-called national technical means. Yet it seems clear that the Warsaw Pact states, including the USSR, might be more willing to accept inspection of their forces outside the USSR than of Soviet forces on Soviet territory. They have suggested as much, informally.[5] If this is true, and an adequate inspection scheme can be nego-

5. Barry M. Blechman and Mark R. Moore, "A Nuclear Weapon Free Zone in Europe," *Scientific American*, 248(4):35 (Apr. 1983).

tiated, then a controlled mutual thin-out in Central Europe, leading ultimately toward short-range system elimination, can presumably be organized.

If that were done or even begun, publics, governments, and forces here and in Europe should feel safer—not a trivial outcome.

* * *

QUESTIONS AND ANSWERS

Q (Hugh Annet, Trenton State College, New Jersey): Do you believe the Soviets would genuinely like equality in retaliatory capability? Do you feel that there is a genuine will on their side?

A: The Soviets, like most governments, are stuck between competing purposes. The question is not, Are you for something or against it? Rather it is, Are you for this, and if so, how well would you pursue it if it cost you something in another area? As far as Europe or arms control is concerned, I believe the Soviets need to project the idea that there has been movement toward the success of what they call socialism, what Brezhnev used to call the socialist commonwealth. With this success they fulfill a series of ideological purposes, which they have had since the beginning of their society; this is what legitimatizes it, what gives it its moral underpinning. What value do they ascribe to that, as against the impossibility of actually conducting nuclear war, recognizing the differences between nuclear war and conventional war? The trade off between those sets of values is, I would say, in the direction of attempting to avoid nuclear war while stoutly pursuing what influence they can on the other track. What this turns into, in practical terms in arms

control, is a policy of active negotiation, tiny concessions, great advertisement of each concession, and a requirement for a great deal of patience. I would say they have demonstrated that they are serious about pursuing arms control, without having demonstrated entirely clearly that they are serious about arms control outcomes in all areas.

COMMENT (La Rocque): Every country has two policies, the declared policy and the real policy, and sometimes they are in consensus. It does not make much difference anymore as to who is sincere, who is insincere, who is ahead, who is behind. We can both destroy each other, and it simply does not make much difference. But I do not think we ought to hang around and speculate. We ought to test the Russians. In 1981 the Russians introduced a treaty to the United Nations to bar all weapons in space. Our government will not talk about it. I do not know if the Russians are sincere, if such a treaty can be verified, or if it is propaganda. But I would like our government to sit down with the Russians and see. I would like our government to say that on 1 July 1984 we are going to stop testing nuclear weapons and will not explode any more, as long as the Soviets do not explode any more. On 2

July we would find out how serious they are, and how serious we are.

COMMENT (Schwartz): I would agree that it is well worth the effort to test out Soviet intentions. But to guess at Soviet intentions before we have some clear view—and it is an extraordinarily closed society—involves real complexities. A couple of weeks ago, an article by Flora Lewis of the *New York Times* discussed the Soviet reaction to the Baruch Plan—this would have been late 1945 or 1946—to hand over all U.S. nuclear weapons to an international agency that would administer nuclear power. The United States would essentially give up its nuclear weapons. Apparently Mr. Baruch said, "What we really want to do here at the end of this war is to establish a basis of equality between our two countries." The Soviet response was quick and chilling: "We are not interested in equality. What we are interested in is having a free hand to pursue our national interests." There are two sides, at least, to reading Soviet intentions. But I would certainly be willing to test them out the way Admiral La Rocque suggests.

Q (Fred Greenwald, Norristown, Pennsylvania): We have the Pentagon, which has the responsibility for preparing for war and winning war. We have the service academies, which are preparing men and women to work in our armed forces to defend us. Why has there been so little support for the concept of a peace academy, one that Senator Daniel Inouye's task force reported on over a year ago?

A: Forgive me for taking issue with you directly. This is an ancient chestnut. One of the issues is, What in blazes would one do with the graduates of the peace academy? West Point produces second lieutenants who in the fullness of time become lieutenant generals, if they do terribly well. The Foreign Service Institute of the Department of State produces vice-consuls who become ambassadors, ministers, and what have you. It is hard to believe that an institution of the kind you describe has a proper role as an educational institution. There has been some thought about turning such an institution into a clearinghouse, either for information that takes issue with some official positions, or to do what the Arms Control and Disarmament Agency is supposed to have done over the years, to make some form of public case for arms control. The trouble is that these two ideas of what such an institution might do have never clearly been reconciled, and I think that is one of the reasons it continues to languish.

COMMENT (Greenwald): The United Nations has recognized it, and an academy for peace has been established in Costa Rica.

ANNALS, *AAPSS,* **469,** September 1983

Western Europe: Cycles, Crisis, and the Nuclear Revolution

By CATHERINE McARDLE KELLEHER

ABSTRACT: In the 1980s European policies regarding the use and control of nuclear weapons will reflect two different developments. The first is the scope and duration of the current debate about nuclear deterrence and defense, which has dominated public discussion since NATO's decision to deploy intermediate-range nuclear missiles. Less obvious is the second, the emerging agenda concerning the requirements and limits of British and French nuclear independence, the program of nuclear modernization, and the goals of arms control negotiation in Europe. Crucial to the outcomes will be the evolving views of new European leaders and the policy choices of the United States.

Catherine McArdle Kelleher is professor in the School of Public Affairs at the University of Maryland. Educated at Mt. Holyoke and MIT, she has written widely on problems of European security and policies toward the use and control of nuclear weapons in Western defense. She has served as a consultant to government agencies on issues of security and arms control, and was a member of the National Security Council staff in the first years of the Carter administration.

NOTE: This article draws on research conducted, together with William K. Domke and Richard C. Eichenberg, under a grant from the Ford Foundation's International Security Affairs Program.

91

I N 1983 there is no more dramatic evidence of the paradoxes of the nuclear revolution in warfare than the range of policies and popular attitudes held in Western Europe. The most cursory attention to media reports suggests that the leitmotif is the rejection of all things nuclear—nuclear weapons, nuclear energy, doctrine of deterrence based on nuclear risk. For the last three years the streets of the major West European capitals have seen demonstrations, protests both peaceful and violent, petitions and political mobilization, and the emergence of effective, mass-based antinuclear organizations outside the domain of customary politics. The number of participants equals the largest popular outpouring of the postwar period; the tenacity of the popular protest and the stridency of the demands for change almost match those surrounding the primary postwar concern for individuals—employment and the search for continuing prosperity. Responses to opinion polling have reached levels of opposition to nuclear weapons not seen since the late 1950s.

In the welter and noise attending the antinuclear movement, it is easy to miss several other developments in European policies and politics that will affect the pattern of nuclear capabilities in the decades to come. Both nuclear haves and nuclear have-nots face critical choices in three areas: (1) the requirements and limits of nuclear independence in the 1980s and 1990s; (2) the adaptation of existing nuclear and nuclear capable forces to new technologies; and (3) the procedures and potential for the control of nuclear weapons, in Europe and throughout the world. The choices to be made on these issues are not completely mutually exclusive, nor are the asso-

ciated political and military costs easily predicted or isolated from other more general foreign policy calculations.

This article will touch on each of these three areas and suggest the issues raised and the options each of the Western European states has developed to pursue its policy goals, political and economic as well as military. But it will start with what is most important of all: the context in which these choices will be made, the milieu and the present dominance of the antinuclear movement in popular perceptions and attitudes. In many senses this is what will frame the choices to be made by these states in at least the near term and touch upon the basic axioms of the postwar international system.

THE ANTINUCLEAR CONTEXT:
PROTESTS AND PARADOXES

Perhaps the most important aspect of the antinuclear movement is the basic assumption upon which it builds: the use of nuclear weapons on European soil will wreak levels of damage and death inconceivable even to those who experienced the devastation of World War II. The reason lies in part in the character of postwar European society—thickly settled, economically interdependent, reliant on sophisticated technology and complex industrialization for daily existence, and therefore extremely vulnerable. A second cause is the vast quantities of nuclear weapons now held on European soil or reserved elsewhere for use in either defense or attack on European targets.[1] The broad-

1. For the Western side alone, the present estimate of warheads stored on European soil is approximately 6000 or more. This does not include warheads that may be brought to Europe in

est analysis shows storage of a destructive potential far beyond that wielded by all combatants from 1939 to 1945. And the general trend has been to a greater and greater cumulation of nuclear capability, by the European states and their principal ally, the United States, as well as their major opponent, the Soviet Union.

However low the risk of nuclear conflict may be, no European state, as indeed no national state, can now secure the defense of its population or territory from nuclear attack. The existing British and French nuclear forces lie far behind the forces of the United States and the Soviet Union in both number and capability. Mobilization of all available resources for a possible European force would, in the view of many analysts, lead at most to rough nuclear parity, quite apart from the problematic political integration and questions of military credibility involved. Dependence on the nuclear guarantee of the United States is therefore an unavoidable reality; reliance on a strategy of deterrence, on continuing avoidance of war at any level in Europe, is the basic political choice.

The question heard repeatedly over the past three years is, What is the cause for dramatic antinuclearism now? None of these assertions is new or involves new calculation of threat or risk.[2] Both the expert community and the attentive foreign policy publics have been aware of the dangers of nuclear conflict since the 1950s. The initiated saw the results of the Carte Blanche exercises or the Ivy League scenarios; the publics engaged in the protests known as *Kampf dem Atomtod* or the Campaign for Nuclear Disarmament (CND) or the traditional Easter marches. Should there have been any public question on the calculation of potential damage, the early 1970s saw the publication of the damage estimates of the von Weiszäcker group or repeated showings of the BBC's *The War Game*. And while still somewhat dependent on the American forum for detailed weapons data, there have been several generations of writers, journalists, and analysts in each European country committed to the exploration of issues relating to security and nuclear weapons.

Causes

Speculation about the sources for the present unrest are many; conclusive evidence on which to choose among competing explanations is far more rare. One theory, espoused both in Europe—for example, by Willy Brandt and others in the Socialist International—and by members of the Reagan administration, is one of a "knowledge gap" or "generational effect."[3] Broadly stated, the primary cause is seen in the emergence into political life of a generation that expects continuation of prosperity and the detente of the 1970s as the normal state of international affairs. Whether through lack of education or lack of leadership, this group—roughly

the event of conflict, or those designated for systems presently deployed outside of Europe but with assigned responsibilities for European targets.

2. For one account of the German experience in the 1950s, see my *Germany and the Politics of Nuclear Weapons* (New York: Columbia University Press, 1975).

3. A more analytic statement of this hypothesis can be found in Stephen F. Szabo, ed., *The Successor Generation: International Perspectives of Postwar Europeans* (London: Butterworths, 1983), pp. 43-75.

25 to 40 years of age—sees any addition to Western, and often Eastern, nuclear capabilities as unnecessary and probably immoral as well. The basic balance has been set; the facts of Europe's military division are less important than the political and economic moves to offset or overcome the resulting tensions and separation. The Soviet build-up is not questioned; what is not acknowledged is any specific new political or military consequences flowing from these increases in the 1970s. And whatever the Soviet Union has done, the West should not carry out its decision of 1979 to deploy new long-range theater nuclear forces, the 572 Pershings and ground-launched cruise missiles (GLCMs). To do so is to threaten stability, or sometimes to create yet another occasion of risk to be overcome or contained.

There is a considerable body of writing, particularly by Europeans and American Europeanists, that supports this explanation. At the simplest level, the largest number of those 1 million or so who marched in Bonn, in Amsterdam, and in London were younger than 40; so are many of the antinuclear spokespersons in the major European political parties. Related research by Stephen Szabo and Ronald Inglehart shows a broad shift in generational values on all major public policy issues, and an expressed willingness of those interviewed in public opinion polls to take political action consistent with these beliefs.[4] On issue after issue, the concern is with the quality of individual lives, a concern for social and political justice, and a commitment to change past patterns of class, caste, and privilege. The doctrines and

the dicta of the past establishment are always to be subject to question and close scrutiny—whether these concern the cold war, the primacy of international commitments over domestic economic and social priorities, or the inviolability of defense budgets and governmental secrecy.

But there is also much to indicate that this is not a complete explanation or even perhaps a primary cause. Observation of public protests as well as the scrutiny of, say, the membership rolls of the new European Nuclear Disarmament (END) coalition reveal a substantial number of partisans older than 40 and another group of what must be called the settled middle class. There is even a small but notable group of leaders and activists who observed the first cycle of nuclear protests in the late 1950s—1956-59 on the Continent, 1955-61 in Britain—but have become mobilized only over the past four or five years. Moreover a number of studies suggest that there is far less uniformity of belief, or even policy preference over a spectrum of issues than the theory of generational change suggests. The more than 55 percent of those polled in England, Germany, and Holland who oppose the stationing of long-range theater nuclear forces (LRTNF) in Europe, for example, obviously encompasses a number of societal groups and age cohorts.[5]

Perhaps the greatest amount of unexplained variance is composed of the differences in both the range and the intensity of antinuclear sentiment across

4. Ibid.; Inglehart, *The Silent Revolution* (Princeton: Princeton University Press, 1975).

5. An extensive analysis of these and other trends can be found in David Capitanchik and Richard Eichenberg, *Public Opinion and Defence,* Chatham House Papers in Foreign Policy (London: Routledge and Kegan Paul, 1983).

the major West European states. Pierre Hassner has argued persuasively in terms of a divergence in the European traditions of northern Protestants and southern Catholics.[6] Even in those countries in which there is an ecumenical character to the antinuclear movement—notably Holland and to a lesser degree the Federal Republic of Germany (FRG) the dominant influences seem to stem from the generalization of the Protestant heritage of individual responsibility and the search for moral justice in the primary activities of this world.

Still left unexplained is the case of France, where the antinuclear weapons movement has attracted few supporters and has yet to reach even a limited level of organized activity inside or outside the party political arena. The election of a socialist government, protentially at least somewhat more receptive to antinuclear sentiment, has had little observable effect; the attempts of other national movements to stimulate a greater French response have also met little success. The vast majority of the French population continue to support nuclear weapons as the principal security instrument for their own country and, in contrast to other European populations, to show only a limited increase in concern about new risks of nuclear war. Moreover every effort was to be made to retain the advantages flowing from France's special nuclear position on the Continent.

Perhaps one overarching factor behind all of these variations is what I call the cyclical nature of the Western debate about nuclear policy and control.[7] Involved are really three separate but interacting cycles: (1) the American domestic debate, which is the product of budgets, elections and technological imperatives; (2) the American-European or Atlantic debate, in which the issues are most often questions of the sharing of risk, of burdens, and of control; and finally (3) the domestic debates within each European state, which are influenced by tradition, location, and the pressure of domestic demands. Most often these cycles are interactive but not simultaneous; that is, they affect one another but are separate in timing and effect. For much of the history of the North Atlantic Treaty Organization (NATO), for example, there has been a lag between the American debate and Atlantic confrontations of at least 18 months; the experience of the LRTNF decision of 1979 suggests a similar time period between NATO deliberations—largely the High Level Group meetings of 1978 and early 1979—and national discussion, at either the cabinet or the parliamentary level.

What has happened over the past four or five years is the explicit interaction and thereby intensification of these three cycles. The effect was all the more dramatic given the relative quiet of the 1970s and the era of benign neglect of nuclear control issues through American involvement first in Vietnam and then in Watergate. The continuing work

6. Perhaps the earliest statements of this argument appeared in his discussion paper prepared for the Woodrow Wilson Center Security Program of the Smithsonian Institution, Washington, D.C., in 1981.

7. For a more extended discussion of the specific historical interactions over NATO's intermediate-range nuclear weapons plan of 1979, see my "The Present as Prologue: Europe and Theater Nuclear Modernization," *International Security,* 5 (4): 150-68 (Spring 1981).

of the Nuclear Planning Group allowed for ongoing expert discussion and the narrowing of at least technical differences. Once President Carter placed renewed emphasis on defense within NATO, and then more generally on American defense preparedness, the American and Atlantic cycle of discussion began simultaneously.

Two further factors brought interaction to a new high: first, the self-imposed delay of the cycle of technological improvement and modernization in the face of the last stages of Vietnam—for example, delay in the Pershing update or the updating of obsolescent battlefield munitions and weapons; and second, the political impact in every European polity of the neutron bomb fiascoes of 1977-78. Involved was not only a new level of political outreach and organization among protestors but also the first public exposure, in over a decade, of the absence of nuclear issues from cabinet debates even among coalition governments, and the problems posed by the chronic uncertainty of the many actors involved in the American debate on nuclear issues. The stridency of the Reagan administration and its completion of the more conservative, militant trend in defense emphasized during Carter's last two years merely acted as the final catalyst to fuse the three debates, and to magnify—to a degree seen last in the early 1960s—popular fears and opportunities for direct public mobilization on nuclear issues.

The effect was most dramatic in those countries and among those groups that had the most at stake in these cycles of debate.[8] The FRG's vulnerability ap-

peared in all areas—as indeed had always been true when a major shift in American military strategy or force structure was in process, as in 1954, 1962, or even 1974. Chancellor Schmidt's weakness within his own party as well as in the governing Social Democratic/Free Democratic (SPD-FDP) coalition only made the situation more significant. Britain was involved, given both the strong ideological and political links— particularly between Thatcher and Reagan, who glory in the same opponents —and the set of defense realignments Britain was then facing, especially in the nuclear area.

The Netherlands was from the outside perhaps the least predictable participant. But given the priority it has always accorded German political stability in the postwar period as well as several unique developments in political and social-religious trends in the 1970s, the stake of the Dutch governments and of Dutch political activists was obviously considerable. France, on the other hand, was clearly outside the Atlantic circle and was linked only through its domestic political commitment to contain any German disruption of the European balance. Threats to Germany's integration within the NATO defensive structure, whether from within the FRG or from outside, were to be quickly and decisively countered; and the United States, the primary guarantee of German good behavior, was to be supported.

Consequences

What will be the long-run effect of this mobilization of opinion and action against nuclear weapons? A number of

---

8. The exception here is Italy, which reportedly was the only NATO nation that had actually had a parliamentary vote on possible deployments on Italian soil prior to the formal NATO vote of December 1979.

observers, including several influential voices within the Reagan administration, suggest that the movement will parallel the course of the CND efforts of the late 1950s. This would mean several years of intense activity and expanding popular support, followed by periods of apathy and frustration, declining attention and activism, dwindling finally to acts of political theater and a small core of true believers. One official interviewed in 1982 drew the analogy with the antiwar protestors of the American sixties, who ultimately settled down, and wanted to buy houses, too.

Less cynically, others asserted the difficulties of sustaining any mass movement, particularly on an issue involving extreme risk and few simple solutions. Their prediction was that once the LRTNF missiles have actually arrived, once the NATO governments have actually acted, protests will decline and opinion will subside. The short-term result may well be substantial political alienation and a lack of meaningful debate on future nuclear issues—as was true in the years after the *Kampf dem Atomtod*. But the protestors, a minority even in Holland, will fade from public view and the views of the inarticulate majority, who seemingly believe in the maintenance of the most favorable nuclear balance possible and in continued reliance on nuclear deterrence, will again prevail. These historical parallels are thought-provoking but not necessarily conclusive.

A critical variable is unquestionably the behavior of the Soviet Union and the way it will affect domestic opinion. It is wrong to attribute more than a small fraction of the impetus for the antinuclear movement to Soviet agitators or direct Soviet intervention; at times Europeans have seen the Soviets and

national communist parties scrambling to keep up with relatively unorganized actions.

Moscow, however, has shown considerable sophistication in exploiting every possible opportunity to conduct a campaign of smiles, and shows every indication of continuing to do so—whether in arms control initiatives, receptivity to visiting delegations and letters from peace-loving children, or in fanning the on-going Atlantic disputes about appropriate approaches to trade and future arms limitation. The era of detente and the forging of new economic links during the 1970s have given the Soviets new channels of access to every European polity—far different from the frozen ties of past phases of antinuclear mobilization—1956-58 with memories of Hungary and Berlin, for example. And while events in Poland remain a grim reminder of the realities of Soviet control, the Soviets so far have been able to keep channels open and to avoid any direct action that would catalyze West European opinion against them or invite West European reprisals.

A factor that may point toward a decline in the domestic political effectiveness of the antinuclear forces is the generally conservative trend in recent national and local elections. The most publicized case, the German national election of March 1983, seemingly produced a mixed result: the entry of the antinuclear Greens into the parliament and the continuation of the Christian Democratic-Free Democratic (CDU/CSU-FDP) coalition under Kohl. Attention to the degree of the conservatives' victory and the magnitude of the loss suffered by the SPD, which sought to capitalize on the antinuclear sentiment demonstrates, however, a significant negative trend. Parallel developments were observable in the skirmishing for the British general election that was held in 1983 and led to a Thatcher victory; trends in Holland and Denmark are less strong, but may be seen as partially related.

The consequences in the short run are threefold. First, these victories signal the triumph of status quo policies—as, in Germany, the pursuit of both arms modernization deployments and arms limitation agreements—at the official level. Second, while protests and active opposition will clearly continue, these governments and the particular leaders are less vulnerable to the claims of antinuclear activists than was a Helmut Schmidt or even a Van Agt at an earlier period.

Third, and perhaps most important, these governments will be less disturbed by Reagan hard-line rhetoric on military preparedness and on verbal confrontation with the Soviet Union. Europeans across the political spectrum feel more comfortable when not confronted by superpower hegemony.[9] In his 1977 speech to the International Institute for Strategic Studies, Helmut Schmidt was warning against a superpower agreement, eventually Strategic Arms Limitation Talks (SALT) II, which did not take adequate account of European interests. Moreover the cycle of the Atlantic debate over the new American military build-up is now more than half-accomplished; Washington's tone has become more muted, and new startling statements about limited war and nuclear doctrine are far less frequent than in Reagan's first year in office.

9. For one sharp statement of this view, see Klaus Bloemer, "Freedom for Europe, East and West," *Foreign Policy*, 50: 23-38 (Spring 1983).

Last of all, the strength of future antinuclear movements may also be related inversely to speed and extent of Western economic recovery. Lowered economic expectations and unprecedented unemployment levels gave rise to expressions of societal unease in all sectors, particularly among the young, who seemed to face the most uncertain future. Their availability for political mobilization on national political issues of all types may well decline as chances for employment or for career development increase.

In the short run, however, much will depend on the events of 1983, both at the official level and in the streets. All current indications are that deployment will begin on schedule, and that whatever the shape of a final East-West agreement on arms limitation, some LRTNF missiles will indeed be stationed in Western Europe. Opposition to nuclear weapons may then focus on three emerging areas of national choice and alliance decision—nuclear independence, nuclear modernization, and nuclear control.

THE CURRENT
NUCLEAR AGENDA IN EUROPE

Remarkably, in the midst of this debate, Britain and France are embarking on the third generation of their independent nuclear deterrents. Both developments will be costly; both will involve opportunity costs for conventional readiness and capability. Perhaps most important of all, both national programs represent continuity with the political-military assumptions of the 1950s that led to the initial search for nuclear independence from the United States.

Nuclear independence:
the next phase

The British program is the most advanced and the best publicized. The decision to acquire Trident to replace the aging British Polaris submarine fleet is an acknowledged hallmark of the Thatcher government; every indication is that Trident and the subsequent decision to obtain the American D-5 warhead would be the last items Margaret Thatcher would abandon even under severe budgetary pressure. Together with coastal air and naval defense of the British Isles, a sea-based deterrent constitutes an inviolable pillar of the conservatives' definition of national security.

Opposition spokesmen, particularly from the Labour party under Michael Foot's leadership, put forward very different proposals. Labour's election manifesto essentially called for unilateral nuclear disarmament; some in the new Social Democrat-Liberal alliance stress their willingness to forego Trident in the face of any serious Soviet initiative in the Strategic Arms Reduction Talks (START) or revival of the SALT II agreement. Neither party stressed the value of a new multiple independently targetable submarine-launched ballistic missile (MIRVed SLBM) force as a deterrent against either enemy attack or Allied abandonment. And the cost, absorbing—as it reportedly will—all the funds for new equipment for the Royal Navy through the 1990s, appears both prohibitive and counterproductive.

A substantial proportion of the British peace movement is already motivated by a desire to stop Trident as well as the American intermediate-range nuclear forces (INF), to be stationed on British soil. Yet in this respect they run counter to the broad tide of British opinion; most recent opinion polls show that between 55 and 70 percent of those interviewed favor the maintenance of an independent nuclear force.[10] The specific details may not be known; the strategic rationale, in terms of either deterrence or defense, may be unknown. But popular support for a national force remains strong, even in times of economic adversity.

Similar trends are observable in France, even though the national debate on the next nuclear generation has hardly begun. Popular support for the *force de frappe* remains high; nuclear independence has received an even greater emphasis under the socialist Mitterand than it did under Pompidou or Giscard d'Estaing. The new *loi de programmation,* the five-year plan governing the evolution of French force structure, has not yet been released. Available evidence suggests that there will be a decided reallocation of resources to the nuclear force, perhaps even as high as the 45-50 percent of the budget designated by de Gaulle. Included will be a spectrum of forces: new tactical systems as well as additional submarines and modernization of both the air and missile arms. The cost once again will be borne by the conventional forces, particularly the ground forces, which will experience equipment stretch-outs as well as direct manpower reductions.

The context of this decision is very different, however, given the lack of a significant antinuclear movement in France beyond that concerned with eco-

10. See, here, the articles on the various national debates in Capitanchik and Eichenberg, *Public Opinion and Defence.*

nomy and the perils of nuclear power. Analysts suggest that parliamentary debate will be fairly routine, and the opposition minuscule.[11] Even the French decision to begin production of neutron warheads has brought little sustained criticism from the general public, although debate within the military over this and over budgetary issues has been almost constant for the last five years. The debate remains that of experts and participants, not involving those who challenge the consequences, let alone the assumptions, of Gaullist insistence on national nuclear independence.

Elevation to the status of national symbols may well ensure that neither the British nor the French force will undergo radical change in the forseeable future. Two factors suggest possible pressures for modification. The first, undoubtedly, is the 1983 Andropov proposal that existing and modernized European forces will by the 1990s be the approximate equivalents of the 240 or so Russian SS-20s now deployed against European targets. Soviet interest in including these systems in a strategic nuclear limitation regime is not new; it was argued during the negotiations for both SALT I and II. Yet there is a new specificity to Russian demands, as well as a new appeal to the fears of the European nonnuclear states. Present British and French assertions about national independence and separability are almost sure to come under increasing criticism, especially if negotiations fail to result in an acceptable INF agree-

ment before the actual Pershing and GLCM developments.

A second factor to watch is the vague stirring of European defense cooperation, at least at the declaratory level.[12] The discussions are often conducted in terms of code words or phrases from the past: the need for greater consultation on political security, on joint initiatives, on the eventuality of a European defense pillar to balance that provided by the United States, on specialization, or—the French favorite—on the revival of the concept of a Western European defense union. Most supporters recognize the intractability of the nuclear control issue—the degree of joint planning, if not control, that would have to be implemented and even shared with the still nonnuclear Germans, and the smaller Allies. But the idea is clearly appealing; and as recent research in four European countries suggests, there are some elites who see a European drawing together as the only defense against an increasingly unpredictable American ally, which is under mounting economic and party-political strains to begin withdrawing from its European security commitments.[13]

Nuclear modernization: the uncertain calculus

A quite different catalogue of questions concerns how modernization of existing nuclear systems will proceed in

11. Perhaps the most complete examination of the present French defense debate is David Yost's *France and European Security,* Adelphi Paper Series (London: International Institute for Strategic Studies, 1983, forthcoming).

12. A reflection of this is Hedley Bull, "European Self-Reliance," *Foreign Affairs,* 61(4): 874-92 (Spring 1983).

13. These are the results of the first phase of the Ford project, cited in the author's Note and reported in *Sicherheit—zu Welchem Preis?* ed. Catherine M. Kelleher and Wolf-Dieter Eberwein (Munich: Gunther Olzog Verlag, 1983).

the 1980s and at what cost, political and military. At earlier points these questions would have been left solely to military planners and experts, on both NATO and national levels. But the pitch of antinuclear sentiment and the resulting dispersion of information about national nuclear involvement may well make these choices far more visible and controversial.

At issue are many of the calculations that have dominated American discussions of tactical nuclear warfare since the early 1970s. The Allied nuclear capable force posture in Europe is largely the product of discrete decisions reached in the late 1950s and early 1960s under a very different U.S.-Soviet strategic balance and at far lower levels of Soviet nuclear capability in Eastern Europe. The goal was for each Allied state to participate in a spectrum of nuclear capability—battlefield systems, midrange missiles, and nuclear capable aircraft. The intervening period has largely been a program of progressive improvement of systems—for instance, better battlefield munitions—or direct replacement in kind, with relative stability in numbers deployed and the level of warhead stocks held. Perhaps the only clear shift has been the decision to reduce the share of each national air force dedicated to nuclear as well as conventional missions, in the interest of greater conventional readiness.

The current political and military context suggests a number of interrelated questions and possible tradeoffs. First, if there is broad interest, such as in Holland, in reducing reliance on nuclear weapons, what are the implications for the present levels and readiness of conventional forces? Will these be increased, which would require an unlikely rise in national defense expenditures? Will there be a restructuring of existing forces to fulfill more missions, but at more or less the same level of military expenditure?

A number of current suggestions turn on new combinations of standing forces and larger, better trained reserves with continuing responsibilities for active defense.[14] Involved would be not only political decisions and perhaps longer reserve commitments, but also some reconsideration of the specifics of forward defense and resistance as close to the inner-German border as possible. Others see the solution to greater conventional effort at stable cost in available new technologies—precision-guided weapons to be used both against battlefield and second-echelon targets. Still another group of proposals stresses the return of longer terms of service for regular forces as well.

Even harder to answer are the broad questions of strategy and political commitment. Is it necessary for each state, at least those charged with responsibilities for central front defense, to share in the required nuclear capability? Is this a political necessary, that is, sharing in the risk involved to demonstrate commitment to Allies and opponent alike? Or does it turn on more practical implications for the conduct of an integrated defense under common NATO command? Obviously this would affect the major force contributions of Germany and the United States, but what about the smaller forces assigned by Holland

14. For one discussion of these questions, see the European Security Study Project Report, *Strengthening Conventional Deterrence in Europe: Proposals for the 1980's* (New York: St Martin's Press, 1983).

or Canada? And what impact would this have on national roles in NATO's nuclear decision making—in the setting of nuclear use guidelines, for example, within the Nuclear Planning Group?

Nuclear control:
limits and negotiations

Modernization choices impinge directly on the prospects for nuclear arms limitation in Europe, a goal that has attracted substantial popular support throughout the last decade. The past few years, however, have seen dramatic upswings in fears about the imminence of nuclear war, on both the elite and the popular level. There is therefore more perceived urgency about, and greater political aspirations for, the several related negotiations about nuclear arms control—the INF talks, the START discussions, the proposed Conference on Disarmament in Europe (CDE), and the ongoing Mutual and Balanced Force Reductions (MBFR) round.

Again the pattern of concerns is not new, but the consequences in terms of future options and popular mood are newly significant. Perhaps the most obvious worry is whether to continue the bargaining chip strategies of the past. For example, will the beginning of INF deployments, scheduled now for 1984, be the signal for the start of serious negotiation on mutual limits? Or will the relative stakes in both SS-20 and Pershing-GLCM deployments by then be so great as to prevent limitation or to allow no clear stopping point? And what of the domestic political costs?

A second type of strategy choice turns on Western decisions about the best bargain now to be sought, given the changes in military balances and in popular attitudes. Is it still in the Western interest to offer a reduction in nuclear capable systems in exchange for decreases in Soviet conventional forces, as it was in the mid-1970s? Would a revival of MBFR's Option III, for example—the exchange of obsolescent, controversial battlefield nuclear warheads for Soviet tanks—still represent a desirable tradeoff? Would this become more attractive in the West if expert doubts became more widespread that battlefield systems would ever be released for use before being overrun?

A third set of problems reflects what many Europeans now see as the inevitable tension between the global interests of the United States and the regional stability concerns of the European Allies. Should there be global ceilings for warheads or launchers, as the Reagan administration has proposed for intermediate nuclear forces? How should regional subceilings be arrived at? What are the appropriate calculations about relative sacrifice? Is it indeed possible in effect to fold together negotiations about strategic nuclear systems, necessarily global in scope, and those concerned with theater balances, as the INF talks presently are? Is there not otherwise the danger—highlighted by Chancellor Schmidt in the now famous 1977 speech—of loosening alliance linkages and risking the opportunity to develop integrated negotiation packages that satisfy the interests of all the Allies?[15]

CONCLUSION

In the final analysis, neither the popular mood nor the agenda of questions

---

15. The Schmidt speech is reproduced in *Survival,* 20 (1): 2-10 (Jan.-Feb. 1978).

constitutes a new or immutable obstacle to a continuation of the status quo in terms of European nuclear policy or politics. There is, experienced observers assure current leaders, every reason to expect a lessening of the dramatic aspects of the antinuclear movement in northern Europe. And the emerging nuclear agenda is not unlike questions that have been successfully bypassed or subject to only partial solution for the past two decades.

Most important of all, the policy outcomes will depend in largest measure on two factors that are not yet predictable. The first is the degree of leadership that national governments will exercise. For much of the past decade, they have been weak, Center-Left coalitions, often divided on issues of security and economic policy. The current conservative wave will face problems and choices at least as difficult. But there is at least a probability that these coalitions of the Center-Right will suffer fewer internal divisions, enjoy the benefits of some degree of economic upswing, and find the lead of a Margaret Thatcher worthy of experiment.

The second imponderable is the role that the United States will choose to play. Nuclear policy in Europe has always had as much to do with American initiatives and intentions as it has with some abstract model of the requirements of either deterrence or defense. The set of decisions that Washington will make—about doctrine, deployments, and the sharing of risk and control—will continue to set the parameters for European choice and concern. At the very least this should make for a decade more approaching the style and content of the Atlantic pattern of the 1950s than that seen in what now seem the halcyon 1970s.

West German Perspectives on Nuclear Armament and Arms Control

By GALE A. MATTOX

ABSTRACT: The NATO decision of 1979 to modernize its nuclear arsenal has prompted an intense and divisive political debate over security policy in the Federal Republic of Germany. The divergence of public opinion reflects uncertainty over the U.S. commitment to European security; uneasiness over the possibility of limited war in Europe and the continuing Soviet deployment of the SS-20; and dissatisfaction with the progress of arms control. These concerns have heightened public attention to all aspects of NATO doctrine, conventional strategy, and arms control. However, despite a shift by the Social Democratic Party in the 1983 electoral campaign on the question of intermediate-range nuclear force modernization and some success by the Green candidates on an antinuclear platform, the prospects for reforging the consensus are encouraging. Chancellor Kohl recognizes the need to reestablish broader public support and will attempt to avoid further deterioration of the consensus, even if U.S.-German relations suffer in the short term. The discussion will probably increase support for a NATO strategy that is less dependent on the nuclear threat but does not forfeit the U.S. nuclear guarantee.

Gale A. Mattox, assistant professor of political science, U.S. Naval Academy, received her Ph.D. from the Woodrow Wilson School of Government and Foreign Affairs, University of Virginia. She worked in the Foreign Affairs and National Defense Division, Congressional Research Service, and has taught at Mary Washington College and Trinity College. Her primary research area is U.S.-European-Soviet relations, with emphasis on NATO affairs and West German politics. She has spent several years in Europe conducting research and lecturing.

104

THE impressive and clear consensus on security policy experienced by the Federal Republic of Germany (FRG) for more than 20 years has deteriorated. Not since the rearmament debate of the 1950s and the 1959 adoption by the Social Democratic Party of the Godesberger Programm[1] has the agreement between the major parties faced such serious challenge. Dissension since the 1950s has been limited to extremist groups. Even the disagreement by the Christian Democratic Union (CDU/CSU) over the policy of *Ostpolitik* adopted by the governing Social Democratic/Free Democratic (SPD/FDP) coalition in the early 1970s, though it may have challenged the previous foreign policy consensus, did not challenge the fundamental tenets of security policy.

The primary cause of deterioration has been the plans for increasing the level of nuclear armament in Western Europe, especially the 1979 North Atlantic Treaty Organization (NATO) decision to modernize intermediate-range nuclear forces (INF) with 108 Pershing IIs and 464 cruise missiles, in order to counter the increasing level of nuclear arms in the East, represented by the recent SS-20 deployments. While the electoral success of the Green movement for the first time in the 1983 national elections represented only 5.6 percent of the vote, it is a striking mani-

festation of public antinuclear sentiments.

In the fall of 1983 the Federal Republic may be facing its most divisive issue, with the scheduled plans to deploy 18 Pershing IIs in Germany by December if the U.S./Soviet INF negotiations in Geneva do not succeed. The Greens are now pledged to nonviolent but unquestionable opposition, and it is unknown how opponents within the other parties will react to the modernization. As the opposition numbers increase, so will the potential for violence. Whether the disagreement over security policy will be enduring or ephemeral remains unclear, but it could well destabilize the NATO alliance as well as Germany.

This prediction may prove overly gloomy, but there is a factor that could produce an equally gloomy outcome for U.S.-German relations unless U.S. policymakers appreciate it. That factor is the role Chancellor Helmut Kohl can be expected to assume. Contrary to the prevailing American interpretation, Kohl will make every effort to avoid a direct confrontation with the opposition on the INF issue, even if his position may differ at times from official U.S. policy. While this may not necessarily mean an irreparable U.S.-German split over the issue of INF modernization or any other armament decisions, it could mean a serious strain. Neither the U.S. administration nor most other Western governments attempted to hide their pleasure over the Kohl election. But despite the more clearly favorable sentiment within the CDU/CSU for the 1979 NATO decision, the U.S. and the West must resist the temptation to become complacent about the security issues confronting the FRG chancellor.

1. The Godesberger Programm was adopted by the Social Democratic Party in 1959; it renounced the earlier Marxist basis of the SPD and former foreign policy objective of military neutrality if necessary to achieve reunification. Kurt Sontheimer and Hans H. Roehring, eds., *Handbuch des politischen Systems der Bundesrepublik Deutschland* (Munich: R. Piper and Co. Verlag, 1978), p. 541.

In the area of security, Kohl may be expected to pursue German interests, interests that will include at times opposition sentiment. No one recognizes as clearly as the chancellor that his election was not a blanket endorsement of the NATO nuclear modernization program. Within a week after Kohl's electoral victory in March, he had demonstrated this in his remarks on the INF negotiations. In order to reassure President Reagan during a trip to Washington that Bonn would remain committed to the 1979 decision, the chancellor commented that Germany would "do what we promised to do if there is not agreement [in the INF negotiations]," but he also added that "we are not eager to have these missiles, not at all."[2]

To understand the present discussion of security issues, it is important to understand the framework in which German security policy has been formulated since World War II, and to review the current debates over nuclear armament and arms control that have led to the new and potentially considerable divergence in German views on selected security issues. The manner in which these debates are resolved will, in turn, affect the course of U.S./FRG relations and potentially even the Atlantic alliance.

A FRAMEWORK FOR SECURITY

The basis of West German security is NATO. In fact there is probably no other nation in Europe so wedded to NATO. Unlike the British and French, the Germans have renounced an independent nuclear capability. Under the terms of their membership in 1955, all

FRG troops are integrated into NATO, and the Western European Union stipulates specifically the permissible ceiling of troop levels at 498,000 in peacetime, 1.2 million in wartime.

This total commitment to NATO enjoys the support of all the major parties and has also had wide public support. Even in a period of public dissatisfaction with the decision to deploy modernized nuclear forces on German soil—opposition as high as 60 percent[3]—support for NATO has increased and is at one of its highest levels since World War II.

This support for NATO pervades German society. Despite their opposition to rearmament and membership in NATO in the 1950s, the SPD is today a strong supporter of the alliance as are the CDU/CSU and FDP. Perhaps the most striking illustration of the shift by the Social Democrats is Helmut Schmidt. Despite his vote against German entry into the alliance as a young parliamentarian in the 1950s, he became an unwavering advocate of NATO during the 1960s. There is even conditional support by the antinuclear movement for NATO. The Green party, however, prefers an Austrian-style nuetrality.[4] Although there is now a clear consensus for German membership in NATO, there are

2. Steven R. Weisman, "Kohl Assures Reagan on U.S. Missiles," *New York Times,* 16 Apr. 1983, p. 3.

3. This figure is from an unpublished report done for the federal government and cited in *Der Spiegel,* 37:1 (3 Jan. 1983). This study by the Kohl government in fact also showed that 55 percent of the country doubted that the United States and Russia were negotiating seriously. William Drozdiak, "Bonn Parties Wavering on Arms Talks," *International Herald Tribune,* 11 Jan. 1983, p. 1.

4. While many in the broader antinuclear movement would accept a NATO with less dependence on nuclear weapons, the Green party would prefer an Austrian-style neutrality to an alliance with the United States (80 percent). Stephen F.

differences about how to assure deterrence effectively without provoking Soviet attack.

Initially the NATO strategy of massive retaliation appeared to provide a simple and inexpensive deterrent. SPD reservations about alliance membership primarily reflected concern for the question of German reunification and not opposition to NATO strategy. The United States was vastly superior to the Soviet Union in nuclear capabilities, and even when the superpower balance shifted to mutual assured destruction, the U.S. strategic nuclear guarantee remained a premise of European security.

The U.S. decision to introduce into NATO a policy of flexible response—of graduated reaction to a Warsaw Pact or Soviet aggression—was not received enthusiastically. It envisioned reliance on conventional defense, use of tactical nuclear weapons if that failed, and use of central U.S. nuclear forces only as a last resort. Conventional or theater nuclear response might win negotiating time to stem the conflict, but in either case would devastate German territory.

Although flexible response was adopted largely through German assistance in 1967 as NATO strategy and, to an extent, at the cost of French membership in NATO, the German acceptance of the concept has been at best hesitant. The FRG force posture with its emphasis on *Vorne Verteidigung*—a policy of forward defense close to the border—substantiates this hesitancy. *Vorne Verteidigung* is designed to prevent an extended conflict on German soil. Although this is seldom articulated offi-

cially, the Germans oppose conceiving flexibility in NATO response in terms of a long and destructive war on their territory.

This reflects an even broader German concern that limited nuclear war might be possible in Europe, more specifically in the Federal Republic. That concern has surfaced repeatedly in various public debates since World War II. For the German population it would be an understatement to say that the concept of limited nuclear war is unsettling. Unfortunately those popular fears were fueled by remarks made in the opening days of the Reagan administration, by both President Reagan and Secretary of Defense Caspar Weinberger. Without passing judgment on the intent of those remarks, it is obvious that they intensified public nervousness over the concept of limited war. During the same period there was persistent mention of Pentagon reports on war-fighting scenarios; for the German public, security necessarily excludes war fighting.

Furthermore, the remarks had been preceded by a generally uneasy atmosphere, prompted in the mid-1970s by growing concern about the credibility of the American strategic nuclear guarantee. Given the nuclear parity between the superpowers codified in the Strategic Arms Limitation Treaty (SALT), did flexible response really still include U.S. central strategic forces if the Warsaw Pact appeared likely to overrun Europe, or was the nuclear guarantee now meant to limit the conflict to Europe? Former Secretary of State Kissinger's speech[5] in 1979 at the Palais d'Egmont in Brussels questioning the Amer-

Szabo, "Generations and Changing Security Perspectives in West Germany" (Paper, Washington, DC, 1983); see Table 3 based on EMNID survey reported in *Spiegel,* 1981.

5. "NATO—The Next Thirty Years," photocopy (Remarks at Palais d'Egmont, Brussels, 1 Sept. 1979).

ican strategic guarantee was less than comforting to the Germans.

It was not that the most recent debate was the first instance of nervousness over the U.S. commitment. Indeed those uncertainties have been voiced with almost predictable regularity for over three decades. But it is clear that comments by prominent American officials together with the changed strategic equation between the superpowers rekindled European concern. In a world of strategic parity, the choice for the U.S. president might actually be Hamburg or Washington. Would the U.S. decision to defend Hamburg now be as clear as it seemed before the Soviets threatened Washington?

Several factors during the last decade had prompted divergences in the German public over aspects of the present NATO strategy and doctrine. First was uneasiness over U.S. commitment to the security of Europe in a new era of strategic parity, and the concomitant fear of the possibility of a war limited to European or even German territory. Second was the uneasiness since 1976 over the increased Soviet threat at the intermediate-range nuclear level posed by the new SS-20 missile. Third was public frustration with the lack of U.S. attention at the outset of the Reagan administration to the INF negotiations, which were seen by the Europeans as an equally important part of the 1979 NATO decision to pursue a dual-track approach of arms control as well as modernization. Fourth was nervousness over the possible effect on the Soviets of the impending deployment of the new NATO weapons, to begin in December 1983 in Great Britain, Italy—ground-launched cruise missiles—and Germany—Pershing IIs.

Whereas the government would normally confront and attempt to allay the public concerns through official policy initiatives, the dissolution of the 13-year SPD/FDP coalition in September 1982, and its replacement by a CDU/CSU/FDP coalition, complicated the process. An electoral campaign encourages the formulation of alternative rather than common positions, and the political circumstances of 1982-83 threw the Federal Republic into its most important election campaign since 1969.

Rather than striving for public consensus as in their former roles within the government, the Social Democrats attempted to distinguish themselves from the CDU/CSU/FDP government position, and thereby attract voters disenchanted with the possible NATO modernization plans, by offering an alternative position on the missile issue with an emphasis on arms control. In particular they asserted the need to articulate German interests in the INF negotiations. The fall of the Schmidt government had been due less to the security debate than to economic policy, and the SPD consciously chose to wage the 6 March national election campaign over security policy. Although the polls have indicated that the voters ultimately voted their pocketbooks, the missile issue clearly was the focus of the electoral campaign.

In the fight for voters, SPD support for the two-track decision—which had been unequivocal under Schmidt—was reversed. This marked the abandonment of the national consensus. Whether that damage may be repaired or whether only new, even dramatic, changes in the German position on current NATO strategy will prompt a necessary future consensus, remains an open question.

THE NUCLEAR
ARMAMENT DEBATE

All the developments mentioned promoted broad discussion of several areas of FRG security policy that had not traditionally evoked public interest but had remained the preserve of political leaders and military experts. The discussion has focused on the role of INF, but has also sparked interest in the use and positioning of short-range, battlefield nuclear weapons; the role of conventional forces in flexible response; the policy of first use of nuclear weapons; and primarily in expert circles, the concept of negotiated zones of reduced nuclear forces. This list is not exhaustive but illustrates the considerable range of topics now under debate by a public that has traditionally entrusted security policy to its government officials.

The most controversial and potentially most divisive discussion has been over the role of INF.[6] The argument that originally convinced officials of the need to introduce INF was that it would add one more step to flexible response and therefore add credibility to the NATO nuclear deterrent. Proponents argued that the threat to respond to a Warsaw Pact attack with either short-range nuclear forces—which would have to be used on West European territory—or the U.S. strategic nuclear arsenal was insufficiently credible. An intermediate-level response could assure escalation control and therby add credibility. Particularly if the INF were land-based, they would have the added effect of coupling U.S. and European security more securely.

6. NATO, "Communique of the Special Meeting of NATO Foreign and Defense Ministers," photocopy (Brussels, 12 Dec. 1979).

However, when Han-Jochen Vogel replaced Helmut Schmidt in the fall of 1982 and the need emerged to develop a campaign platform distinguishable from that of its opposition, the SPD withdrew its support for the Pershing II because of its allegedly threatening first-strike capability, deriving from quick flight time and high accuracy. The party expressed concern that a Pershing deployment would put detente at risk and thereby increase the potential for conflict. It withheld a decision on the cruise missiles to be deployed in the Federal Republic in 1986.

The point is not that the SPD unanimously favored missile modernization under Schmidt. To the contrary, it was a topic of considerable, often even sharp, debate in the party meeting held in the spring of 1982. In order to defuse opposition to the official position, former Chancellor Schmidt supported a resolution at that time to delay a final decision on the modernization to November 1983. However, now as an opposition party, any formal withdrawal of support for Pershing modernization would align the Social Democrats with the Greens against the governing coalition. Such a position would not necessarily affect SPD support for NATO, and in fact would most likely be accompanied by an explicit reaffirmation of support for the alliance as the vital basis for German security—albeit with possible conditional dissent on its left wing; but a reforging of the consensus between the major parties on appropriate NATO strategy to assure FRG security would become virtually impossible.

The growth of the Green movement played a primary role in the shift of the SPD on this issue, and there is no question that the antinuclear views of the movement also find resonance even within some segments of the CDU/CSU. Chancellor Kohl will not ignore those sentiments. The antinuclear movement—now represented by the Greens in the German Parliament—is clearly opposed to INF modernization on the grounds that the new deployments would increase rather than decrease tensions, that they would make limited war more rather than less likely; and that they would only fuel the arms race.

The movement has already declared its intention of becoming more vocal as the time for deployment comes closer. There is no question that Kohl will face pressures both from the movement and from his own coalition. There are indications that the position of his coalition partner, the FDP, as well as members of his own party may be volatile in the face of the impending deployments. But even if an arms control solution is found to avoid Pershing deployment, the dilemma of the INF debate is double edged. While the missile deployment appears destabilizing to its opponents, failure to deploy will unnerve those convinced of the need to counter the SS-20. The ability of the alliance to act cohesively would be discredited. For this reason, the INF debate has sparked discussion of related areas of NATO strategy.

One of those areas is short-range nuclear forces. A major problem with these forces is that in the current mode of deployment, a Warsaw Pact aggression could put NATO in a use-them-or-lose-them position. In other words, at the expected swift rate with which the Soviet Union could overrun German territory, NATO and specifically the United States would be forced into using their battlefield nuclear weapons, thus escalating the conflict. The dilemma

is obvious: how far forward should those weapons be based to achieve optimal deterrent value without NATO becoming hostage to its own weapons?

NATO has agreed that modernization of INF will be accompanied by a corresponding number of reductions in tactical nuclear weapons. But even though there is general agreement on the need for a change in basing mode or a reduction of those armaments, there is no agreement on how to accomplish either objective. While the public has become increasingly interested, the issue has not attracted the degree of public debate that has accompanied INF.

Renewed interest in conventional forces after a long period of neglect is a direct result of the search for alternatives to dependence on nuclear arsenals. Both INF and, to a lesser but important extent, battlefield nuclear weapon discussions have raised the specter for all political parties of overreliance on nuclear weapons to deter attack. Could this not be minimized with enhanced conventional capabilities? There has been interest in this issue from all three major parties but also, more significantly, from the antinuclear movement.

In May 1982 reports on conventional forces were released at the same time by the offices of U.S. Senator Sam Nunn, member of the Committee on Armed Services, and CDU defense expert Manfred Woerner, since last fall the minister of defense.[7] The reports were the result of a unique joint effort by the staffs of

7. Sam Nunn, "NATO: Can the Alliance Be Saved?" Report of Senator Sam Nunn to the Committee on Armed Services, U.S. Senate, U.S. Congress, photocopy (Washington, DC, 13 May 1982); Manfred Woerner and Peter Wuerzbach, "NATO's New Conventional Option," *Wall Street Journal,* 19 Nov. 1982.

both officials to devise conventional defense alternatives that would not only reduce the reliance on nuclear weapons, but also shift any future conflict from West German territory to the East. Modernization would be necessary but would involve conventional rather than nuclear armament. Although, as ever, the financial barrier is large, and more attention needs to be directed to building a political consensus, the concepts have attracted interest. They are particularly attractive to those uneasy about the danger of too low a nuclear threshold in the case of conflict. For this reason, a new conventional force posture may hold the greatest potential for reestablishing a German security policy consensus.

A further issue in the recent debates over nuclear strategy is that of the NATO policy of first use of nuclear weapons. This is viewed by most Europeans as an integral part of NATO's deterrent strategy. The best deterrence, it is argued, is to confront the Warsaw Pact policymakers with the possibility that any attack—conventional or nuclear—could evoke a nuclear response. The pact would be faced thereby with an incalculable risk.

In a 1982 article in *Foreign Affairs,* four former U.S. policymakers[8] initiated the debate by proposing a shift in NATO policy to no first use of nuclear weapons, on the grounds that such a declaration would be more credible by avoiding dependence on escalation. There was an immediate bipartisan response from four eminent Germans,[9] who argued against the adoption of a non-first-use policy, for several reasons.

(1) It would decouple the U.S. nuclear guarantee.

(2) There are neither the financial means nor the political consensus for the increase in conventional forces that would be necessary.

(3) It would rob the present strategy of war prevention.

Furthermore, others argued, the moral barriers to conflict in Europe might be lowered. At the time, their opposition was shared by both the SPD/FDP policymakers and the CDU/CSU opposition.

However, the debate has attracted more attention over the past year, primarily as a result of general nervousness over the use of nuclear weapons. It is an unresolved discussion, and several positions have begun to crystallize. The CDU/CSU/FDP coalition remains adamantly committed to possible nuclear first use as vital to NATO strategy; the antinuclear movement advocates a shift to a policy of non-first use, but has not developed a clear policy on compensation by conventional force; and the SPD is split. The official SPD position is to retain the option of possible first use but to avoid early first use.

Other views range from non-first use to a conditional and negotiated agreement on non-first use of both nuclear and conventional forces, with provisions for the agreement to be voided in the event of a transgression by either side of an agreed zone along the East-West border.[10] In fact, a non-first-use policy that would thin out Soviet troops in any

8. McGeorge Bundy et al., "Nuclear Weapons and the Atlantic Alliance," *Foreign Affairs,* 60(4):753-68 (Spring 1982).

9. Karl Kaiser et al., "Nuclear Weapons and the Preservation: A German Response to No First Use," *Foreign Affairs,* 60(5):1157-70 (Summer 1982).

10. Nunn, *NATO: Can the Alliance Be Saved?* p. 25. This is also a later phase in the report by Senator Nunn, which would presuppose a substantial increase in NATO conventional capabilities.

manner along the border might be attractive to the population generally. While NATO and FRG policy remains clearly one of possible first use, it is interesting to note the growing assumption that the policy will inevitably change.[11]

A final and hotly contested proposal in the recent debate has been the Palme Commission Report,[12] advocating a nuclear free zone of 150 kilometers on each side of the border, which would permit but decrease the conventional force presence. The report has been flatly rejected by the government, but has stirred interest in some segments of the SPD and is attractive to proponents of lowering the nuclear threshold.

The unprecedented level of public discussion of these issues, the entry of 27 Greens into the Bundestag, the divisions within the SPD, and polling data on opposition to INF deployments even within the constituency of the CDU—all these developments reflect the fissures in the security consensus of the last quarter century. There is one area, however, where progress could repair these fissures or at least prevent them from widening. That area is arms control.

THE ARMS CONTROL DEBATE

If there is one emphasis in the German white paper on defense, *The Security of the Federal Republic of Germany and the Development of the Federal Armed Forces,*[13] and one issue that

11. Hedley Bull, "European Self-Reliance and the Reform of NATO," *Foreign Affairs,* 61(4):874-92 (Spring 1983).

12. Olaf Palme, chairman, Independent Commission on Disarmament and Security Issues, *Common Security: A Blueprint for Survival,* rpt. U.N. General Assembly Disarmament Commission, Doc. A/CN.10/38 (8 Apr. 1983).

13. FRG Ministry of Defense, *Weissbuch 1979. Zur Sicherheit der Bundesrepublik Deutschland*

transcends party lines, it is the joint importance of deterrence and detente. Whereas the Harmel Report is almost never mentioned by Americans, it is almost always mentioned in official and unofficial German remarks on NATO. The Harmel Report adopted by NATO in 1967 specifically assigns the alliance the dual responsibility of deterrence and detente.[14] As interpreted by the Germans, arms control is an integral part of detente. A signatory of the Non-Proliferation Treaty and a committed nonnuclear state, the Federal Republic is most concerned with the progress of arms control in the three general areas of strategic nuclear forces, INF, and conventional forces.

Despite the interest in these various forums, the Germans well recognize that they are only observers. The most direct participation occurs in the Mutual and Balanced Force Reductions (MBFR) talks in Vienna, conducted between representatives of NATO and the Warsaw Pact on conventional forces. The German contribution is direct and an important component of the Western position. The chief German concern has been to establish equal force ceilings for both sides while avoiding national force levels that might have adverse effects on Western troop strength, should a unilateral reduction occur sometime in the future. In MBFR, as in the debates at the Conference on Security and Cooperation in Europe dealing with troop issues, the Germans have emphasized the importance of confidence-building measures as steps necessary to subsequent agreements and real controls or reductions.[15]

und zur Entwicklung der Bundeswehr. (Bonn: Der Bundesminister der Verteidigung, 1979).

14. Ibid., p. 13.

15. The Federal Republic has also been interested in the convening of a Conference on Disar-

The negotiations on arms control of nuclear arsenals are occurring exclusively between the superpowers, but with Allied consultation. Whereas SALT had purported to deal only with strategic systems—an assertion not entirely factual—two separate forums were created for discussion of strategic systems and intermediate-range nuclear systems. Of the two forums—the Strategic Arms Reduction Talks (START) and INF—the latter obviously has greater direct consequences for the Europeans. This is even more true with the pressure of the projected 1983 deployment—and thereby enhanced importance—of INF.

However, one should recall the Alastair Buchan Memorial Lecture at the International Institute for Strategic Studies by Chancellor Schmidt in 1977, pointing to the failings of SALT with regard to European systems.[16] His concern was assuring that strategic arms reductions were not negotiated without regard for the European theater. Those remarks were in large part the result of insufficient sensitivity to the Europeans in SALT. This is not to put the blame squarely on either side; the Americans must learn to consult as much as the Germans must learn to assert their interests. But those involved in START would do well to remember the lessons of SALT. For the Europeans, the strategic-tactical nuclear link is critical and finely balanced.

The INF negotiation confronts the Germans with the most pressing issues for arms control. It is this negotiation that has prompted the German nuclear

debate and the divisions on security policy. The dual-track decision reached by the NATO alliance in 1979 was an attempt to reduce the threat posed by the new Soviet SS-20 systems through negotiations, if possible, and an INF modernization with Pershing II and ground-launched cruise missiles in 1983, if the negotiations proved unsuccessful. The fact that all FRG political parties have been committed to the arms control track, and that this track was more crucial to European governments than to Washington, is often overlooked in the United States. The U.S. presidential election year was under way, ratification of SALT was uncertain, and the country's mood had clearly shifted in favor of a stronger defense posture. The U.S. stance with regard to INF was a reflection of those factors.

As a result, commentary by U.S. officials initially differed markedly in emphasis from European remarks when addressing the decision.[17] This was obvious even during the discussions prior to the December decision. The Special Group was formed in Spring 1979 at the suggestion of the Germans specifically to address the arms control element of the modernization decision. With pressure from the Europeans, not only was modernization linked to arms control, but the decision itself also presumed ratification of SALT as a condition to modernization. The difference between the U.S. and European approaches became even more marked after the Soviet invasion of Afghanistan. While the Europeans shared in the U.S. condemnation

mament in Europe as a means of including the non-Allied European nations such as France. Again their initial proposals have focused on confidence-building measures.

16. "Speech before the Annual Meeting of the IISS," *Survival,* 20(1):2-10 (Jan.-Feb. 1978).

17. It is interesting and revealing, for instance, that not one of the major U.S. broadcasters mentioned the arms control track in its initial reporting of the 12 December 1979 decision by NATO, and concentrated instead on the modernization track.

of the invasion, their approach to the incident has been clearly different.

For the Germans who believe that East-West negotiations have a moderating effect on the East and the Soviets, the withdrawal of SALT from Senate consideration as well as the hiatus in INF negotiations—from the beginning of the Reagan administration to the announcement that the U.S. was prepared to enter into INF negotiations—appeared interminable. The proposal made by Reagan in a public address on 18 November 1981 was the particular brainchild of the Dutch and Germans. Termed the zero-zero proposal, it proposed that the West not deploy its scheduled INF in exchange for Moscow's agreement to dismantle its SS-4s, SS-5s, and SS-20s. The present FRG government position has remained strongly supportive of the dual-track approach as well as the zero-zero proposal and the subsequent interim proposal for an equal warhead ceiling and a common objective of eventual reductions to zero-zero.[18]

While all major political groups have supported the Reagan arms control efforts and the objective of zero INF systems in Europe, the consensus on the deployment of half of the dual-track decision has disintegrated on the issue of the Pershing II. Even the FDP coalition partners at their annual convention in January reserved final judgment on the

"merits of stationing U.S. missiles on West German soil in light of the results of the Geneva disarmament negotiations."[19] While the Greens have totally rejected any Pershing II or cruise missile deployments, the SPD has signaled its opposition only to the Pershing II. Those Pershings are to be sacrificed for substantial SS-20 reductions, and the SPD has indicated that negotiating deadlines should not be considered sacrosanct.

There has been considerable interest in the tentative deal explored by negotiators Nitze and Kvitsinky during their famous walk in the woods in the summer of 1982. That proposal was reported to have set equal INF ceilings not to include the Pershing II. It was rejected by both sides, but it remains attractive to many Europeans who liked the idea of permitting both a modernization that was not as threatening to the Soviets as the Pershing and an arms control agreement that would halt the SS-20 deployments, which continue at the rate of one a week.

THE FUTURE OF FRG SECURITY POLICY?

The longer-term consequences of the deterioration of the consensus on security policy are unclear. No longer under the pressures of responsibility for governing, the Social Democrats will probably veer left for some time before reestablishing an internal equilibrium that could offer voters a sober alternative to the present center-right coalition. Although the Greens represent only 5.6

18. If the reports are correct, it was on the advice of Chancellor Kohl that President Reagan modified his original interim proposal, limiting both sides to 100 launchers, no more than 300 warheads, to a proposal in which the Soviets could choose any number between 0 and 572. Walter Pincus, "Arms Talks Positions Hardening," *Washington Post*, 1 May 1983, pp. A-1, 4.

19. German Information Center, "FDP Convention Produces Surprise Results," *The Week in Germany*, 4 Feb. 1983, p. 1.

percent of the population, they captured 23 percent of the first-time voters and will not be ignored by the more established parties. The Greens may be expected to play a significant role in influencing the security debate.

Resolution of the debate will be determined in the final analysis by the major parties. The response by the SPD to the INF issue and to the Greens will again provide (1) a cohesive policy that a larger proportion of the populace can support, or (2) an intense, even dangerous alienation. However difficult it may prove, the facts of politics will require that an equilibrium eventually be struck. Just as the Christian Democrats recognized—and even, to a large extent, adopted—the concept of an *Ostpolitik* that encouraged more extensive East-West contacts, the Social Democrats will also adapt.

In spite of this pessimistic assessment, there are some important aspects of German political life that should assure a reestablishment of the consensus. A point that is neither really understood nor appreciated in the United States is the degree to which Chancellor Kohl will attempt to avoid any deterioration of the long-standing agreement on FRG security policy and specifically arms control. Kohl recognizes that his March national mandate represented primarily voter dissatisfaction with the prevailing economic situation in the Federal Republic, and not unreserved agreement on security. The security debate was not resolved in March. In fact the public appears to continue to show a preference for avoiding any deployments, if possible.

Unless approached with an understanding of the pressures under which Kohl will be operating, the United States could find that the result of his efforts to mend his national consensus in turn strain U.S.-German relations. Despite the seemingly large concurrence of interests between the U.S. administration and the Christian and Free Democrats, there remains a fundamental difference in their respective approaches to dealing with the Soviets. With a border on the East and relatives in the Eastern bloc, the Federal Republic will continue to emphasize that, in addition to a strong defense posture, the best way to reduce tensions and the threat to Western security is through working relations with the Soviet Union.

Above all, Chancellor Kohl's first loyalty will be to the German public, even when public sentiment sometimes contradicts a policy direction taken by the U.S. government. Nowhere has this been clearer than in the positions taken by the chancellor on both the issue of the U.S.-USSR negotiations on INF, where he is encouraging U.S. flexibility on arms, and the issue of a superpower summit. The German pressure on the United States for a Reagan-Andropov summit meeting may also be attributed to a strong conviction of the need to maintain a dialogue with the Soviets. The future course of U.S.-German relations will reflect the manner in which these issues and others—such as defense budgets, East-West trade, even West-West trade—are handled, particularly in the area of security policy.

The longer-term prospects for German security policy will be influenced by a number of factors. The INF decision will have, and in many regards has already had, ramifications beyond the question of modernization. Over the next few years the public debate in the Federal Republic can be expected to broaden even further to address the issues of nuclear armament and arms control in greater detail. It is unclear whether those debates will move the present government as well as the opposition in the direction of the Greens. However, it is clear from the debates that the focus of discussion will move away from a NATO strategy highly dependent on the nuclear threat, and toward a strategy that could raise the nuclear threshold and lower the potential for a nuclear exchange in Europe.

One possible option in this respect would be a shift to greater dependence on conventional forces. In some of the plans now under discussion, the strategy would shift conflict from West German to East German territory by targeting second- and third-echelon forces. The problem of insufficient manpower could be partially allayed with projected improvements in conventional arms. The concept has sparked the interest of all the major parties and the Green movement, each for its own reasons.

This is not to ignore the fact that there are a number of potential political and financial constraints that need to be examined more closely. However, those constraints would not be insurmountable if there were broad agreement on the need to accord priority to conventional force improvements. Such a solution could at once reestablish the common ground for FRG security policy that Kohl is seeking, provide the necessary internal party compromise for the FDP and SPD, and offer the Greens a tangible indication of official response to their concerns over nuclear weapons. If the German public also found attractive the concept of decreased dependence on nuclear weapons in favor of increased dependence on conventional forces, it could prove a good basis for the forging of a new political consensus in German security policy.

*   *   *

QUESTIONS AND ANSWERS

Q (Dario Scuka, Oxon Hill, Maryland): The European economic situation has changed drastically. What is your conception as to the impact of economic prospects on the European military situation?

A: The Germans are trying to raise the nuclear threshold, and one of the areas they are moving into is conventional forces. But looking to that area for an answer raises important economic problems. It is very expensive, more expensive than the nuclear alternative, and economics is going to play a big role. How concerned are we, and how much are we willing to pay to allay those concerns? It has recently been suggested that this would require a minimum 4 percent increase in defense spending, at a time when the European countries are not meeting their 1977 commitment to the 3 percent increase. It is going to call on all their resources, and it will take a kind of political commitment that has not really been reached.

ANNALS, *AAPSS*, **469,** September 1983

The Soviet Approach to Nuclear Weapons: A Historical Review

By MAJOR GENERAL WILLIAM E. ODOM

ABSTRACT: The Soviet approach to nuclear weapons shares very little with the American approach and a great deal with the way the Soviets adopted new military technologies such as aviation and motorization after World War I. Popular Western misperceptions have been reinforced by policy debates in the Soviet press that have been more apparent than real. More compelling evidence is found in the evolution of their military forces and doctrine. This evidence indicates integration of nuclear weapons in a combined-arms approach at the strategic, operational, and tactical levels designed to achieve military objectives, not to maintain deterrence through mutual vulnerability and escalation control. The emergence in the 1980s of a large Soviet force structure to fit their doctrinal view of nuclear war presents the West with a qualitatively new defense problem for the foreseeable future.

William E. Odom, major general and since 1981 assistant chief of staff for intelligence, U.S. Army, has served as military assistant to the assistant to the president for national security affairs (1977-81); associate professor of social sciences and research officer, U.S. Military Academy (1974-77); and assistant army attache, Moscow (1972-74). He received his Ph.D. in political science and M.A. in Russian area studies from Columbia University, and has received many decorations, including the Defense Distinguished Service Medal, the Legion of Merit, and the Meritorious Service Medal.

WE do not know the full details of the evolution of the Soviet approach to nuclear weapons. Soviet officials whose views count for policy-making have not provided the rich discussions of the topic so common among their U.S. counterparts. A precise account of the growth and content of Soviet views, therefore, is not possible, but we can infer the general contours from considerable circumstantial evidence of three kinds.

The first kind of evidence is the historical record of how the Soviets have approached other new technology for weapons, particularly after World War I. That gives us a basis for judging the extent to which they have dealt with the nuclear era in a different or similar fashion.

Second, the Soviets have aired theoretical views about the nature of nuclear weapons and their relation to war and politics. While we may not want to take such utterances at face value, it is possible to determine their compatibility with other kinds of evidence. The greater the compatibility, the more credibility we can attribute to them.

Third, we have growing evidence of how the Soviets build their nuclear forces and the employment doctrine they teach for the use of those forces. Such actions cannot be wholly unrelated to Soviet views of nuclear weapons and in fact are probably the most compelling evidence.

The emerging picture of the Soviet view has little in common with popular views in the West. While accepting the revolutionary character of nuclear weapons for modern warfare, the Soviet leadership has proceeded on the traditional assumption that war, even nuclear war, must be made subordinate to pol-icy; that nuclear war might well break out; and that Soviet forces must be designed, organized, and trained to fight successfully under nuclear, chemical, and biological battlefield conditions.

Most important, while nuclear weapons can be decisive in the initial phases of a war, they alone are not adequate for victory. All branches of service and weapons systems must be integrated doctrinally for a combined-arms approach to war. As the Soviet military theorists see it, nuclear weapons affect dramatically not only the strategic but also the operational and tactical levels of warfare. Far from being unthinkable, nuclear warfare requires enormous doctrinal attention, material preparation, special training, and psychological toughness. Finally the vast resources allocated for nuclear war preparations in line with Soviet doctrinal dictates suggest a seriousness about the matter only vaguely appreciated in the West.

The Soviet leadership did not come to this view suddenly. Their doctrinal perspective has evolved as a dialectical interaction of three sources of influence: their traditional approach to military problems, based heavily on the experience of World War I and World War II; the physical characteristics of nuclear and other modern technology; and Western development of nuclear weapons and forces—Western military technology more than Western doctrine and force structure. The consequence has been the emergence of Soviet military capabilities that threaten to change fundamentally the nature of East-West relations, and a qualitative change in the military balance. Its effect on political relations is yet to be fully appreciated. But that is to reflect on the future; our purpose here is to review the evolution of Soviet views on nuclear weapons and warfare. Let us turn to the first kind of evidence, the traditional Soviet approach to revolutionary change in weapons technology.

THE SOVIET APPROACH TO NEW TECHNOLOGY FOR WAR

It is not widely appreciated the extent to which Soviet political and military leaders saw that World War I technologies —aviation, poison gas, motor vehicles— had wrought a dramatic change in the nature of war. The Soviets had been through the trauma of the first modern industrial mobilization on a massive scale during the war with Germany and the civil war. They faced isolation in the international arena at a time when they felt technologically inferior to and threatened by the West. Flush with victory, the young Red Commanders turned their minds to developing a revolution in military doctrine to fit the ideological imperatives of Marxism-Leninism.[1] And they followed Western military theorists, showing particular but critical fascination for their views on air power, chemical weapons, and industrial preparations.

For a few years this intellectual development filled the pages of Red Army journals and the writings of Trotsky, Frunze, Svechin, Shaposhnikov, Tukhachevskii, and others. To the extent that it had an early synthesis, it is to be found in two works by M.V. Frunze: "A Unified Military Doctrine" and "Front and Rear in War of the Future,"[2] brief tracts that summed up the critical tasks for Soviet military policy in the interwar period.

Key for Frunze was the nature of future war. In his view the world of military affairs had reached a new threshold. The front would no longer be the only locus of combat. Air power made the state's entire rear vulnerable to attack. Chemical weapons would make bombing all the more terrible, and motorization would permit deep mobile operations.

For the fledgling Soviet regime and its bankrupt economy, building capabilities to fight such a war was nothing short of daydreaming, in the minds of many. Although Trotsky accepted much of Frunze's view of the nature of future war, he lacked Frunze's enthusiasm to begin building a military establishment to conduct it. Yet the West's industrial and technology base seemed quite capable of providing such military power in the near future. Frunze expressed a clear understanding of Trotsky's point that building an industrial and technology base came first, and he was quite explicit that military requirements should determine the priorities of such development.[3] In retrospect, it seems that Stalin embraced much of what Frunze preached. Military factors probably had more to do with the structure of the First Five Year Plan than is generally realized.

In the realm of military operations and tactics, Svechin, Shaposhnikov, and Tukhachevskii carried the task with

1. Dmitri Fedotoff White, *The Growth of the Red Army* (Princeton, NJ: Princeton University Press, 1944).

2. *Izbrannye proizvedeniia* (Moscow: Voen-izdat, 1957), pp. 4-21, 133-42.

3. See my *Soviet Volunteers* (Princeton, NJ: Princeton University Press, 1973), pp. 40-49, for a discussion of this debate over the implications of new military technology.

remarkable brilliance. By the early 1930s, Tukhachevskii had demonstrated that an entire regiment could be dropped by parachute at one time. By 1936 he had revised the concept of deep operations to mean 50 to 100 kilometers at one stroke.[4] Soviet industry, in the meantime, produced the T-34 tank, which won the reputation as the best tank in World War II. Although the Soviet aviation industry did not perform as effectively, it continued to receive the highest development priority.

The event of war in 1939 vindicated much of the Soviet military thinking. Deep operations and bombing became common; the rear did prove part of the combat zone; and the Soviet judgment that airpower alone could not win a war proved valid.[5] A combined-arms approach, the Soviet preference, was imperative. The American Strategic Bombing Survey of Germany after the war was substantial evidence of Soviet wisdom on that account. German war production continued to increase even under Allied bombing. For Soviet tacticians, bombing made sense primarily in support of ground operations, not as a separate operation—a view that later would hold for nuclear weapons.

Two key points emerge from this brief historical review. First, the Soviets found themselves confronted with a revolution in military technology and doctrine but without the means to implement it easily. Second, while several Western theorists insisted that strategic air power would be wholly decisive, the Soviets never entertained that view seriously. It would be important but could not relegate combined-arms operations to irrelevancy. The frightening new weapons had to be integrated with all forces for combat at the operational and tactical as well as strategic level.

At the end of World War II, the Soviet military leadership found itself in a position strikingly analogous to the one they occupied in the 1920s. A new triad of technologies was revolutionizing the nature of warfare: nuclear weapons, rocketry, and cybernetics. Again they were behind in research and development (R & D) and left with a war-torn industrial base.

Because of Stalin's ironclad censorship, we know much less about how the Soviets analyzed the new challenge than in the 1920s, when the military professional journals recorded the competition of ideas fairly faithfully. By the mid-1950s, however, nuclear weapons were being discussed in *Red Star* and other Soviet newspapers. The theme was not their impact on military science and doctrine but rather public education about nuclear effects and how to mitigate them. Though they were presented as powerful weapons, the emphasis was survivability.[6] A great deal of reasonably accurate data were published about radiation doses, protective shelter, and proper mental toughness to deal with the impact of a nuclear strike.[7]

4. David M. Glantz, "Soviet Operational Formation for Battle," *Military Review*, 63:2-12 (Feb. 1983).

5. See A. Lapchinskii, "Vozdushnaya voina bydushchego," *Voina i revolutsiia* (Moscow: Voenizdat, 1931), bk. 3, pp. 3-15, for a Soviet critique of Douhet.

6. G. C. Reinhardt, "Atomic Weapons and Warfare," in *The Red Army*, ed. Riddell Hart (New York: Harcourt, Brace, 1956), pp. 420-51.

7. Leon Goure, *Civil Defense in the Soviet Union* (Berkeley: University of California Press, 1962).

This policy of popular literacy in matters of nuclear effects has been sustained to the present in the USSR and even made mandatory in elementary and high schools. It stands in curious contrast to the American approach, which, beginning in the mid-1960s, encouraged illiteracy about nuclear effects and prophylactic measures. The consistency of the Soviet policy cannot be discounted as a clue to official thinking. Western empirical analysis of the Soviet popular civil defense literature supports the technical details it teaches, even if the overall estimates of survivability are too optimistic.[8]

Parallel with silence on the military implications of nuclear weapons, R & D went ahead with surprising speed. By 1949 a bomb had been exploded. In 1957 *Sputnik* demonstrated that the USSR could soon produce intercontinental ballistic missiles (ICBMs). Bomber developments copied early U.S. models, first the B-29 and later the B-47. And in 1959 a new branch of service, the Strategic Rocket Forces, was created.

In 1962 Marshal V. D. Sokolovskii's celebrated *Military Strategy* appeared. Revised in 1963 and 1968, it has become the most comprehensive Soviet statement on the nature of nuclear war. After Stalin's death, Soviet officers began publishing articles that treated some aspects of the nuclear weapons problem, but none as extensively as the Sokolovskii volume. Playing a role analogous to Frunze's "Unified Military Doctrine" and "Front and Rear," it is a synthesis of the work of many military specialists, summing up the thinking in the military academies, the General Staff, and classified journals.

Its conceptual approach to analysis is highly reminiscent of Frunze's. It begins by defining the nature of future war in which "rockets and weapons of mass destruction" would be used. It describes the character anticipated for the nuclear battlefield. It points out the likely impact on the scope and depth of operations and the kinds and sizes of forces that would be required, the realities that combined arms doctrine would have to take into account. Unlike much writing in the West, it draws heavily on historical experience from World War I and World War II. Emphasizing continuity, it also stresses what is new and what must be done to deal with the novel aspects of new weaponry. Its outline of requirements for future Soviet Armed Forces bore little resemblance to the forces in being in the 1960s. It was a road map for force development, just as Frunze's tracts had set forth the direction for future force and doctrinal development rather than articulating a doctrine for existing military capabilities.

The similarity of the Soviet approaches to new military technology in the post-World War I and post-World War II decades is quite strong. It is critical for understanding the weakness of the arguments in the West that the Soviet military leaders did not take the nuclear issue seriously until after Stalin's death, and that they then were far behind the thinking in the West. The conviction that the Soviet analysts were behind persists in many Western quarters.[9] In fact it was popular to speak of

8. Leon Goure, *War Survival in Soviet Strategy: Civil Defense* (Miami: Center for Advanced International Studies, 1976).

9. Lawrence Feedman, *The Evolution of Nuclear Strategy* (New York: St. Martin's Press, 1981), pp. 58-59.

"raising the Soviet learning curve" during the first round of Strategic Arms Limitation Talks (SALT I).[10] No academic military treatises on deterrence theory appeared in the Soviet Union, and talk of the destruction of mankind was limited to occasional statements by senior leaders, notably Malenkov and Khrushchev. As will be shown presently, statements by party leaders were taken to mean that military hawks and civilian doves were debating nuclear policy in the USSR. In retrospect, this seems unlikely. Not only was the USSR not stagnating in the area of thought about nuclear weapons, it was developing the issue along its own unique lines at a rapid pace, considering the long period of Soviet industrial and R & D reconstruction.

THE SOVIET DEBATE ABOUT NUCLEAR WAR

To consider the second kind of evidence, much has been made of a limited number of statements and articles about nuclear war by high-level Soviet military and political officials. Quotations can be found that seem to vindicate all sides of the debate in the West. Indeed it would be surprising if there were no differences of opinion, and it may well be that military doctrine got caught up in those debates. Only a small number of officials, however, have had sufficient access to information on nuclear weapons to participate cogently in such discussions. Would they have carried their differences into the open press?

The answer depends on the political circumstances at the time. In the post-Stalin succession struggle, differences

among competing factions appear in retrospect to have crept into public debate. In the Brezhnev years there was greater control over publication of serious policy disputes that were congruent with political factions. At both times it has proved difficult to know whether proponents of particular public views held them for tactical reasons or from genuine conviction.

For example, in 1954 Malenkov insisted that a major war would bring the "destruction of world civilization." Khrushchev took the opposite view—that a world war would mean the victory of the Soviet Union and socialism. A short time later, Khrushchev could be found emphasizing that war is no longer "fatalistically inevitable." After the Cuban missile crisis, the Chinese entered the Soviet debate, chiding Khrushchev for claiming that nuclear weapons have changed the relationship between politics and war, that war is no longer a continuation of politics. This would mean, the Chinese said, that there is no longer any difference between just and unjust wars.[11] More than a decade later, in 1974, Brezhnev told the Polish Sejm that "in recent years such a mass of weapons has already been stockpiled to make it possible to destroy every living thing on earth several times."

Khrushchev's statements have been taken by some to mean that he preferred a minimum-deterrence strategy and a reduction of general purpose forces. Brezhnev's statement has been interpreted as a warning to his own military spokesmen who, at about the same time, were proclaiming the political utility of nuclear weapons, the validity of the Leninist theory of just and unjust wars, and

10. John Newhouse, *Cold Dawn* (New York: Holt, Rinehart and Winston, 1973), p. 4.

11. Radio Peking, in English, 31 Aug. 1963.

the victory of socialism in the event of a world war. Put in the political context in which both Brezhnev and Khrushchev spoke, it is equally, perhaps more, cogent to interpret their words as political tactics. Aiming at international audiences, not domestic military staffs, they sought resonance in the West, which they got, not changes in Soviet military programs, which did not occur. It certainly would not be wise Soviet policy to pursue a consistent policy line of nuclear saber rattling. That could encourage the very Western response the Soviet military does not want: a sustained set of North Atlantic Treaty Organization (NATO) military programs to deal with the growing Soviet nuclear arsenal.

At a lower level in the Soviet hierarchy two series of public exchanges were far more explicit, the first in the mid-1960s between retired Major General Talenskii and Lieutenant Colonel Rybkin. Talenskii put it bluntly: "In our days there is no more dangerous illusion than the idea that thermonuclear war can still serve as an instrument of politics, that it is possible to achieve political aims by using nuclear weapons and at the same time survive."[12] Rybkin countered Talenskii by name, asserting that "to maintain that victory in nuclear war is in general impossible would not only be untrue theoretically but dangerous from a political viewpoint."[13] Colonel Sidelnikov echoed Rybkin's critique the same month in *Red Star* with the charge that "some people" were ignoring the dangers of war by arguing that the maintenance of large armed forces was unnec-

essary. Others attacked Talenskii as well, and his side of the issue found no other vocal support.

Again in 1973 and 1974 there were public exchanges concerning the size and nature of necessary Soviet forces. Military authors Major General Milovidov and Rear Admiral Shelyag voiced the one line, while Georgii Arbatov, Aleksandr Bovin, and G. A. Trofimenko of the USA Institute in Moscow made the counterarguments. Milovidov and Shelyag criticized the so-called quantifiers who wanted to determine force levels by mathematics rather than by traditional dialectical methods. The primacy of politics over military technology, even in the nuclear age, remained their tenet of faith. Arbatov and his colleagues spoke of the suicidal nature of nuclear war and quoted Clausewitz against the military spokesmen.

Marshal Grechko and Marshal Kulikov put themselves on record in 1974, firmly on the side of the Leninist and Clausewitzian view of war and politics. This of course was the same year that Brezhnev warned about the size of nuclear arsenals during his speech to the Polish Sejm, and Kosygin told his election district about the dangers of the nuclear arms race.

It is easy to see all these public statements as part of an open domestic debate over the nuclear issue and defense budgets. A look at the institutional positions of the authors, however, throws doubt on this interpretation. Milovidov and Shelyag are members of the faculty of the Lenin Political-Military Academy. They write for the education of the Soviet officer corps, particularly its political education. Arbatov and his staff at the USA Institute have long cultivated an American constituency. They are

12. "Poslednaya voina: nekotorie razmyshleniia," *Mezhdunarodnaya zhizn,* 5 (May 1965).

13. "O kharaktere yadernoraketnoi voine," *Kommunist vooruzhenykh sil,* 17 (Sept. 1965).

well read in Western literature on nuclear weapons and strategy. Their knowledge of Soviet military affairs is dubious at best, as they do not enjoy access to Soviet military circles. Their task is to know and to influence Western, not Soviet, opinion. It is entirely possible that they were posing in their statements, that the debate was in fact a calculated sham.

Statements by Brezhnev, Kosygin, and other high party officials did not refute the Milovidov-Shelyag line directly. They did not treat the ideological issues raised by the military writers. Rather they spoke of the dangers of the arms race, a point most appropriate for the arms control and detente policy they were pursuing. It is not clear, therefore, that they were indeed parties to the debate. In fact the whole affair looks more like a well-orchestrated campaign designed to deal with different audiences without creating confusion within the USSR. Soviet military programs, doctrine, and training were proceeding on a course quite at odds with the Arbatov line, a line given gentle reinforcement by Brezhnev and Kosygin. Had that been the only line, confusion could have arisen in the regular political education of the officer corps as to the real essence of detente and arms control. Much of the officer corps, unlike the larger Soviet public, knew the direction of Soviet military doctrine and programs. They needed a political-ideological line that fit the military realities.

Shelyag sounded a theme that is critical for the Soviet regime: the morality of a nuclear war in which everyone perishes. How can any such war be just, whatever its purpose? Shelyag answered that while a nuclear war would be highly destructive, everyone would not be destroyed. In fact the socialist camp would achieve victory. In that case, it would be just, serving a moral purpose. None of the military spokesmen advocated nuclear war. They simply insisted that it would not mean the end of mankind because of the strength of the Soviet Armed Forces and Soviet nuclear weapons. Implicitly they were agreeing with the 1963 Chinese critique of Khrushchev's utterances on the nature of nuclear war.

This is not a trivial point. To accept the alternative view would be to turn Marx and Lenin on their heads, giving technology primacy over politics, denying a voluntarist role for policymakers. True, a mechanistically determinist interpretation of Marx held sway in many Marxist circles, most notably among the Mensheviks in Russia and much of European Social Democracy in the nineteenth century. But even Marx envisioned political consciousness by the revolutionary masses, and Lenin insisted upon designing a concept of a highly voluntarist political party to ensure that political consciousness would be a basis for mass action. From a Leninist viewpoint, Arbatov and his colleagues were clearly in serious ideological error. Brezhnev and Kosygin never went that far, nor has any other major Soviet leader, except possibly Malenkov and Khrushchev, neither of whom made his heretical views prevail. Nor is it clear that any of these apparently errant Marxist-Leninists really believed their own non-Marxist-Leninist utterings with more than tactical conviction. Neither is the point trivial for Western policy and opinion makers. Have nuclear weapons transcended politics, removed political choice in the affairs of war?

Our interpretations of the thin Soviet literature on the relation of nuclear weapons to politics have tended to be so inextricably intertwined with our own domestic debates about nuclear weapons policy that what little insight they may offer has been blurred, distorted, or wholly lost. At best, we can only see through that glass darkly. For greater clarity we must turn to other glasses.

THE CHARACTER OF SOVIET FORCE DEVELOPMENT

The third kind of evidence of Soviet views of nuclear weapons is the character of Soviet force development. Open source information on Soviet forces and weapons is far from complete, but publications such as the *Military Balance,* updated annually by the International Institute for Strategic Studies in London, give a fairly clear view of the emerging profile of weapons and forces. The Department of Defense publication of *Soviet Military Power* in 1981 and 1983 filled in that profile considerably. In the 1960s, before the full momentum and direction of Soviet force development was unambiguously clear, it was possible to debate about what form and substance it would take. In the 1980s there is less basis for such debate. Even those analysts who took the most conservative view—estimating large Soviet military growth projections in the 1960s and early 1970s—turned out to be on the low side when the evidence came in on actual Soviet military programs. While words on policy and doctrine for nuclear weapons are quite cheap, weapons, troops, and equipment are not. The question follows, therefore, Whose words on nuclear weapons seem more in line with Soviet force structure? Those of Arbatov, Trofimenko, and Bovin? Or those of Sokolovskii, Shelyag, Milovidov, Grechko, and Ogarkov?

It was widely believed by Western military analysts and defense officials in the 1960s that the Soviet nuclear force structure goals were parity with the United States. Secretary of Defense McNamara chose the criterion of assured destruction as a budget measure of how much is enough for nuclear forces. He did not expect the Soviet land-based ICBM force to grow beyond 1054 launchers, the size of the U.S. force. In fact by 1975 approximately 1600 ICBM launchers were in the Soviet force. As qualitative improvements were pursued, the number dropped to about 1400, but the number of warheads on the fourth-generation ICBMs—SS-17, SS-18, and SS-19—increased dramatically because they can carry more warheads than earlier generations.

Not only did numbers increase. Accuracy also improved so that the latest-model SS-18 and SS-19 enjoy a hard target kill capability, accuracy sufficient to destroy U.S. ICBM silos. At the same time, evidence appeared that Soviet launchers have a reload capability. Additional missiles may be stored and used in surviving ICBM silos for subsequent launches after initial exchanges.[14] From the U.S. doctrinal view of nuclear weapons employment, these were surprising developments. Strategic stability between the two superpowers, it was believed, derives from mutual vulnerability. The growing Soviet arsenal could conceivably be launched first and effectively destroy the U.S. land-based ICBM force, and would be large enough to retain a reserve of accurate warheads for subsequent attacks on other targets in the United States. Such a Soviet force clearly exceeds what Western analysts judge necessary for deterrence.

14. Department of Defense, *Soviet Military Power* (Washington, DC: Government Printing Office, 1983), p. 21.

Further evidence is accruing to suggest that Soviet forces will not stand still at the parity level. Not only has a new ICBM of the MX variety been tested, but a small mobile ICBM is also in the test phase.[15] Small mobile ICBMs of course change the prospects of survivability dramatically. They cannot be pretargeted before a conflict breaks out. They simply do not fit the concepts of Western deterrence theory unless both sides forgo strategic defensive programs.

Although it was widely assumed that the Soviet commitment to the ban on antiballistic missiles (ABMs) in the SALT I treaty meant a commitment to abandon strategic defense, Soviet behavior belies that belief. The Soviet civil defense program has proceeded on a countrywide scale. Deployments include over 10,000 missile launchers with over 12,000 missiles located at over 1000 air defense sites. Progress in low-altitude air defense has been considerable. ABM radars and interceptors have been deployed within the limits of the treaty, giving the USSR an edge in the event of a breakout from the treaty. Hardening and redundancy in the military and political command and control have gone ahead with surprising speed.[16]

Soviet programs for cruise missiles, strategic bombers, and improved submarine-launched ballistic missiles show equal vitality, but the ICBM and strategic defense programs alone are difficult to explain as anything less than a serious capability for waging global nuclear war. Force developments, however, do not stop there, but go right down to the tactical level.

The theater weapon, the mobile SS-20, continues to be deployed at a rapid rate—351 with 1053 warheads are now extant—giving the USSR a large nuclear capability with great accuracy against Europe, the Far East, and the Persian Gulf region.[17] At operational and tactical levels—front, army, and division—short-range ballistic missiles with nuclear warheads have long been deployed. Now they are being modernized for greater accuracy and mobility on the battlefield. Nuclear capable frontal aviation and artillery are also receiving significant attention in Soviet programs.[18]

Not as well understood, but integrally related to these tactical delivery systems, is the character of Soviet ground forces. Tanks were recognized early on as highly survivable in a nuclear environment. They could lean into nuclear fire support for offensive operations. But tanks need infantry, artillery, and air defense to achieve combat success. Accordingly in the 1960s the Soviet Army began converting its infantry to motorized formations in armor-protected fighting vehicles. Artillery and air defense weapons have followed this pattern. Today many Soviet divisions are equipped with almost fully protected tank, infantry, air defense, and artillery units. Their armored vehicles have interior protective characteristics to reduce the risk of exposure to radiation and chemical and biological weapons.[19]

This sketch of Soviet force development is incomplete, but it does highlight the Soviet view of nuclear weapons. The cost of this preparation is not trivial. It is inconceivable that it just occurred from bureaucratic momentum in the defense industries and the military staffs. In fact Colonel Oleg Penskovskii tells us that

15. Ibid., p. 18.
16. Ibid., pp. 27-30.

17. Ibid., pp. 36-37.
18. Ibid., pp. 37-40.
19. Ibid., pp. 38-40.

some parts of the military establishment did not welcome it.[20] It meant dramatic changes within the Soviet military. It involved a transformation of the officer corps, significant new organizational changes for command and control, and fundamental decisions in industrial development and R & D. To find a rationale for this radical transformation, we must look at the transition in Soviet military doctrine.

THE TRANSITION IN
SOVIET MILITARY DOCTRINE

Soviet military writers are precise in their use of "military doctrine." They define it as a state's unique, officially accepted system of views on war and the armed forces used in them. It must take into account the political, social, economic, and geographical peculiarities of the particular state.[21] We should not, therefore, expect it to follow Western patterns.

As already mentioned, the possibility that nuclear weapons had transcended politics caused no little concern within Soviet political and military circles. It may well be that for a time in the 1950s the policy-significant Soviet elite took this possibility seriously. Perhaps Khrushchev did try to turn Clausewitz and Lenin on their heads, subordinating politics to weapons. The fact that officers published classified articles dealing with the possibility suggests that the top leaders had not come down clearly from the beginning.

Parallel to the apparent debate at the level of senior leadership, the USA Institute, and the Lenin Military-Political Academy, a more textured discussion was clearly under way within military circles by the mid-1950s. Although R & D had gone ahead full speed under Stalin for producing nuclear weapons and rockets, a number of military writers complained in the de-Stalinization period that not enough thought had been given to the proper doctrinal implications of such weapons for force design and operational art. Major General Talenskii, editor of the classified journal *Voennaya mysl'*, called there for a discussion in September 1953, insisting that Stalin's "permanently operating factors" were not adequate theoretical development of the implication of nuclear weapons.[22]

Publicly this internal concern with nuclear weapons became known as the "revolution in military affairs," but it did not parallel the Western dynamic that led to "deterrence theory." Instead it followed a path described in Marshal Rotmistrov's article in *Voennaya mysl'* in 1958, which asserted that indeed there is a new military age at hand. Rather than emphasizing the unwinnability of nuclear war, Rotmistrov insisted that "Possessing powerful weapons of destruction, Soviet military strategy is now capable of fulfilling great missions quickly and achieving a drastic change in the military-political situation."[23] He spoke of the implications for operational art and tactics, for second-echelon forces and reserves, of highly mobile operations under nuclear conditions.

20. *The Penskovskii Papers* (Garden City, NY: Doubleday, 1965), pp. 233 ff.

21. *Dictionary of Basic Military Terms* (Moscow: Voenizdat, 1965; rpt. U.S. Air Force, Washington, DC: Government Printing Office, n.d.), p. 37.

22. Harriet Fast and William F. Scott, eds., *The Soviet Art of War* (Boulder, CO: Westview Press, 1982), pp. 123 ff.

23. Ibid., p. 140.

Finally Rotmistrov put nuclear weapons in historical perspective. Prior to World War I, new military technology had influenced only tactics; tanks, and aviation, appearing in World War I and World War II, influenced not only tactics but also operational art—that is, a much larger geographical area of combat. Nuclear weapons, he insisted, influence all three levels—strategy, operational art, and tactics—the full range of global warfare. Western deterrence theory differs fundamentally from this approach in that it tends to treat operational art and tactics as irrelevant in the event nuclear weapons are used, placing serious military attention only on the strategic level.

In January 1960 before the Supreme Soviet, Khrushchev and his minister of defense, Marshal Malinovskii, placed great emphasis on the formation of a new branch of service, the Strategic Rocket Forces. The next year at the Twenty-first Party Congress, Malinovskii announced that any world war unleashed by "imperialist aggressors" would inevitably take the form of nuclear-rocket war. Once again citing the new Strategic Rocket Forces, he called for remaking Soviet military art and retraining personnel, especially officers. Finally he called attention to the reduction in active duty military personnel.[24]

Many in the West at the time viewed this new Soviet military policy as a belated coming around to more advanced Western assessments of the implications of nuclear weapons. Khrushchev, some believed, was choosing a minimum-deterrence strategy. Certainly Western writings were closely followed in the USSR, and they may have stimulated tendencies to emulate Western strategic logic, but clearly those tendencies failed

to gather much support, if any serious consideration at all.

Raymond L. Garthoff, Herbert Dinerstein, and Thomas Wolfe followed this "revolution in military affairs" in the USSR at the time.[25] Their close scrutiny of the Soviet literature attuned them to the particularistic Soviet perspectives, and many of their judgments look sound in retrospect—judgments too frequently ignored by deterrence theorists and defense analysts, who accept too uncritically the superiority of Western theory on nuclear war and overemphasize the discontinuity in Soviet military ·thinking created by Stalin's death. A former Soviet officer now in the West describes his perplexity at what he read of Western doctrine while serving with the General Staff. He believed that it must have been dreamed up "to reassure nervous old-age pensioners." As U.S. force deployments unfolded in line with the doctrine, he reports that it was "greeted with the greatest delight in the Kremlin and by the General Staff."[26]

The analytical work for changing Soviet military policy would emerge in print in 1962 as Marshal Sokolovskii's *Military Strategy,* hardly a treatise in support of deterrence theory. Although not definitive on the precise scenario nuclear war would take, it did lay down parameters for strategy, operational art, tactics, and force development. Nuclear-rocket war would allow for great mobility in shifting military force rapidly. That would require dispersion of forma-

24. Ibid., p. 158.

25. Garthoff, *Soviet Strategy in the Nuclear Age* (New York: Frederick A. Praeger, 1958); Dinerstein, *War and the Soviet Union* (New York: Praeger, 1959); and Wolfe, *Soviet Strategy at the Cross Roads* (Cambridge, MA: Harvard University Press, 1964).

26. Victor Suvorov, *Inside the Soviet Army* (New York: Macmillan, 1982), p. 161.

tions to prevent damage by enemy nuclear strikes, but it also would require rapid concentration of forces to affect the correlations of forces at points and times decisive for offensive operations. Surprise and the initial period of a war took on new significance. Also, the professional and moral quality of officers and troops would be critical for troop control.

How do we interpret the reduction in forces that Khrushchev carried out and his great emphasis on the rocket forces? Did he indeed lose out in an attempt to implement a minimum-deterrence strategy? Reading Sokolovskii, one can easily reach that conclusion. But it is well to remember the analogy between the 1920s and the 1950s before concluding that Khrushchev and his marshals were at odds on policy. The large Red Army had been demobilized in 1921-23 against considerable internal resistance. The senior military leadership realized that the cost of a large standing force structure would make it impossible to afford the military modernization program they believed imperative in light of new military technology.

Stalin took a similar approach in the 1940s, reducing Soviet forces dramatically in order to afford reconstruction and the development of nuclear and rocket weapons. Had he lived, he undoubtedly would have followed Khrushchev's policy with additional reductions, particularly within the officer corps. Soviet officers from World War II did not possess the level of technical education necessary to deal with the new weaponry. A new generation of officers had to be trained. The same undertaking began in 1923 with the Red Commanders sent to the War College, later to become the Frunze Academy. In the post-World War II period, the educa-

tional imperative was much stronger and applied as well to enlisted personnel. In the 1950s and 1960s, officer pre-commissioning training increased from one or two to five years, and the literacy level of troops went up no less dramatically. The peasant manpower base has shifted to an urban base, not as fully as the Soviet leadership would like, but dramatically nonetheless. Far from a minimum-deterrence strategy, Khrushchev and the military leadership were committing the USSR to a long-term force build-up to be based on the character of future war as defined by Sokolovskii's collaborators.

If we reflect on the Soviet force structure that has come into existence in the past two decades against this interpretation of Soviet military policy decisions of the 1950s and early 1960s, then Soviet military programs look logical. Nuclear weapons do change the requisites of military art but not the fundamental relationship between politics and war, and changes implied by new doctrine are easy to find in Soviet military capabilities.

DOCTRINAL CHANGES AND FORCE STRUCTURE

One of the most distinctive changes that evolving Soviet doctrine dictates for force structure concerns the level of war stocks and ready forces that should be maintained in peacetime. That issue was extensively examined in the 1920s in light of the experience of European powers in 1914. They had not planned for economic mobilization; they expected a short war to be fought with extant war reserves. Some Red Army theorists argued that much larger peacetime stocks would be essential in the future. Others argued that the economic burden of such a policy would be too high. A better alternative would be a militia system of industry in which the entire economy could be quickly brought to military production, if not just before hostilities, then in the early months of a war. Trotsky, Frunze, and Voroshilov—the commissars of war—all came down more or less on the same side: put as little capital into war reserves as prudence allows and give priority to building a large industrial base that can mobilize swiftly in wartime. Thus the Red Army did not enjoy an abundance of equipment and weapons until the late 1930s. When the war started, an industrial mobilization plan did take effect, albeit with mixed results at first. And eventually, with U.S. aid, Soviet war production surged.

The Soviet answer in the nuclear era is different. The requirement for rapid industrial mobilization remains, but because of the possibly decisive nature of the initial period of war, forces in being at the beginning of hostilities are far more critical than in the past.[27] This line of reasoning has been consistent in Soviet writings on doctrine. Accordingly Soviet force structure and war matériel have steadily grown in the 1960s and 1970s.[28] The levels in many categories are three or four times as high as NATO levels and still growing. This enormous allocation of resources certainly makes no sense in light of popular Western views of nuclear deterrence doctrine, but from the viewpoint of Soviet military writing on the nature of nuclear war it is imperative.

27. See, for example, V. E. Savkin, *Osnovnye printsipi operativnogo isskustva i taktiki* (Moscow: Voenizdat, 1972), p. 368.
28. *Soviet Military Power,* p. 63.

Another distinctive change in force structure that also makes sense from the Soviet doctrinal viewpoint is the offensive character of the forces. Sokolovskii's volume describes war in which "weapons of mass destruction" require great dispersion of forces to limit damage to them. At the same time, it argues that nuclear weapons allow and require great mobility and concentration of military power. How are these apparently incompatible criteria possible to obtain simultaneously?

Dispersion is obtained by deep echelonment, stretching formations out far to the rear of the line of contact with the enemy. Concentration is obtained by high-speed offensive maneuver, advancing at the rate of 60-100 kilometers per day. That rate of attack creates a rapid accumulation of forces at the line of contact for breakthroughs and penetrations deep into the enemy's rear where he is less likely to employ nuclear weapons because of the proximity of his own forces and population. As mentioned earlier, tank units inherently have this kind of mobility and armor protection from nuclear effects, but infantry and artillery have not traditionally enjoyed the same advantages.

Thus in light of Soviet doctrine, the dramatic transformation of Soviet ground forces over the past two decades—giving armor protection and motorization to infantry, artillery, air defense, and other branches of combat support—becomes understandable. It is also clear why armored vehicles have been provided with additional protective liners against nuclear and chemical effects, why decontamination units have been made organic to all fighting formations. Colonel Savkin in 1972 elaborated in considerable detail this synthesis of new military technology with the doctrinal requisites of the nuclear battlefield.[29] Savkin is not exceptional in this regard.[30]

In the 1960s, before Soviet forces had been fully armored and motorized, there was little indication in Soviet doctrinal literature to suggest a conventional phase. Now that the Soviet modernization process is well advanced, there is more discussion of a conventional phase enduring for days and weeks. And as John Erickson explains, the Soviet command does not have to face a nuclear/ conventional choice, but rather has both choices as conditions may dictate. John Hemsley adduces much evidence for the same conclusion.[31]

This evolution in Soviet doctrine and forces continues, much the way it did under Tukhachevskii in the 1930s with the concept of deep operations. C. N. Donnelly has recently recorded its latest development in the concept of the operational maneuver group.[32] With the higher possible speed of armor forces and attack helicopter support, Soviet tacticians seem to believe that they can push larger forces deeper into NATO's rear in the first days of conflict. Not only do such operations promise to paralyze the defense, but they also lean into nuclear fire support, which can be delivered several hundreds of kilometers deep with

the new and more accurate tactical ballistic missiles found at the division, army, and front organization levels.[33]

Marshal Ogarkov, chief of the Soviet General Staff since 1977, appears to have provided the impetus for this modification in doctrine to achieve greater offensive speed. He argues that doctrine must keep up with new technology. Pauses of several days between frontal operations, as was the case in World War II, can be reduced to no pause at all if modern technology is fully exploited.[34] He expresses great concern for better command and control, for the "theater of military operations" level of command, the critical level for future war. One gets the impression that Ogarkov is saying that the Soviet military cannot rest on what it achieved in the 1960s and 1970s but must keep up the pace in the 1980s and 1990s, not only in offensive capabilities but also in strategic defense of the economy.

Western deterrence theorists might well ask what difference all this concern with tactics and operational art will make if strategic nuclear forces are used. Western understanding of the operationalstrategic nexus for theater war is not highly developed, but Soviet military leaders have devoted considerable thought to it. Joseph D. Douglass and Amoretta M. Hoeber, relying heavily on Soviet classified writings that have become public in the West, show an evolving Soviet strategic nuclear forces doctrine with roots in Sokolovskii's basic

29. *Osnovnye printsipi,* pp. 229-65.

30. See, for example, many others cited by John Erickson, *The College Station Papers, 2: Soviet Combined Arms: Theory and Practice* (College Station: Center for Strategic Technology, Texas A&M University, 1980).

31. *Soviet Troop Control* (Oxford: Brassey's Publishers, 1982).

32. "The Soviet Operational Maneuver Group: A New Challenge for NATO," *Military Review,* 63:43-60 (Mar. 1983).

33. See *Soviet Military Power,* pp. 37-38, for details on the new SS-21, SS-22, and SS-23 tactical missiles.

34. *Always Ready to Defend the Fatherland* (Moscow: Voenizdat, 1982), pp. 33 ff.

characterization of nuclear war.[35] And what we know of Soviet strategic force development lends added credence to such analysis. ICBM reloadable silos, small ICBM development, strategic air defense, and a large ABM R & D program make sense for a military establishment that holds the doctrinal view— explored by Douglass and Hoeber—that war at the strategic nuclear level is to be managed in order to gain and hold the strategic initiative for phases after the initial period.

HOW THE EVIDENCE STACKS UP

To understand what all this adds up to, let us review the three kinds of evidence indicated at the beginning as available to shed light on our topic.

First, the Soviet approach to new military technologies after World War I and World War II reveals more parallels and continuities than are usually recognized. There are dramatic differences in some of the policy conclusions from each period, but the Soviet approach to nuclear weapons and rocketry appears to share more with their own interwar experience with aviation and motorization than with Western deterrence theory and assured destruction standards for force levels.

Second, the record of Soviet theoretical discussions of nuclear weapons is mixed. It can be argued that some Soviet figures share Western assumptions about the implications of nuclear weapons for war outcomes.[36] But close

35. *Soviet Strategy for Nuclear War* (Stanford, CA: Hoover Institution Press, 1979).

36. For an example, see Robert L. Arnett, "Soviet Attitudes Towards Nuclear War: Do They Really Think They Can Win?" *Journal of Strategic Studies*, 2:172-90 (Sept. 1979).

examination of the context of apparent Soviet debate over opposing approaches can lead to the opposite conclusion. Even if a Western-min 'ed faction in Soviet policy circles is granted, its effect, if any, seems to have been marginal. Its opponents have consistently captured more space in the press, a monopoly of textbooks for officer education, and greater access to the Soviet domestic audience.

Third, the record of Soviet force development and nuclear weapons employment doctrine shows a unique Soviet approach, clearly in line with the approach to new military technologies in the 1920s. It was slower in emerging in the postwar decades, not finding articulate public expression until the early 1960s. Since that time, however, it has advanced methodically, elaborating the details of a combined-arms operational art with appropriate weapons, equipment, and training. This approach shows great respect for the revolutionary character of nuclear weapons, demonstrated by staggering allocations of resources to all branches of military forces to make them usable in the event of a nuclear war.

WHAT DOES THE EVIDENCE REALLY MEAN ABOUT THE SOVIET VIEW OF NUCLEAR WEAPONS?

Ambiguities in the evidence will continue to allow for different conclusions about what the Soviets really think. It does seem, however, that a lot of concrete Soviet behavior, expressed in the development of weapons and forces, narrows significantly the diversity of compelling conclusions. The view widely held in the 1960s and 1970s that the USSR would essentially follow the U.S. lead, that the technical imperatives of nuclear effects would make them see a war-fighting capability as a pointless goal, is no longer tenable. Even if it is pointless—a fact not yet proven by experience—Soviet leaders clearly do not see it that way. They are investing their scarce resources on the probability that it is not pointless.

Such a Soviet view does not necessarily mean that Soviet leaders are looking for an opportunity to use their nuclear war-fighting capability. We should take them quite seriously when they say that they want to avoid nuclear war. But we should also pay equally serious attention to the implications of the great Soviet emphasis on the necessity of efforts to prevent nuclear war.

The West has not challenged the Soviet postwar sphere of influence and territorial acquisitions. At the same time the USSR has continuously challenged the postwar Western international order—cautiously for the most part, but with their own military forces in the case of Afghanistan and with surrogate military forces in other instances. The danger of nuclear war comes from Soviet challenges to the international order, not from the weapons themselves. Furthermore, U.S. nuclear forces have been tailored for retaliation and defense, not territorial offensive operations. Precisely the opposite is true of Soviet nuclear forces. Doubtless, Soviet leaders prefer to reach the objectives of their definition of "peaceful coexistence"—another form of the international class struggle—without resort to world war. But it would be "adventurism," to use their term, to continue to challenge the West politically in Europe and with arms and surrogate military forces in the Third World without also having the capability to prevail in nuclear war if by some mis-

calculation it comes to that. Furthermore, having that kind of potentially usable force is bound to affect the political and psychological resistance of the West over time.

The Soviet approach to nuclear weapons in this regard creates a qualitatively different task for Western defense than in the first three decades of the postwar period. As long as U.S. nuclear forces were clearly superior to Soviet forces, U.S. employment doctrine was most likely to dictate the scenario a nuclear conflict would take. But as Soviet nuclear and other military capabilities have become equal and in some regards superior to NATO forces, the Soviet General Staff is likely to be able to impose its own scenario for such a conflict. That would seem to be not simply an intercontinental nuclear exchange but also a high-speed ground offensive, conventional if possible, supported by nuclear fires if deemed essential, to seize Europe in a few weeks, months at most. Similar ground offensives in the Far East and Southwest Asia might well be included, notwithstanding the effects of U.S. strategic strikes on the USSR.

The popular Western image of controlled or limited nuclear war has been one of small exchanges between the U.S. and the USSR. There is no place in the Soviet view for this kind of warfare. Indeed it makes no sense because it would involve the use of forces for only subjective, not objective, military purposes. That should not, however, be taken to mean that the USSR would launch the majority of its nuclear forces in one large strike in an uncontrolled fashion. Initial strikes would be large but only a part of the Soviet arsenal, and they would be aimed at changing radically the correlation of forces so that

Soviet combined-arms offensives could succeed dramatically. We should expect large reserves of Soviet nuclear forces held for subsequent phases of the war. Soviet writings make little attempt to define the duration and precise character of those phases.[37]

Clearly, popular Western views of controlled and uncontrolled nuclear exchanges are incompatible with Soviet views of the meaning such terms might have. In their view all forms of nuclear war would be controlled in an operational sense. They would involve the interrelationship of combat in several theaters of war and at all three levels—strategic, operational, and tactical. As noted earlier, the Western view tends to discard the theater operational and tactical levels as inoperative when the strategic level comes into play, and the only theaters seem to be the homelands of the two superpowers. There is no sign, however, of a controlled homeland-to-homeland concept of nuclear war based on tacit or explicit understanding of rules with an opponent. There is on the contrary a strong concern with controlled use of nuclear weapons to change the correlation of military forces early in a conflict, to gain and retain the strategic initiative, and to coordinate military operations with diplomacy aimed not at enemy governments but at so-called progressive political groups within enemy states.

If Soviet diplomacy and active measures in the West can prevent the United States and NATO from having more than minimum-deterrence nuclear capabilities, then it is not inconceivable that the initial period—to use the Soviet concept—of a world war could lead to the Soviet occupation of the European theater and possibly one or both of the other major contiguous theaters without significant projection of U.S. ground forces to their defense.[38] The cost would be a large nuclear blow to the Soviet homeland, but if the alternative were ignominious retreat in a crisis, the territorial and potential political and economic gains might seem worth forcing the U.S. to give up its powerful alliances on the Eurasian rimland. In the subsequent phases of such a war, could the United States remain a serious opponent? Could it attract and hold allies, even in the Western hemisphere? Could it deal with and defeat pro-Soviet groups in allied states?

Such a scenario could be relegated to the level of fantasy entertained only in the Lenin Military-Political Academy in previous decades when the United States persisted in asserting military superiority. In the decades ahead it cannot be dismissed, because Soviet force development, guided by such fantasy, has progressed far enough to give it a vague element of reality. We cannot wait for the definitive history of the Soviet approach to nuclear weapons, based on the Soviet General Staff archives, to make up our mind about its essential character. The evidence is already sufficient to provide a rather clear understanding, and the implications for Western defense are far too critical to indulge in dilatory debate about what is disturbingly obvious.

37. See Douglass and Hoeber, *Soviet Strategy for Nuclear War.*

38. See Suvorov, *Inside the Soviet Army,* pp. 163-67, for a former Soviet officer's view on these points.

* * *

QUESTIONS AND ANSWERS

Q (Charles Courtney, Drew University, New Jersey): You indicated that it is un-Marxian to let technology dictate political thinking. I would submit that it is also counter to our democratic humanistic traditions to have technology dictate our political thinking and political actions. I would like a response to my observation that in fact in both societies technology is dictating our political thinking and action.

A: I do not think we have the choice to reject that technology, to pretend it does not exist, nor do I think we will get a political agreement to do away with it. The Luddites did not succeed. I do not know of a society that succeeded in putting the technology genie back in the bottle once it got out. The task becomes how you deal with it and what kind of costs you are willing to pay.

COMMENT (Churchill): One aspect of problem technology is the way it tends to control what we take to be significant in our reasoning about the problems of nuclear war. I would point to the alarming dangers of expertise itself. I think all citizens should participate more directly in decision making concerning nuclear weapons. Expertise suggests to me an overriding tendency to try to see these problems entirely in terms of evidence and facts, leaving out of account the fact that factual situations do not come tagged, "This is significant," and "This is not significant." These problems depend rather on the way we conceive the issues, the conceptual, logical basis on which we deal with them.

ANNALS, *AAPSS,* **469,** September 1983

The Position of the USSR on
Nuclear Weapons and Arms Control

By YEVGENIY N. KOCHETKOV

ABSTRACT: The Soviet nuclear doctrine is to prevent nuclear war. Nuclear power in the hands of the USSR is a means of defense against nuclear attack. The Soviet Union has officially renounced first use of nuclear weapons and expects other nuclear nations to follow suit. Progress in the negotiations on strategic and European nuclear weapons can be achieved only on the basis of the principles of equality and equal security. The Soviet Union will do everything to keep the present strategic parity with the United States and will not allow the United States to gain nuclear superiority. Among the most urgent tasks of today is to prevent an extension of the arms race into outer space. Given goodwill, common sense, and the right principles, the USSR and the United States can cooperate successfully in the area of arms control and disarmament.

Yevgeniy N. Kochetkov has been first secretary of the USSR Embassy in Washington, D.C., since 1980, with responsibilities for international security issues and arms control and disarmament aspects of USSR-U.S. relations. He served in the Soviet consulate in New York in 1979, was for several years the executive secretary of the Soviet component of the USSR-U.S. Consultative Commission and held various positions in the Soviet delegation at the SALT II negotiations. A graduate of the Moscow school of diplomacy, he was assigned to the U.S. desk in the USSR Ministry of Foreign Affairs, and from 1966-72 was a simultaneous interpreter at the U.N. General Assembly and Security Council.

NOTE: This article was generated from an oral presentation that was given by the author in his capacity as an employee of the USSR government. The contents of the article are, therefore, in the public domain.

A better understanding of the Soviet nuclear doctrine requires first of all an understanding of what it is not. Our doctrine is not to win a nuclear war, not to prevail in a nuclear war, nor to restore by nuclear means deterrence on terms favorable to the Soviet side. In other words, the Soviet military and nuclear doctrine is to make nuclear war not possible at all. We do not visualize any nuclear demonstration shots for intimidation, nor any limited, protracted, or all-out wars. In our thinking, war simply must never happen.

To achieve this objective, to enhance security and maintain peace, we believe that the best means are detente and ultimate disarmament while preserving rough parity in nuclear strength between the USSR and the United States. Deterrence by the threat of an ever-increasing military force only increases the danger of nuclear calamity.

This parity developed in the early 1970s and has given the world a good measure of stability. The Soviet Union is determined to preserve it. Yet the USSR is not having any more nuclear weapons or other arms than are absolutely necessary to maintain parity. Compelled to counter the continuing military build-up and threats from the outside, the Soviet Union has built a powerful yet purely defensive capability as a forceful warning to aggressors. Soviet nuclear power is a means of defense against nuclear attack.

Of special significance in this regard is the fact that the Soviet Union has officially renounced first use of nuclear weapons. On 21 December 1982 Yuri V. Andropov said, "The unilateral commitment of the Soviet Union not to use nuclear weapons first was received with approval and hope over the world. If our example is followed by the other nuclear powers, this will be a truly momentous contribution to the efforts of preventing nuclear war." In January 1983 the Warsaw Treaty countries proposed concluding a treaty between the North Atlantic Treaty Organization (NATO) and the Warsaw Treaty Organization on the mutual nonuse of armed force and the maintenance of peaceful relations. We believe it to be a good initiative.

Under these circumstances no one can say that the possession of nuclear weapons by the USSR is meant to threaten or pressure anyone, for any political purpose. Our position on this issue is clear. On 21 December 1982 Yuri A. Andropov also said, "A nuclear war—whether big or small, whether limited or total—must not be allowed to break out."

HISTORY OF ARMS RACE

To understand the Soviet perspective better one should try to see the world through Soviet eyes. The Soviet Union has been beset with wars in its relatively short history as a socialist country. In the 66 years of our history, 30 have been given to wars and periods of reconstruction. All of these wars came from the West, from the world of capitalism.

After World War II the world had to live through a period when atomic weapons were actually exploded, when the H-bomb was built and when the Soviet Union was surrounded by a string of nuclear bases and directly menaced with the use of nuclear weapons against it. Let us trace the arms race further. The United States was the first to introduce nuclear weapons into Europe, to build bombers with nuclear weapons and nuclear aircraft carriers, to build in massive numbers intercontinental ballistic missiles, including solid fuel missiles. The United States was the first to launch submarines with nuclear weapons, and to start deploying multiple independently targetable reentry vehicles (MIRVs) on nuclear weapons.

Those who favor further increases in weaponry sometimes base their arguments on allegations that in the 1970s the United States was sitting on its hands, while the Soviet Union was racing. A consideration of the facts exposes the fallacy of this contention. Indeed during this period the United States acquired 550 new multiple warhead Minuteman III missiles; deployed new multiple warhead Poseidon ballistic missiles on Poseidon submarines; started building new, more capable strategic Trident submarines; upgraded Minuteman III warheads by beginning deployment of new reentry vehicles to replace existing ones, doubling their destructive power; deployed new nuclear attack missiles aboard B-52 bombers; and initiated production and deployment of air-launched cruise missiles. During that period the MX missile and B-1 bomber were developed, and neutron bomb production was started. What is next? Binary chemical weapons? The introduction of the MX missile accompanied later by numerous new so-called small intercontinental missiles in various basing modes? The arms race is also being pushed into space, with the proclaimed intention of deploying anti-ballistic missile (ABM) systems, space arms, laser weapons, and so on.

To be sure the Soviet Union was not standing pat in the 1970s. It had a lot of catching up to do, considering the fact, for instance, that in 1960-65 the ratio of nuclear warheads was 10 to 1, to the Soviet disadvantage. It has been claimed here that much more could have been done by the United States during that period but was not, because of the alleged desire to show restraint and encourage reciprocity. Yet it is clear that whatever was done or not done by the United States was the result of deliberate military, technological, or financial choice. For example, if the B-1 bomber production plans were initially canceled, it was because someone wanted to get the more advanced Stealth bomber faster. Now both the B-1 bomber and the Stealth bomber have turned up on the military programs.

It should be pointed out at the same time that Soviet proposals designed to curb the arms race—for example, not to MIRV ballistic missiles, not to engage in building new large nuclear submarines, and other offers of that nature—were turned down by the United States.

PRINCIPLES OF ARMS CONTROL

What have both sides tried to do in the past in the area of arms control? There was a period in Soviet-American relations when the United States seemed to recognize that the security of one side could not be increased through an incessant build-up of arms at the expense of the other side's security. There are in fact two possible approaches to the problem. One is to go on increasing the number and sophistication of weapons and, therefore, the danger of war. The other is to try arms control. The Soviets insist on the latter.

In the beginning of the 1970s both sides decided to operate from mutually agreed basic principles, which were incorporated in certain agreements. These were equality and equal security:

equality in the sense that there is rough overall parity between the two sides, albeit with dissimilar forces, and that neither side should strive for nuclear superiority; equal security in the sense that limitations and reductions of nuclear weapons should be carried out in such a manner that the security of neither side would suffer, with all factors of the strategic situation taken into account.

Once both sides started operating on these principles, they were fairly successful. Their efforts culminated in the Strategic Arms Limitation Talks (SALT) I agreement, the ABM Treaty, the treaties on the limitation of underground nuclear tests and on nuclear explosions for peaceful purposes, and finally the SALT II Treaty. But as soon as the United States departed from these principles, the arms control process was seriously damaged and deteriorated badly.

The arms limitation and reduction process should also be viewed against the backdrop of current U.S. policy toward the Soviet Union, which may be characterized by four major elements. First, there is an all-out effort to pressure the Soviet Union, to try to interfere in its internal affairs, even to question the legitimacy of its system, to initiate all kinds of crusades to isolate it politically, and to damage it economically with all sorts of sanctions. Second, there is an attempt to rearrange the world arbitrarily into various spheres of interest; to proclaim certain regions to be of vital interest to the United States with no regard for the vital interest of those regions' people. Third is a clear desire to achieve military superiority over the Soviet Union, although this is sometimes called a margin of safety. Fourth is, of course, a heavy offensive propaganda campaign against the Soviet Union, portraying it as the embodiment of evil in the world, and as a country not to be trusted to comply with its obligations under agreements—hence, all the innuendos and accusations, such as the alleged Soviet use of chemical weapons, and so on.

The result was a very ominous pause in the arms control process—the SALT II Treaty was suspended and not ratified; the threshold nuclear tests limitation treaty and the peaceful nuclear explosions treaty were left unratified. A number of talks—on a complete and general test ban treaty, the banning of chemical weapons, reducing the military activity of both sides in the Indian Ocean, limiting conventional arms transfers, banning antisatellite activities and placement of weapons in space—were all suspended unilaterally, and not by the USSR, which stands for their resumption.

For almost a year and a half there was no arms control process at all. The world was just waiting for the United States to be ready to talk. Then came all sorts of extraneous linkages as conditions for talking, and still later the United States decided to resume negotiations with the Soviet Union in Geneva on European nuclear weapons and strategic nuclear weapons. It was immediately obvious, however, that the proposals advanced at those talks were totally nonnegotiable to the Soviet Union. The tested principles of equality and equal security were discarded. Instead attempts were made to talk to the Soviet Union from a position of strength. Our partner in these talks set out to achieve military superiority over the USSR, and its arms control policy was subordinated to the requirements of further military build-up.

LIMITATION AND REDUCTION
OF STRATEGIC NUCLEAR ARMS

START, the Strategic Arms Reduction Talks, as presented in the United States proposal, was a no-starter from the beginning. The U.S. proposal is to cut ballistic missile warheads by one third, with no more than half of those missiles to be left on land-based missiles; to cut ballistic missiles on both sides to one-half the present U.S. level; to cut throw weights of both sides' missiles down to equal levels.

This sounds fine, except if one looks at the asymmetrical forces of the two sides, and if one knows that for geographical, technological, and historical reasons Soviet nuclear forces are 70 percent in land-based missiles, while 80 percent of the U.S. arsenal is submarine-launched ballistic missiles and heavy bombers. By any calculation the Soviet Union under this approach would have to reduce two times more ballistic missiles and would be left with 1.5 times fewer delivery vehicles, if bombers are counted, and with almost three times fewer nuclear weapons on such launchers. As for land-based missiles, the Soviet Union would have to give up 90 percent of those and all its heavy missiles.

The result for the United States would be that it could probably reduce some old land-based missiles and some missiles on old submarines, which it has begun replacing with new ones anyway. But the United States would be free to go ahead with all ongoing programs— MX missiles, Trident II-D5 missiles, B-1 bombers, Stealth bombers, and so on. In other words, all that is now planned would be left intact. And there will still

be thousands upon thousands of U.S. nuclear cruise missiles of various kinds, as the United States began deploying them operationally on strategic bombers. Thus the START proposals, as they stand, are nothing but a prescription for the continuation of the arms race. One cannot expect the Soviet Union to restructure its forces in ways suitable to the other side. We are in the business of negotiation to curb the arms race and to reduce existing weapons, not to give the arms race new dimensions.

The Soviet Union proposes to cut weapons fairly, on the basis of equality and equal security, across the board; to go down, at least as a beginning, to 1800 delivery vehicles, counting everything— land-based missiles, submarine-launched missiles, and strategic bombers. Cruise missiles must be banned. Another part of the Soviet proposal is that at least while negotiations are going on, a freeze should be put on nuclear arsenals of both sides, as common sense would have it. It must also be pointed out that new nuclear arms should be limited, reduced, and prohibited before they present really difficult problems of verification.

The Soviet proposal for the START talks is thus very logical and fair to both sides. If implemented, it would withdraw from the arsenals of both sides about 1000 nuclear launchers; the number of warheads will be reduced substantially to lower equal levels.

If, however, the arms race goes on unbridled, if the first-strike MX missiles are deployed together with other planned new missiles, countermeasures will have to be taken. The MX missile will have to be answered with a similar missile; a long-range cruise missile will have to be countered with another long-range cruise missile, which the Soviet Union, as is known, has begun testing.

SPACE SHOULD BE USED
FOR PEACEFUL PURPOSES

Announcements have been made of U.S. plans to develop and deploy so-called strategic defensive weapons or comprehensive ABM systems. These systems only sound defensive; in fact they represent an attempt to acquire first-strike potential and to use such means to destroy the existing strategic forces of the Soviet side. When the USSR and the United States discussed their first strategic weapons agreements, it was recognized that the strategic offensive and strategic defensive arms were inseparably linked, and that only mutual restraint with regard to the antiballistic defense would make it possible to achieve progress on the limitation and reduction of strategic offensive weapons. That was precisely the reasoning behind simultaneously concluding the ABM Treaty and the SALT I agreement on the limitation of strategic offensive arms. Disruption of the link between strategic offensive and strategic defensive arms would certainly open the floodgates to a runaway arms race in all directions.

One of the most burning and urgent tasks of today in this regard is to prevent an extension of the arms race into space before it is too late. The Soviet Union suggested concluding an international treaty banning the deployment of weapons of any kind in outer space, and in fact submitted a draft of such a treaty to the United Nations in 1981. Now the United States is assigning space-based military technology an even greater role in its strategic plans than before. Thus the critical moment is coming. Either the interested parties will sit down and negotiate, or the arms race will spill over into space, with disastrous consequences.

MEDIUM-RANGE
NUCLEAR WEAPONS IN EUROPE

The subject of medium-range nuclear weapons in Europe deserves special consideration. Introduction of new American Pershing II and cruise missiles would certainly make the situation in Europe and the world extremely threatening and destabilizing. Not for nothing do some people in the West call 1983 the year of the missile.

Let us look at the European situation. At present there is approximate parity between the USSR and NATO countries in medium-range nuclear delivery systems. Each side has roughly 1000 such systems, while NATO enjoys a 1.5 advantage in nuclear charges deployed on those systems. Back in 1976 the Soviet Union began a process of modernizing its medium-range weapons in Europe, withdrawing old missiles, proportionally in greater numbers, and replacing them with newer ones in the same category. The result is that there are fewer Soviet missiles in Europe today than before the modernization was begun. The mission of the Soviet missiles in Europe has been and remains the same: it is not to threaten anyone in Western Europe, but rather to counterbalance the nuclear weapons of NATO, including numerous medium-range forward-based American systems, such as nuclear delivery aircraft ground- and air-based in proximity to the borders of the Soviet Union and other Warsaw Treaty countries.

The U.S. position in the Geneva talks on the subject is represented in the so-called zero option, which in fact entails neither zero weapons nor real options. It does not eliminate the U.S. nuclear weapons already in Europe, nor is it an option for the Soviet side at all. According to the U.S. position, the USSR will simply have to eliminate unilaterally all the medium-range nuclear weapons it has in Europe as well as in Asia—that is, those weapons it currently has to counterbalance the corresponding arsenals of the United States and its allies. Consider too the so-called intermediate option offered in addition to the zero option. The zero option tells us, "Disarm unilaterally while I keep my similar weapons intact." The new U.S. proposal says, "You will reduce and I will build up by adding to my and my allies' present nuclear inventory in Western Europe new, dangerous, and destabilizing weapons—the Pershing II and cruise missiles."

The Soviet Union is ready to reduce its nuclear weapons in Europe if the United States and NATO reduce theirs too. The Soviet position in this regard speaks for itself. The Soviet side is prepared to have absolute zeroes in nuclear weapons with the United States and NATO in Europe—absolute zeroes, no nuclear weapons at all, whether medium-range or tactical. This Soviet proposal is officially on the negotiating table.

If that proposal is too radical, the Soviet Union is prepared for another alternative, to cut both sides' medium-range nuclear systems in Europe by two-thirds, down to 300—in other words, to cut them substantially, both missiles

and nuclear delivery aircraft. Thus the Soviet Union would keep only 162 missiles, the equivalent of the NATO—Great Britain and France—level, with lower equal levels of nuclear delivery aircraft, 138, on both the Soviet and NATO—the United States, France, and Great Britain—sides.

In a nutshell, the USSR is not seeking to possess a single missile or airplane in Europe more than the number at the disposal of NATO. It is ready to negotiate to achieve equality of nuclear arsenals in Europe, both in delivery vehicles and in the nuclear charges on those vehicles. What could be more fair? To facilitate progress, the USSR unilaterally placed a moratorium on further deployments of new missiles in Europe, and in those parts of Asia from which it could reach targets in Western Europe; and it is adhering to that moratorium.

A very important point must also be emphasized: there is a marked difference between present Soviet and U.S. nuclear forces in Europe. The USSR does not have medium-range nuclear systems in Europe capable of reaching targets on U.S. territory. On the other hand, all U.S. forward-based nuclear systems have a direct strategic meaning to the Soviet Union, as they sit close to its borders and are meant to strike its territory. The United States already has an important strategic advantage in this sense.

If, however, advanced first-strike Pershing IIs—which are designed to hit deep inside Soviet territory with almost no warning time—and long-range cruise missiles—which can stealthily reach targets in the Soviet Union—are deployed in Western Europe, countermeasures will have to be taken to put U.S. territory in a similar position, as well as countermeasures with regard to the countries that would allow such new American missiles on their territory.

Of course, there is another way—the way of goodwill and negotiations based on principles of equality and equal security.

THE FUTURE

Intensive material preparation for war, with expenditures of hundreds of billions of dollars, yields a growing danger of nuclear war. The position of the Soviet Union is based on the premise that building new arms is the way not to increase security, but only to make it even more fragile. Both sides should return to the track they were correctly following before—that is, limitations and reduction of nuclear arms, based on equality and equal security. We call for normal relations between the USSR and the United States, with mutual respect, no threatening rhetoric, no attempts to question each other's legitimacy, no preaching of animosity and hatred.

The Soviet Union and the United States had one common enemy in the past they successfully conquered together, and that enemy was fascism. Their common enemy today is the possibility of mutual destruction in a nuclear war. Given the political will, common sense, and an understanding of our mutual interest, which is above all to prevent nuclear war, both sides should be able to emerge victorious.

ANNALS, *AAPSS,* **469,** September 1983

The Case for Disarmament:
Some Personal Reflections on the
United States and Disarmament

By CHARLES C. PRICE

ABSTRACT: Nuclear war would represent an unparalleled catastrophe for civilization. Even preparation for it wastes resources, drains the world economy, breeds hatred, fear and suspicion, degrades moral principles, and demeans respect for human life. The United Nations has proved inadequate to prevent war. Arms control is merely an effort to manage the war system, not to end it. Deterrence is bound to fail eventually, and U.S. military policy has already shifted to preparation for nuclear war. In a 1961 Joint Statement of Agreed Principles for Disarmament Negotiations, the United States and the USSR agreed (1) to abolish all national military establishments, (2) to strengthen the United Nations for peacekeeping and conflict resolution, and (3) to establish an International Disarmament Organization with the right of unrestricted access to monitor the agreement. After two decades of U.S. obstruction, it is time to establish a vigorous U.S. effort to elaborate and update the Agreed Principles as the foundation for an effective, acceptable alternative to war. The development of effective institutions to establish disarmament in a peaceful world and to manage the economic, political, and social challenges of the increasingly interdependent world community demands active and dedicated attention.

Charles C. Price, B. A. Swarthmore, 1934, Ph. D. Harvard, 1936, served as professor of chemistry at Illinois, Notre Dame, and Pennsylvania, at the latter two as department head. He was president of the American Chemical Society in 1965 and received its awards for Pure Chemistry, Creative Invention, and Distinguished Public Service. Concern with the threat of nuclear war has brought him leadership roles with the World Federalists, the Federation of American Scientists, and the Council for a Livable World, and board service with the American Association of the United Nations, the Commission to Study the Organization of Peace, and the U.S. Commission for UNESCO.

I N presenting the case for disarm- ament, I would first declare that disarmament alone is an unrealistic goal. It makes sense only if and when we are willing and able to replace war and the threat of war as the arbiter of international disputes by an effective and acceptable system of law and order at the international level.

A second assertion is that arms control has not been a step in this direction but is merely an effort to manage the war system, not to replace it. As a way to a peaceful world it is thus a snare and a delusion.

A third crucial assertion is that deterrence cannot be relied on to prevent war indefinitely. Evidence of this is the U.S. shift from deterrence to planning for nuclear war, initiated by President Carter and accelerated by President Reagan.

The risk of the failure of deterrence leading to all-out nuclear war and the destruction of human civilization is simply an unacceptable risk. Achieving an effective and acceptable alternative to war is thus an absolute necessity, regardless of the difficulties that may be involved.

PERSONAL CONCERNS

Over the past 35 years I have devoted considerable time and effort to a variety of organized endeavors to minimize the risk of nuclear war and eventually to replace the war system with a civilized system of law and order. My activities have included leadership roles with the Federation of American Scientists, the World Federalists, and the Council for a Livable World. In addition, I have served on the boards of the American Association for the United Nations, the Commission to Study the Organization

of Peace, and the U.S. Commission for the U.N. Educational, Scientific and Cultural Organization (UNESCO). These activities have led to a number of interesting and revealing contacts with various facets of our government in Washington.

I have come to the sad conclusion that time and again during the past two decades, important initiatives and even negotiated treaties that would have significantly limited the military activities of the United States and the USSR have been undermined by power- ful forces in the United States. There are facile rationalizations for these actions, but it seems clear that a major real reason, sometimes even frankly stated, is to protect jobs and profits in the military-industrial complex. Certainly these obstructionist activities have not increased the security of American citizens from nuclear annihilation.

The purpose of this presentation is to summarize some of the facts and public information that have led me to this unhappy conclusion. Recognition that by no means all of the onus for the dire threat we face belongs to the Soviet Union may, it is to be hoped, rekindle efforts to encourage our government to constructive action to find effective and acceptable alternatives to the war system.

SOME HISTORICAL NOTES

During the Eisenhower and Kennedy administrations there was an atmos- phere of hope and progress, especially after the death of Secretary of State John Foster Dulles ended his brink- manship policies. His successor, Christian Herter, a world federalist, made speeches strongly enunciating the need to shift from reliance on mutual assured destruction to a system of civilized international law and order.

One of the promising early actions of the Kennedy administration was the establishment of the Arms Control and Disarmament Agency (ACDA). The passage of legislation for this purpose was assisted in part by the help of volunteers provided by the World Federalists. Working under Senator Hubert Humphrey's aide on disarmament, Betty Goetz, it was possible to get the ACDA legislation approved in time for Kennedy to announce it at the 1961 U.N. General Assembly. John J. McCloy, as disarmament adviser to Kennedy, also provided major help in securing passage of this act.[1] In Section 2, the act states

An ultimate goal of the United States is a world which is free from the scourge of war and the dangers and burdens of armaments; in which the use of force has been subordinated to the rule of law; and in which international adjustments to a changing world are achieved peacefully. It is the purpose of this Act to provide impetus toward this goal by creating a new agency of peace to deal with the problem of reduction and control of armaments looking toward ultimate world disarmament.[2]

Section 3(a) states,

The terms "arms control" and "disarmament" mean the identification, verification, inspection, limitation, control, reduction, or elimination, of armed forces and armaments of all kinds under international agreement

including the necessary steps taken under such an agreement to establish an effective system of international control, or to create and strengthen international organizations for the maintenance of peace.[3]

In pursuit of these goals, John Kennedy appointed McCloy, a distinguished New York lawyer and former U.S. high commissioner for Germany after World War II, to negotiate with the Russians on eliminating the threat of nuclear annihilation. In the short space of five months he and his counterpart for the USSR, Valerian Zorin, reached a remarkable—in fact revolutionary—accord in 1961, the Joint Statement of Agreed Principles for Disarmament Negotiations. It was endorsed unanimously by the U.N. General Assembly. Its main provisions were that the goal of negotiations should be

— the elimination of all national military establishments, leaving only lightly armed militia for internal police purposes;

— the endowing of the United Nations with the proper authority to settle disputes peacefully and with a peace force able to deter any illegal use of force internationally; and

— the establishment of an International Disarmament Organization with the necessary capabilities, including the right of unrestricted access for on-site inspection, to assure all nations that the agreement was adhered to.

The United States and the USSR submitted draft treaties to accomplish

1. U.S., Congress, House, Committee on Foreign Affairs, Subcommittee on National Security Policy and Scientific Developments, *Hearings on the Arms Control and Disarmament Agency,* 93d Cong., 2d sess., 24 Sept.-3 Oct. 1974 (Washington, DC: Government Printing Office, 1974), pp. 1-18.

2. Ibid., pp. 232-33.

3. Ibid., p. 233.

these aims, and negotiations were begun. It must be stated that the U.S. draft treaty was hastily prepared by a small working group including Louis Sohn, of Harvard Law School, and Betty Goetz, then on Senator Humphrey's staff. Both drafts proposed three stages, each involving the elimination of one-third of the armaments, to reach the goal of general and complete disarmament. Both were somewhat vague in describing the international institutions required for the completion of stage three. Progress was made in defining a number of basic articles of a treaty to achieve the goals of the Joint Statement.

A significant controversy arose over the timing of inspection. The Russians were quite willing for international inspectors to inspect and certify the junking of all weapons removed from their arsenal in pursuance of the agreement, with complete inspection of all former military weapons when disarmament was complete. The United States, with some reason, felt that this was inadequate since there was no assurance that junked weapons would not be secretly replaced. We therefore insisted on completely open inspection of the entire military establishment from the beginning.

To break this deadlock, Louis Sohn came up with the idea of zonal disarmament, which was formally proposed by the United States. The idea was that each side should divide its territory in any way it saw fit into, say, 10 defined zones. Then lots would be drawn to see which zone on each side was at that point to be completely disarmed and completely inspected. When this was finished, the next zone would be selected by lot for similar treatment, and so on. The first Russian reaction was *nyet*. However, after a few

months the Russians had filtered the proposal through their complex bureaucracy and said that they would accept it as a basis for negotiation. Unfortunately by this time President Kennedy had been assassinated and Lyndon Johnson was secretly preparing to escalate the war in Vietnam. The United States withdrew from the negotiations.

U.S. OPPOSITION TO THE McCLOY-ZORIN AGREED PRINCIPLES

This position was rationalized by Arnold Wolfers and others in *The United States in a Disarmed World: A Study of the U.S. Outline for General and Complete Disarmament*.[4] This book, from one of the university branches of the military complex, is a completely unbalanced argument based on all the possible disadvantages resulting from the worst-case situations in a disarmed world. It does not compare any of these relatively trivial drawbacks with the devastation of nuclear war, the only logical end result of the alternative it supports, continuing the arms race. It also of course minimizes all the benefits that would accrue to the United States in a disarmed and more cooperative world.

Shortly after Richard Nixon took office as president, the Russians formally proposed that the negotiations for general and complete disarmament as defined by the Joint Statement of 1961 be renewed. President Nixon refused. I was so dismayed by this refusal that I

4. *The United States in a Disarmed World: A Study of the U.S. Outline for General and Complete Disarmament* (Baltimore, MD: Johns Hopkins University Press, 1966).

went to see Dr. Fred Iklé, then head of the ACDA, to find out why the United States would refuse to negotiate for an agreement that would

— disarm our potential adversaries;

— end the waste of resources and inflationary spending of the arms race;

— end the degradation of moral principles and respect for human life resulting from massive nuclear arms poised to kill hundreds of millions of people and leave a devastated and poisoned globe for the survivors; and

— kindle hope for a world of increasing cooperation, in which our energies could be devoted more constructively to justice, welfare, and realization of the human potential with which we are all endowed.

I was shocked even more when Dr. Iklé, a product of the military-industrial complex, stated that I was naive: we had never intended the Joint Statement to be taken seriously. It was just propaganda to counter Russian propaganda!

I then arranged to see William Foster, head of the ACDA when the negotiations with the Russians on the Joint Statement were actually taking place. After listening to my dismay that the statement was only propaganda, he finally shook his finger at me and stated emphatically that Jack Kennedy and he had been completely sincere in their pursuit of the goals it proposed. He then paused for a moment of reflection and said that he must add that before the Russians agreed to the Joint Statement, he had no problems from the Department of Defense. After that, however, this most difficult negotiations were not

with the Russians but with the Pentagon. If he was not trying to tell me that the Pentagon was out to sabotage agreement, I do not know what he was trying to say!

In testimony from the Council for a Livable World at the House of Representatives Hearings on the Arms Control and Disarmament Agency, 24 September - 3 October 1974, we urged that since billions were spent for arms research and development, at least millions should be spent on research and development for alternatives to arms. This proposal of 0.1 percent of the military budget for developing alternatives to war was also made at Senate hearings, drawing favorable comments from Senators John Sparkman and Charles Percy. As a result, additional money was in fact appropriated for the ACDA for such long-range planning, but it was diverted by Dr. Iklé to other purposes.

U.S. SENATE HEARINGS
ON THE 1978 U.N. SPECIAL
SESSION ON DISARMAMENT

In the fall of 1977, some of us were concerned about the lack of initiatives proposed by the United States for the 1978 U.N. General Assembly Special Session on Disarmament. A conversation with Senator Claiborne Pell led to a hearing by his Subcommittee on Arms Control, Oceans and International Environment on 13 April 1978. The government witnesses were the Honorable Charles W. Maynes, assistant secretary of state for international organization affairs; Lawrence Weiler, special coordinator for the U.N. Special Session on Disarmament; and Adam Yarmolinsky, counselor to the ACDA. The main testimony presented by these three had to do with procedures and items that other nations were pushing for action at the Special Session on Disarmament. Very little was said of any U.S. proposals for action.

The presentations by Kay Camp for the Women's International League for Peace and Freedom, William H. Kincade for the Arms Control Association, and Edward C. Luck for the U.N. Association offered effective arguments for many arms control steps that the United States ought to advocate at the special session. The main thrust of my presentation, for the Council for a Livable World, was that while arms control measures may be helpful, the only real relief from the threat of nuclear war would be a change from a war system to a civilized peace system at the world level.[5] Specifically, I urged

— the establishment of the goals defined by the 1961 Joint Statement as active working goals for the United States government;

— the devotion of at least 0.1 percent of what we spend on arms to the research, development, and planning needed to reach these goals; and

— that as a step in this direction, the United States support the French, Dutch, and Sri Lankan proposals for a U.N. Disarmament Agency to help such planning and to monitor existing and new arms control and disarmament measures.

5. U.S., Congress, Senate, Committee on Foreign Relations, Subcommittee on Arms Control, Oceans and International Environment, *Hearing on the U.N. Special Session on Disarmament,* 95th Cong., 2d sess., 13 Apr. 1978 (Washington, DC: Government Printing Office, 1978), p. 56.

Senator Pell had asked the three government witnesses to remain for the four nongovernment presentations and then invited them to comment. Mr. Yarmolinsky commented briefly on the proposals of Kay Camp, William Kincade, and Edward Luck.[6] He then sat down. Senator Pell then asked for comment on the proposal about a U.N. Disarmament Agency. After briefly replying that they were studying these proposals, Mr. Yamolinsky again sat down. Senator Pell continued:

Senator Pell. How about reviving the McCloy-Zorin approach? Do you see that being done?

Mr. Weiler. Mr. Chairman, as far as a commitment to general and complete disarmament, that will clearly be affirmed in the new special session. As far as negotiation—

Senator Pell. Excuse me for interrupting there, but do we as a nation really want general and complete disarmament?

Mr. Weiler. As a nation, we have committed ourselves—as a government, at least—ever since the McCloy-Zorin agreement, we have committed ourselves to that. Now, that implies a very considerable amount of reorganization of the world security system which frankly no one has a clear idea how to bring about.

Senator Pell. A country with 1 million bodies could be overrun by a country with 100,000 bodies if it doesn't have any weapons.

Mr. Weiler. In various past U.S. proposals concerning general and complete disarmament, there have always been provisions, as you proceed through the various stages, for the development of improved international peacekeeping arrangements. It is a difficult intellectual problem there, how you begin to

6. Ibid., pp. 63-64.

get hold of that. There will be discussions over long-range objectives that will take place under the general rubric of comprehensive negotiating program, which will be discussed, in addition to specific negotiations that may be laid out in the program of action. . . .

Mr. Price. Is it pertinent to make a comment?

Senator Pell. Please.

Mr. Price: I was intrigued very much with what Mr. Weiler had to say about the McCloy-Zorin. I agree it is difficult. I think what he said, though, supports exactly what I am trying to propose and what I proposed a few years ago to this committee, which is the urgent need to do some serious research and planning to solve those problems. The fact is, for the last 15 years, we have done nothing consciously to try to solve those problems.

I would think what he had to say in fact, supports the idea that we do need to devote some effort and resources to trying to come up with solutions or we are never going to make any progress in achieving what is a goal of this country, general and complete disarmament.[7]

It seems appalling that the bureaucrats responsible for U.S. planning for the Special Session on Disarmament had to be prodded by Senator Pell even to comment on general and complete disarmament, and then admitted that it was a U.S. policy goal but was so difficult that they did not even want to think about it, let alone do anything to promote it.

SOME OTHER U.S. REACTIONS TO DISARMAMENT PROPOSALS

In addition to these personal experiences, many items from the news of the day have reinforced my view of the U.S.

7. Ibid., pp. 64-65, 71-72.

position on serious disarmament measures. Years ago, when a complete nuclear test ban was being negotiated between the United States and the USSR, the United States rightly insisted that some on-site inspection of suspicious events was highly desirable. We further proposed that up to seven such on-site inspections be allowed in each nation each year. The USSR at first flatly refused. Finally, however, they made a major concession and proposed that such on-site inspection would be acceptable, but only three per year. The United States refused to budge from its seven-per-year stance—a compromise on five would have seemed obvious— and a major chance to limit the arms race and establish the principle of on-site inspection was lost. Glenn Seaborg, then chairman of the Atomic Energy Commission, in 1982 publicly expressed regret that the United States did not accept a reasonable compromise to achieve an inspected total ban on nuclear test explosions.

In the more recent negotiations on a complete test ban, negotiators have reached agreement on a treaty providing for 12 automated monitoring stations inside the territories of each of the signatories, with international on-site inspection of suspicious events detected by the monitors. The United States has balked at this proposed treaty. A major article in the *Philadelphia Inquirer* reported that the principal reason was that the nuclear weaponeers were totally opposed to any complete ban on nuclear test explosions.

An article on Zbigniew Brzezinski in the *Philadelphia Inquirer* for 18 May 1980 quoted him as stating that one of his major accomplishments in office was "the decision to move ahead with the MX missile as a first-strike weapon."

Perhaps this claim by Brzezinski helps to explain the sad news reported in the *Philadelphia Inquirer* on 24 May 1979. The article stated that President Carter had rejected a Soviet proposal to include in the Strategic Arms Limitation Talks (SALT) II a ban on all new missile systems by either side. The reported reason was to get support for SALT II from hawk senators committed to the MX missile program. A member of the SALT II negotiating team was quoted as saying that the day this Soviet proposal was turned down was "a day of infamy for the United States."

SOME CONCLUSIONS

One can only speculate about the reasons for U.S. opposition to working for the stated goals defined by the Joint Statement of 1961. It is clear that opposition from the military-industrial complex has been the major factor. One obvious reason is that achievement of these goals would be a major threat to job security and profits from arms programs. To protect its interests, the military-industrial complex has promoted to influential positions many individuals with strong anti-Russian obsessions while it has denigrated the appeals for moderation by the many distinguished Americans who have served in the military complex, such as Thomas Watson, Cyrus Vance, George Kennan, Grenville Clark, Admiral Gene La Rocque, McGeorge Bundy, and Robert S. McNamara.

These various reflections of U.S. policy leave me with the sad conviction that our government is so obsessed with military options that it has not only ignored, but for nearly 20 years has actively opposed, any effort to find an alternate, more civilized, and more moral basis for policy options.

Surely the United Nations of today is not such an option. It would be ludicrous if we tried to organize Philadelphia, the City of Brotherly Love, on the principles of the U.N. Charter. The City Council could pass only nonbinding resolutions urging people to stop at red lights, not to rob banks, and so on. There would be no city police, only armed guards for various organizations within the city. The City Council could not levy taxes, only request contributions from constituents. The courts could try cases only if both sides agreed to it. In view of its weakness, it is a wonder that the United Nations has been able to do as much as it has!

It seems absolutely obvious that the implementation of the goals of the 1961 Joint Statement will require a reformed and strengthened United Nations. Instead of bemoaning the fact that such changes are very difficult or impossible as we march like lemmings to nuclear annihilation, it is high time we put a major effort by the best brains in the world into seeing how to accomplish the necessary changes for the shift from the war system to a civilized peace system. It is not necessary to invent new forms of political institutions. It is only necessary to make the determined commitment to establish them at the world level.

The challenge is not to develop new ideas, for there are many excellent ones. The challenge is to develop the firm commitment to decide which are the most likely to succeed and to build the political will to get on with the job. It is encouraging to note that some 600 members of parliaments from around the world have joined the Parliamentarians for World Order, an organization dedicated to promoting such a transformation of the United Nations.

UPDATING THE
McCLOY-ZORIN ACCORD

While the McCloy-Zorin Joint Statement of Agreed Principles for Disarmament Negotiations envisaged an enhanced role for the United Nations in peacekeeping and conflict resolution, neither the accord[8] nor the implementing treaties submitted by the United States[9] and by the USSR[10] proposed the necessary reform and strengthening of the United Nations for it to become an acceptable and reliable alternative to war. This failure to come to grips with this difficult problem has served as one excuse for abandoning the efforts to pursue implementation of the McCloy-Zorin principles.

Agreement to "strengthen instititutions for maintaining peace and the settlement of disputes by peaceful means"[11] is an absolutely critical requirement for the "programme of general and complete disarmament in a peaceful world" as envisaged by McCloy-Zorin. While the principles of the U.N. Charter are a noble statement of purpose to end the threat of war, it is obvious that they fail to endow the United Nations with the authority to accomplish that goal. To be effective and acceptable the United Nations must be reformed and strengthened with defined authority

8. "Text of the Joint Statement of Agreed Principles for Disarmament Negotiations," in *Current Disarmament Proposals,* ed. Harry B. Hollins (New York: World Law Fund, 1964), pp. 189-91.

9. "Outline of Basic Provisions of a Treaty on General and Complete Disarmament under Strict International Control," in ibid., pp. 29-60.

10. "Text of the Draft Treaty on General and Complete Disarmament under Strict International Control," in ibid., pp. 1-28.

11. "Text of the Joint Statement," pp. 189-91.

— to raise its own revenues directly, for example by taxes on international travel, communications, and commerce;

— to make binding decisions within the area of its authority by a responsible majority voting system based at least in part on population and economic factors of member states;

— to enforce such binding decisions based mainly on nonviolent coercion applied directly to individuals and organizations breaking such international law, with limited police power sufficient to maintain international order and to apprehend international lawbreakers; and

— to endow the International Court of Justice and any subsidiary or regional U.N. courts with compulsory jurisdiction to make binding decisions in disputes over international treaties and over charges of breaking international law.

Any agreement to establish such significant authority in the United Nations almost certainly will require a clear statement of legal principles limiting improper exercise of U.N. authority and providing for some limited guarantees of basic human rights, at least with respect to the United Nations; and arrangements for the diversion of a significant fraction of the resources now devoted to war and military establishments to world economic development.

A fundamental principle of enforceable world law must be absolute respect for national boundaries. Any present or future disputes over them are to be settled nonviolently by mutual agreement, by binding arbitration, or by decision of the International Court of Justice. Many boundary disputes related to national military security will become relatively insignificant in a peaceful world.

These principles for achieving disarmament in a peaceful world are basically those proposed in 1962 by Grenville Clark and Louis Sohn in the Draft Treaty Establishing a World Disarmament and World Development Organization within the Framework of the United Nations.[12]

The obvious difficulties in achieving these goals must be measured against

12. "Draft of a Treaty Establishing a World Disarmament and World Development Organization within the Framework of the United Nations," in *Current Disarmament Proposals*, pp. 61-184.

the forlorn hope that nuclear deterrents, diplomacy, and collective security can succeed in saving civilization from nuclear devastation. Hope for a developing human society demands a more successful alternative.

There is no more urgent and important task for you in the fields of political and social science than action on and solutions to the problems in the development of new political institutions to manage the political, economic, and social challenges of the increasingly interdependent world community. First you must make the decision that this is the crucial area for your active concern. Then you can come to grips with how each of you personally can best contribute to this essential effort for human survival.

*   *   *

QUESTIONS AND ANSWERS

Q (Dr. Greenwald, Foundation for International Probation and Parole Practice): There have been several references to alternatives to nuclear war, such as biological warfare. A system less destructive of physical structures could be more selectively destructive of populations. Would you comment on the question of an international criminal court before which nations would be brought as defendants, with the appropriate individuals as representatives, much as we can bring a corporation before the courts with a corporate officer as defendant.

A: My feeling is that the urgent problem we have to solve now is nuclear warfare. Biological warfare could relatively easily kill millions of people. The last world war for that matter killed many, many millions, but it did not

completely destroy the warp and woof of civilization, or poison the world for decades afterward. Since nuclear war does have such destructive capability, and since it is what we are preparing to do, it seems to me the number one problem. If we can get that problem solved, we would have set up the instrumentalities to deal with these other problems, such as biological weapons, along the way. If terrorists or small nations or others try to make use of such means of accomplishing their objectives, they should be subject to trial by an international court that would have competence to try the individuals as well as the nation.

COMMENT (Kupperman): One concern is that small have-not or Third World nations, where there are not lots of people with nuclear weapons, are probably going to go toward biological weapons. Some terrorist groups are reputedly going in this direction already. They can kill an awful lot of people. Biological weapons are easily obtained, in comparison with nuclear weapons. But the point is that you have to look at the use of biological weapons either as an isolated incident, which is terrible enough, or as precipitating the use of nuclear weapons. Therefore there is again a crisis-management problem to be concerned with.

———————

Q (Dr. Stikliorius, Wallingford, Pennsylvania): You mentioned that there should be an international authority that takes care of these matters, to prevent nuclear war. How do you prevent the presence in such an authority of people like Hitler, Stalin, Idi Amin, Qaddafi, or Khomeini? You said too that there should be an international court. You do not have to be a lawyer to know that a court without a sheriff is completely useless. By sheriff, I mean an agent with a physical force and the authority to exercise it. Whom do you suggest as sheriff?

A: If the United Nations is to be reformed and restructured to serve its intended purpose, then there can be an agreement. It should have an international peace force. Any civilized community should have a police force. But I do not think there is any guarantee,

even in this country, that we could not get an Idi Amin or a Hitler as our leader. We came perilously close to it once or twice, and we have had some pretty reprehensible people in our political system. I do not advocate a system of law and order as a utopia. All I am saying is that in civilized human communities, we would be better off to have a system of law and order than to have anarchy.

———————

Q (Dr. Ashman, Lenoir Rhyne College, North Carolina): In view of Cardinal Krol's statement, how do we deal with those groups—whether orthodox Marxist-Leninist, or one of the many fundamentalist Christian groups in the United States—that see things in black and white, where compromise with evil is out of the question? How can they seriously sit down and negotiate?

A: I do not think that we or the Russians have to negotiate agreement on ideology, any more than a baseball game has to be negotiated. What you agree on are the principles, a set of rules to play by, the institutions by which you are going to try to live together. I do not know whether the Russians will be able to accept what we are talking about, but I do not think it requires an agreement on ideology. I do not know whether we will win or lose, but we have a much better chance of winning that way than we do with a nuclear war.

Arms Control Developments

By SENATOR ARLEN SPECTER

ABSTRACT: Interplay between the public, the press, Congress, and the executive branch helps shape American arms control policy. Presidential initiatives set the stage for the negotiating process; the senator cites President Kennedy's 1963 speech at American University, and President Reagan's April 1983 decisions to end the ban on long-term grain sale agreement with the Soviet Union, and to withhold charging the Soviet Union with violations of the SALT Treaty. Such signals may imply a readiness to reach accommodation and may induce a reciprocal signal. Moreover,the senator advocates an early summit of the superpowers. For President Reagan, who in 1984 will be a candidate for either reelection or retirement, 1983 will be the most productive time. A Senate resolution urging a prompt summit was reintroduced by the senator in April 1983. Finally, discussions between individual senators and top officials can affect the direction, tone, and pace of arms control efforts; the senator describes his own discussions with the president and National Security Adviser Clark on the nomination of Kenneth Adelman to head the Arms Control and Disarmament Agency, and on the MX missile.

Arlen Specter was elected to the Senate for a six-year term beginning 1981. He is a member of Appropriations Committee subcommittees on agriculture, the District of Columbia—which he chairs—labor/health and human services, state, commerce and justice, and foreign operations; and of Judiciary Committee subcommittees on juvenile justice—which he chairs—criminal law, and agency administration. He was Philadelphia district attorney, 1966-74; assistant counsel to the Warren Commission, 1964; and served on Pennsylvania's State Planning Board, the White House Conference on Youth, the National Commission on Criminal Justice, and the Peace Corps National Advisory Council.

TODAY I shall address the nuclear arms issue from the political perspective—that is, the focusing of attention, persuasion, and pressure that are the key political factors in achieving arms reduction.

In the last decade we saw insistent U.S. public opinion compel our disengagement from the Vietnam War. In the last week we have seen insistent U.S. public opinion compel the Senate to alter radically the program to withhold taxes on savings accounts. When as much attention is focused on the risk of world destruction as has been focused on the 10 percent withholding on savings accounts, similar concrete results may be expected. In 1982 the Senate spent more time debating subsidies for tobacco than debating the subject of nuclear arms control.

Last October, I spent a considerable amount of the Senate recess traveling across Pennsylvania and visiting college campuses to speak on the subject of nuclear arms and arms reduction. At the University of Pittsburgh on a weekday afternoon at about four o'clock, approximately 150 students appeared. About the same number attended a midweek, midmorning session at Temple University. The numbers were small when I visited Bucknell, Scranton University, the Penn State campus in Middletown, and St. Joseph's University. Several hundred Pennsylvanians visited me last month when the nuclear freeze issue was debated in the House of Representatives in Washington. But as yet the issue of arms control, the prevention of nuclear war, has not caught fire with the American people, as the world may catch fire from nuclear destruction if the issue does not.

PRESIDENT KENNEDY'S
INITIATIVES

Time magazine this week notes John F. Kennedy's speech of two decades ago and focuses on the results of his attitudes and efforts. In 1963 at American University President Kennedy said, "It is sad to read these Soviet statements. But it is also a warning to the American people . . . not to see conflict as inevitable, accommodation as impossible, and communication as nothing more than an exchange of threats."[1] *Time* then notes,

to show his good faith, President Kennedy announced the end of this nation's nuclear tests in the atmosphere. From the words and thoughts of that speech flowed the test ban treaty, a prohibition on nuclear weapons in outer space, the first grain sale to the Soviets, and the first nuclear arms limitation agreement.[2]

In that speech President Kennedy added, "I speak of peace because of the new face of war."[3] Now, 20 years later, the newer face of war demands that we do more than just speak of peace. We must act vigorously and decisively to achieve real peace. Today's weapons of destruction dwarf those of President Kennedy's age. The 16,000 strategic warheads possessed by the two superpowers can reduce both societies and the rest of the world to rubble. But the threat that nuclear arms pose to civilization derives less from the destructive power than from the delivery speed. In under 15 minutes submarine-launched ballistic

1. Hugh Sidey, "The Presidency," *Time,* 25 Apr. 1983, p. 16.
2. Ibid.
3. Ibid.

missiles can deliver thousands of hydrogen bombs. In 30 minutes thousands of land-based missiles can travel from homeland to homeland. Our mutual peril multiplies as superpower tensions increase, and when tensions and weapons both increase, then the danger is compounded.

But the same ingenuity and brainpower that have spawned the power to destroy the world can also inspire ways to allow the world to live in peace. I am optimistic that arms control and arms reduction are possible, and that leadership can come from the United States and President Reagan on these important issues. Today's news reports bring two significant signs of encouragement from the White House.

INDICATIONS OF
NEW INITIATIVES BY
PRESIDENT REAGAN

I refer first to the report that the president has softened his position on the Soviet missile test. The *New York Times* dateline is 22 April 1983:

President Reagan, apparently deciding not to make public charges that the Soviet Union violated the terms of the 1979 strategic arms treaty, today emphasized the difficulty of obtaining "hard and fast evidence" and indicated that the Administration might prefer to approach Moscow through private diplomatic channels.

His comments marked a shift in tone from his statements in a speech in Los Angeles on March 31st when he said there were "increasingly serious grounds for questioning" Soviet compliance with the treaty.[4]

4. Hedrick Smith, "Reagan Softens Position on Soviet Missile Test," *New York Times,* 23 Apr. 1983, p. 3.

The president said, "If you can't get that kind of courtroom evidence, then you can't make the charge of violation."[5] All know that international pronouncements are seldom made with an evidentiary base that would survive in a courtroom. The *Times* goes on to point out,

Evidently responding to pressures from several conservative Senators that he or other top Administration officials accuse Moscow publicly of violations, the President stressed that "it is difficult to establish and have hard and fast evidence that a treaty has been violated."[6]

I suggest, and this will be amplified in the following, that the president's attitude on that subject was occasioned by pressure from senators, but not those referred to by the *New York Times.*

The second subject of considerable significance relates to the president's ending the ban on negotiations for a long-term Soviet grain pact. The front page of the *New York Times* reports, "President Reagan announced tonight [22 April 1983]

that he was ending the ban on negotiations over a long-term grain agreement with the Soviet Union that he had imposed last year out of concern for the political situation in Poland. Mr. Reagan said he was taking the steps to reaffirm our reliability as a supplier of grain to the Soviet Union.

Last July [1982] he said the ban would continue "until the Soviet Union indicates that it is prepared to permit the process of reconciliation in Poland to go forward and

5. Ibid.
6. Ibid.

demonstrates this desire with deeds and not just words."[7]

I submit that these two events are of considerable potential significance, for the negotiations process has frequently been preceded by U.S. insistence that there be a signal from the Soviet Union before there can be significant discussion. One good turn deserves another, and one good signal deserves another. It may be that these signals from the White House are carefully planned to produce other signals in return, which may set the stage for some serious arms reduction talks.

My sense is that these conciliatory indicators may well follow the controversy last April concerning the nomination of Ambassador Adelman as director of the Arms Control and Disarmament Agency.

SENATE CONFIRMATIONS—
THE ADELMAN NOMINATION

The front page of today's *Times* carries the smiling pictures of the president, the secretary of state, and the newly confirmed director and his wife.[8] Those countenances were not smiling 10 days ago when the matter was under deliberation by the Senate, and the early vote counts on the confirmation of Mr. Adelman were grim indeed.

I was among those who were in the grim count. On 21 February 1983 I wrote to the president expessing concern about the nomination of Am-

7. Steven R. Weisman, "Reagan Ends Ban on Negotiations for Long-Term Soviet Grain Pact," ibid., p. 1.
8. Ibid.

bassador Adelman and detailing my reasons. When Ambassador Adelman appeared before the Foreign Relations Committee on 27 January 1983, his testimony was most unreassuring. Millions of Americans saw on television the juxtaposition of his testimony at his first and second appearances, which were directly contradictory. Such testimony would hardly lead to a favorable verdict on his behalf in the most minor of cases, were it to be tried in a traditional U.S. courtroom.

There followed a very intense behind-the-scenes debate on the confirmation of Ambassador Adelman, and those of us in the middle had extensive discussions with the key participants in the Administration, the White House and the State Department.

The president called me on 12 April 1983—and those calls are not confidential but are really for the public record; I spoke about the call when I made an extensive floor statement on Thursday, 14 April 1983, the morning of the vote on Ambassador Adelman. In that discussion there was an opportunity to probe where the president was heading on arms reduction. His assurances seemed to me very encouraging.

The confirmation proceeding also gave me an opportunity to talk to National Security Adviser William Clark personally, and to have his assurance as to the direction of arms talks , and also to talk to Ambassador Rowney and Ambassador Nitze.

In Ambassador Nitze we have a really remarkable negotiator with extraordinary balance and experience; and by so stating I do not mean to deprecate the balance or experience of anyone else by noninclusion. He has been on the international scene since 1946, when he first engaged in lend-lease discussions with the Soviet Union. He has most recently gained considerable fame from his walk in the woods with his Soviet counterpart, where they structured a deal that might have led to a significant break in the impasse on arms reduction. When presented to their superiors on each side of the Atlantic, the deal was decimated rather than ratified, perhaps because of reluctance for either side to go forward without having an assurance in advance, or perhaps the negotiations were too much on the fast track.

In considering the Adelman nomination, I for one was very mindful of the fact that there is vast understaffing in the Arms Control and Disarmament Agency at present, and very mindful that while the Constitution gives the Senate the right to advise, as I did in my letter to the president of 21 February, and the right to consent, when the confirmation matter comes to a vote, it does not give the Senate the power to appoint. It was my judgment and the judgment of many of my colleagues, based on very extensive discussions, that we really should, so to speak, be on with it—permit the president to have his negotiator and permit the process to go forward—to make it absolutely clear that it was the administration's responsibility to succeed, having been given its nominee for the position of director. As one of my colleagues put it, "Now there are no excuses."

On that Thursday morning when the vote was scheduled, I placed a call to Ambassador Adelman, who was in New York and unavailable for a direct meeting. I told him that I had sent him a copy of my letter to the president, which was not complimentary; I therefore thought it appropriate to say that I intended to vote for his confirmation, but wanted to emphasize my view of the role of the Arms Control and Disarmament Agency's director as the advocate for arms control; in conversations with others in the administration I confirmed that this plainly should be his role—the role of advocacy, as distinct from those in the Defense Department who might be on the other end of the predisposition, or in the State Department, who might be closer to the center. Speaking for myself, I added, I expected him to discharge that role with vigor and tenacity; he assured me that he would do so. And when I commented that the casting of my vote would end my participation in the matter, he extended an invitation for further consultation and further involvement in the processes that he would undertake.

WEAPONS DECISIONS—
THE MX MISSILE

The continuing dialogue or debate in Washington on the role of the Arms Control and Disarmament Agency, and on the actions of the president, is significantly colored by recurrent issues that come before the Congress. When the $988 million appropriation for the MX missile was voted on last year, I and many others voted against it, leading to its defeat, not only because of questions of the basing mode, but because of a dissatisfaction at that time with the pace of arms control. The MX is again on our agenda, as is the military budget, and there are many of us who are convinced that we have to be strong if we are to induce the Soviet Union to make meaningful arms concessions, that the dual-track approach is the proper one—that is, strength first, but always coupled with a vigorous effort at arms reduction as well.

It is my judgment that those matters are very much on the president's mind as he evaluates the demand of some of my colleagues in the Senate to accuse the Soviets of a treaty violation. And he has evaluated the request of many to reinstitute the sale of grain to the Soviet Union, as a tool of international diplomacy, above and beyond the interests the American agriculture community has in seeing those sales go forward.

PROSPECTS FOR PROGRESS IN 1983

My own sense is that there is a unique opportunity for a significant breakthrough in 1983, providing we can persuade the president and the premier of the Soviet Union to have a nuclear summit discussion to bring these issues into focus at the highest level.

In April of 1982, in his Saturday speech, the president spoke of his insistence on armaments in order to attain parity. The word was parity, but the music was superiority. That led me to introduce a Senate resolution to call for an immediate summit, on the proposition that there is no such thing as superiority in the nuclear age, and no such thing as parity; that the only reality is inferiority—one power's capacity to be destroyed by another, the Soviet Union by the United States, the United

States by the Soviet Union, either of us by the likes of Qaddafi or the Iraqis; and that the action had to start with the superpowers for a nuclear summit.

When I moved the resolution as an amendment to the Department of Defense Authorization Bill, I was resisted on the issue by Senator Tower, who decried it as a weakening of the American hand and an inappropriate proposition to be advanced in the Senate. Senator Percy, chairman of the Foreign Relations Committee, joined Senator Tower in opposing the sense of the Senate resolution, arguing that there had to be hearings on the issue, notwithstanding my question of what more was there to be heard on such a subject. It was a hard-fought three days, 19-21 April 1982. I deferred pressing for a vote, at the request of Secretary Haig, because of President Reagan's intervening speech in Peoria on the weekend. But the matter came up for a vote on the following Tuesday, 12 May 1982, and a motion to table it was defeated 60 to 30. The resolution was then passed by a vote of 92 to 6.

In 1982 the administration opposed the suggestion for a summit on the grounds that more time was necessary and that the groundwork had to be laid so that we would not have the prospect of hopes raised, abject failure, and hopes dashed. And notwithstanding the affirmative vote of the Senate, there has been no summit.

In anticipation of debate on the Adelman nomination, on 12 April 1983 I again filed a Senate resolution calling for an immediate summit, anticipating that there would be some opportunity to attract the attention of those at the highest levels of the executive branch.

When the president called, within two hours after I had spoken on the subject on the Senate floor, I was able to discuss the issue with him. I was able to say to him, because I had already said so publicly, that I thought his persuasive ability ought to be utilized now; that he appears in person very different from the way he appears in print; but that he was an enormously persuasive person, not only as he has dealt with the Congress but as he has dealt with world leaders. The president's response was that he was interested in a summit but did not think that the time was right. I responded that in 1984 he would be either a president about to retire or a candidate, and would not have the compelling posture he still possesses in 1983.

I had an opportunity to repeat this consideration on 13 April 1983 to National Security Adviser Clark, and on 21 April 1983 to Secretary of State Shultz, when he appeared before the Appropriations Subcommittee. From those discussions it is my feeling that it is realistic to look for a summit in 1983. Not that President Reagan or National Security Adviser Clark or Secretary of State Shultz said that there would be one, but because I sense that they were looking favorably on the matter, assuming that the time were ripe. The events of the grain sale and of the president's not choosing to charge the Soviets with a treaty violation, I think, are very positive signs indeed. I see those as significant signs of a thaw, and if the Soviets respond with similar signs, then I optimistically submit that the stage could well be set for a momentous summit yet this year, 1983.

* * *

QUESTIONS AND ANSWERS

Q: Would you vote for a nuclear freeze if it came before the Senate, and what is the reason for your position?

A: It would depend on the texture of the issue at the time. I voted for a nuclear freeze when the issue was on the ballot in Philadelphia last November, and I thought it was very salutary that there were many referenda across the country to focus public attention and build up that kind of pressure. When the president is making vigorous and reasonable moves on arms reduction—and I do not expect him to make unreasonable concessions—I would not want to tie his hands. If the issue were to come before the Senate next week, as it has come before the House, I would not vote for a nuclear freeze. But if arms talks do not proceed; if Ambassador Adelman does not carry forward a vigorous approach as an advocate, as he committed to do; if there are not efforts by the administration that appear significant, and the matter were to arrive at the Senate in that posture, I might well vote for a freeze. As you can infer, I view the issue of a freeze as a pressure point to give balance and direction to the administration. Such pressure is obviously not binding; the executive is going to do what it choses. I think it is a much more sensible move at the moment to tell the president—to the extent that the Senate and Congress can tell him anything—to hold summit; this is what I am pressing him to do now.

_____

Q: Do you see any possibility of Congress taking more initiative to have some kind of meeting with their Soviet counterparts? Do you see any alternative plan if a summit between Reagan and Andropov cannot work now?

A: Such meetings are highly desirable, have already been under way in a number of directions, and ought to be encouraged, regardless of what happens with the summit between President Reagan and Premier Andropov; I do not think, however, that meetings between members of Congress and their Soviet counterparts can achieve anywhere near the results of a meeting between the executives of each country.

In July 1982, when I traveled to the Soviet Union and visited with Mr. Arbatov and others, Mr. Arbatov expressed great warmth for Senator Baker and Senator Laxalt from a trip they had made a few years before. On my return, I encouraged them to go back. Schedules are very crowded, but I think they will try. Senator Dole traveled to the Soviet Union last November. There was also a very worthwhile conference of Soviet and U.S. scholars at Valley Forge last November, which I attended. National and international attitudes are shaped in a variety of ways, in a fulcrum effect, so I think the meetings between senators and members of the House and their Soviet counterparts are very useful and ought to proceed.

———

Q: If that were to be recognized, it might set the stage for discord between Congress and the White House. But if the White House does not move fast enough in this direction, maybe Congress and particularly the Senate will have to take more meaning as a body.

A: Discord between Congress and the White House is more often a good thing than a bad thing. Strength in our society comes from diversity, from the expression of disagreement and the molding of consensus. The administration frequently argues that we on Capital Hill should not show disunity to the Soviets. My response is that the differences of opinion have to be reconciled, and that they make us stronger. The Adelman confirmation provided a good such opportunity for expression and for advancement of a number of goals. But I do not think it is realistic to expect the legislative branch to perform the executive function. The Constitution was on target in saying we could advise and consent but not direct and control. The president has to make those judgments, and though we can push him hard on it, it finally is his to do. Those rare occasions when congressmen go, say, to Iran and seek to negotiate with the Iranian government—as one did when the hostages were seized—can lead to real problems if there is any formal effort for a legislator to express an executive judgment.

———

Q: What are the maximum benefits we could derive from a summit in this context?

A: I do not know, because the complexities are overwhelming. But I believe we should try. The deployment of the Pershing II and the cruise missiles is a very decisive event for 1983. There have been reports that the Soviets will change their response from launch on attack to launch on warning. With the Pershing II six or seven minutes away from Moscow, the complexion of the world will be very different after its deployment than before. Moreover in 1983 we have a remarkable national asset in President Reagan. He is sincere, he is knowledgeable, and he is trying very hard. The reports about what he has done in his meetings with other world leaders have been very positive. The climate is at a unique low at present, with Andropov calling him "a liar" and "insane", and the president responding with comparative moderation by saying that they have "the empire of evil," ar.d so on. Secretary of State Shultz told me, "President Johnson met Kosygin in a summit at Glassboro and the results were terrible." I said, "There are two differences: this is 1983, and President Reagan is not President Johnson."

ERRATUM

In the May issue of *The Annals,* Ronald S. Scheinman's biographical sketch, on page 78, was incorrectly printed. His title, at the time the article was written, was

> deputy assistant secretary-designate, Bureau of Human Rights and Humanitarian Affairs, in the State Department.

The word *assistant* was dropped by the publisher.

Book Department

INTERNATIONAL RELATIONS AND POLITICS 164
AFRICA, ASIA, AND LATIN AMERICA 169
EUROPE 173
UNITED STATES 178
SOCIOLOGY.. 187
ECONOMICS 203

INTERNATIONAL RELATIONS
AND POLITICS

JOHN BAYLIS. *Anglo-American Defense Relations, 1939-1980: The Special Relationship.* Pp. xxii, 259. New York: St. Martin's Press, 1981. $22.50.

ROBERT M. HATHAWAY. *Ambiguous Partnership: Britain and America, 1944-1947.* Pp. x, 410. New York: Columbia University Press, 1981. $25.00.

Despite differing time-period coverage, these two books on Anglo-American relations agree on two points. One, the relationship can be described as special, and, two, it has been marred by constant misunderstandings, disagreements, and just plain blunders. None of these sources of friction has been serious enough to cause a rupture or even seriously to weaken Anglo-American cooperation over a variety of issues; but they have resulted in everything from ruffled feelings on both sides of the Atlantic to delays in implementing joint policies.

John Baylis's book covers a much broader time span that does Hathaway's, from 1939 to 1980, and thus is obviously more sketchy on individual events. This is not to suggest superficiality; indeed Baylis nicely weaves together the political, strategic, economic,

and technical aspects of the joint defense relationship. He begins with World War II cooperation, which he describes as "extraordinarily close," though marked with disagreement over both European and Asian strategic choice. Discord grows, however, as postwar cooperation falters over the U.S. refusal to share atomic secrets and American reluctance to commit itself to a formal Atlantic defense pact. Cooperation does occur over Korea, though the election of new regimes in both nations in 1952 produces some antipathy between Dulles and Eden over Geneva negotiations of 1954 and especially over British actions in Suez in 1956. Things improve after 1957 as nuclear secret-sharing broadens and both nations cooperate closely over Jordan and Lebanon in 1958. Stresses emerge once again after Kennedy takes office, over cancellation of the U.S. Skybolt missile promised to Britain, and over American pressures upon Britain to support the Multilateral Force over British preferences for an integrated allied air force. Further strains emerged between the two nations when the British refused to assist the United States in Vietnam, much to Johnson's annoyance.

The decade of the 1970s found Britain moving closer to the European continent, joining the European Economic Community and entering into cooperative production on several weapons systems with European partners. Britain was thus more affected by a flurry of U.S. congressional buy-American amendments, which seemed to attempt punishment of these British efforts.

Despite these differences Baylis concludes by suggesting that future U.S.-British defense relations will be close, characterized in part by the recent British plan to buy Trident missiles for their SLBM force.

Robert Hathaway's well-written book more sharply examines British-American war relations between 1944 and 1947. The year 1944 saw differences emerge during the war over monetary and trade agreements, which pitted U.S. desires for free trade against British sterling area preferences. The two also disagreed over wartime goals, particularly over Asia and the Berlin timetable. Moreover there were differences on postwar relations with the Soviets and over U.S. suspicions of postwar British imperial intentions. But Hathaway stresses the trade and aid issues as the most important points of contention, including U.S. efforts to gain British compliance on trade sanctions against Argentina in 1944, an interesting reversal of the 1982 Falklands crisis. Disputes continued on the issue of postwar aid, beginning over U.S. scale-backs of promised aid for British occupation forces and then extending to differences over aid and credit for British postwar economic recovery. Sharp disagreement also erupted over Palestine, stemming from U.S. pressure on Britain to admit European Jewish refugees to the Mandate area, while refusing to admit them to the United States.

These and other disputes are characterized by Hathaway in a statement that could summarize both of these books: "the sharp disagreements . . . were frictions arising from a basic similarity in goals." The differences, both agree, were also the result of the shift in power that characterized the position of the two nations during and after the war, and to the readjustments that these new roles required.

Both Baylis and Hathaway have done thoroughly competent jobs in capturing the complexities of U.S.-British postwar relations, using a variety of primary documents, and maintaining careful objectivity.

DAVID S. SORENSON
Denison University
Granville
Ohio

GEORGE LISKA. *Russia and the Road to Appeasement. Cycles of East-West Conflict in War and Peace.* Pp. xv, 261. Baltimore, MD: Johns Hopkins University Press, 1982. $25.00.

Writing to influence the peacemakers at Versailles in 1919, Sir Halford Mackinder, the founder of modern political geography, uttered his famous admonition: "Who rules East Europe commands the Heartland: Who rules the Heartland commands the World-Island: Who rules the World-Island commands the World." First advanced to the Royal Geographic Society in 1904, the pivot or heartland theory was the subject of intense scrutiny and critical approbation among German specialists in geopolitics during the 1930s. But just as the rim of a rotating disc achieves a velocity—the speed of progress, as it were—several times higher than that of the central pivot, so accelerating technological capacities among the rimlands during the Age of Space render the redressing of Mackinder's Edwardian science appear mystifyingly dated.

This conclusion will be reinforced by perusing the presentation of Professor George Liska, an émigré from the Czech Heartland. Liska argues that there is a difference in the levels of civilization of the present and developing superpowers; that the strategies of land or sea powers is determined by their position; that a volatile bi-power relationship is being superseded by a triangular contest among a declining sea or global power, a thwarted amphibious power standing astride the World-Island, and an emerging land giant culturally antithetical to both. Drawing liberally on the boundless treasury of analogy, Liska argues that long- and short-term cycles—certain to appeal to a stock-owning and market-following elite—suggest that Grand Strategy demands the amphibian power be judiciously encouraged to expand in order to further domestic liberalization and to decompress threatening pressures internationally. The 1939 example of Munich is misleading, except insofar as the Western powers encouraged Germany to attack the Soviet Union; the long-term interests of a maritime power entering into decline require a controlled policy of *apaisement*, without moral overtones, to integrate the Soviet Union into a co-managing role in a recon-structed international system vis-à-vis Asia and a Third World dominated by "local for-ces of anarchism and fanaticism."

Obviously, this book without evidence represents no strategy and offers no analysis; it is an apologetic, in which the—studied—density of prose is inversely proportional to the persuasiveness of the argument. Liska's craftiness in all the catches of special plead-ing would appear to exhaust the current the-saurus of techniques for winning sympathy and extracting provisional agreement on the basis of spurious logic. If the sentiment is from Alexander Blok and certain later neo-Slavophiles, the music is by Georgii Chi-cherin, improvising on the familiar Heart-land motif as reorchestrated by the author: "A typical way of mal-integrating [spirit and power] in the east has been to oscillate between excesses of physical force and intel-lectual fantasies about history and society." Only a sluggish schizophrenic obsession with Russia's destiny can account for the brilliant delusional scheme that blames the Mongols for interrupting Russia's ties with the mari-time West—by sinking the Kievan high seas fleet; ascribing commercial backwardness to mid-seventeenth century dislocations—during the reign of the "Most Quiet" Tsar Alexei when the quasi-parliamentary Assem-bly of the Land evolved the Law Code of 1649 governing commercial organization until the nineteenth century; or faulting Peter the Great for inhibiting the mercantile class—when he adopted mercantilism and gave them a coastline.

Of the suggestion that Soviet outreach toward an economic port on the Persian Gulf is directed toward improving commun-ications with Central Asia, or Siberia, little need be said. Liska's assertion that détente in Europe means that Western Europe can enforce restrictions on freedom in Eastern Europe through economic sanctions does indeed entail "[accepting] the moral obloquy of colluding in the crime of necessary Rus-sian repressions," but this circumstance is allegedly mitigated because guilt "is incum-bent equally or more on those who suffered less." The Pope, for instance? It is perhaps because of his skewed perspective that Liska did not comment favorably on the historical commonplace that since Napoleon's inva-sion, broad reforms in Russia have been stimulated not by external expansion but by military defeats—for example, the abolition of serfdom after the Crimean War, and the abolition of the monarchy after military exhaustion in World War I. It cannot be accidental that he did not draw the obvious analogy between the Soviet invasion of Af-ghanistan and the annexation of Bosnia in 1908 by the dynamic new foreign policy-mover of a semimodernized but backward amphibious Heartland power, Count Aehr-enthal, who is generally credited with wor-sening relations with an eastern land giant and thereby contributing to the preparation for the world war that ended in the amphibi-an's liquidation.

Professor Liska's book may be viewed as a reflection of neo-Nechaevism in interna-tional relations, and will be catalogued avidly, if drowsily, in Peking. The style is inexorably soporific, not to say hypnotic.

N. OTSHCHEPENETS

ARTHUR J. MARDER. *Old Friends, New Enemies: The Royal Navy and the Impe-rial Japanese Navy: Strategic Illusions, 1936-1941.* Pp. xxxii, 533. New York: Oxford University Press, 1981. $49.50.

Arthur Marder went out at the top of his form. Sadly, there will be no volume two to complete this superb first installment of his history of the relations between the British and Japanese navies in the decade 1936-45. The tale he tells here of the naval background to the 10 December 1941 drama off the Malayan coast, and of the Anglo-Japanese encounter itself that day will stand as exemplary of the very best in the stupidly maligned narrative mode. He says in the preface that his ambition was "to tell a story and to tell it well." He certainly knew how to do that. His researches were tireless, his gift with words was marked. Others have questioned the apparent innocence of his "I bring no theories of history to my research and writing" statement, and probably they are right: it is late in the game to make so ostensibly ingenuous a declaration. At the same time, Marder knew perfectly well what he was doing, and his readers will know it too. This is not 'scientific history," and it is not "total history," and it is replete with "events." There will be criticisms and complaints and corrections, but his book will nonetheless remain an enthralling, profoundly informed account of the two navies moving up to the war of 1941.

Marder knew both languages and he pursued his documents and men in both countries. He is frank to admit that his work is stronger on the British side. The materials available in the United Kingdom are unrivaled; in Japan there was much destruction and more reticence. Such was his prestige for his earlier studies of the Royal Navy that admirals and lesser ranks corresponded and talked with him at length in Great Britain. It is evident that he tried something similar in Japan, with some success, but he warns us that cultural and other barriers did not permit anything like the same degree of penetration. All the same, he here offers illuminating parallel accounts of the two navies in the years between the wars, their establishments, their schools, their weapons, their states of mind, their knowledge of each other, and their approaches to an armed struggle that for so long seemed undesirable, unwise, or simply unnecessary. The book is replete, too,

with portraits of the men who made events, ministers and service chiefs of the two nations, mostly laudatory, it is true, but alive and convincing. Given that the post-1941 volume will not appear, some part of all this may now seem overdrawn, but for this there is no help. Sometimes the sheer mass of detail—about weapons, say, or the minutiae of Dartmouth or the Imperial Naval Academy at Etajima—may strike one as a little excessive, but the incremental effect is impressive. We never forget that he is putting in the foundations for a magisterial recounting of the two empires, formerly allies, coming to the fateful break of December 1941. One can only suggest the wealth of evidence surveyed in this study, the generosity Marder shows in sharing it with his readers, and the excitement he sustains, despite the spacious background traced, in working up to the drama of the attack on Phillips's force. It is a masterly performance, both analytical and narrative, in the grand manner. And this superbly informed storytelling, however rare, will help keep plain old-fashioned history afloat, long after a good deal of the desperately dessicated and illiterate little monographs have gone to the bottom once for all.

JOHN C. CAIRNS

University of Toronto
Ontario
Canada

CHARLES REYNOLDS. *Modes of Imperialism.* Pp. viii, 263. New York: St. Martin's Press, 1981. $27.50.

All explanations of imperialism are useful; but some are more useful than others, which is to say that they are useful in different ways. Some serve to pull together certain lectures in a Western Civilization course; others help to increase the guilt load on rich legislators during debates over aid; still others are needed to help the faithful understand that capitalism must shortly collapse, or the opposite. But can we judge them in some verifiable sense according to their relative explanatory power? Charles Reynolds, a philosopher who teaches political science at the University of Durham, and who has written *Theory and Explanation in International Politics,* has used his expertise to explore a very weak spot in the body of our understanding about widely accepted theories of imperialism. While he reposes little trust in any of the competing models he dissects, he has provided us with a powerful set of tools for assessing our own concepts about imperialism. There are other important features of this brilliant study as well. If this book is widely read it could lever the whole debate about imperialism onto a higher plane.

Reynolds begins by outlining his concept of the fundamental differences between views of imperialism that try to be intelligible, in the sense that one can see how the argument hangs together, and those that explain, in the sense that they refer back to a set of generalizations or a theory that has a logical coherence apart from any particular historical events. He further distinguishes between the theoretical mode of argument and the historical mode. The former tests theories according to goodness of fit in actual situations, while the latter tries to understand how a given situation came about by examining the reasons key persons or agents acted as they did.

Each of the next four chapters takes up a major viewpoint on the causes and nature of imperialism: the power-security trap; the economic (Marxist) explanation; the ideological interpretation; and the sociobiological approach. Reynolds feels that these all raise universalist claims to explain imperialism. He makes out a fair case for each by thoroughly exploring its components and also by confronting each with apparently appropriate cases. For example, Soviet hegemony over East Europe is explained in terms of the power-security hypothesis; MNCs are used to test the economic model; Hitler's decision to conquer western Russia is used as a case to test ideological imperialism; and Japanese imperialism in the 1930s becomes a test for the sociobiological approach—man's atavistic, territorialist, aggressive nature.

For those of us who prefer to take our history with a dash of social science, Reynold's treatment of his four cases makes exciting reading, confronted as they are at every step by relevant critiques from theory. This is especially so for the ideological approach, where Reynolds convincingly argues that Hitler's racism was the basic feature in his decision to invade the USSR. But Reynolds seems more interested in theory itself, that is, in the strength of each model to which such cases are referred. Alas, none of these theories stands up to the epistemological probes he employs. For him each theory explored has basic internal flaws. Daunting objections, furthermore, can be raised against any of these cases for testing a given theory. The theories themselves are not truly different or competing, since key points in three of them can be subsumed under the power-security hypothesis: action based on fear—the most important component of the power-security approach—can be demonstrated to be crucial to the other three major views.

We have here, therefore, no short cut on the hard road to understanding the causes and nature of imperialism. Reynolds certainly does not intend to discourage us from pushing ahead; on the contrary. Students of imperialism, if they feel there is more to theorizing than its polemical potential, will agree that Reynolds has not only staked out many pitfalls and wrong turnings, but has also demonstrated some essential baggage for making the trip.

MARTIN WOLFE
University of Pennsylvania
Philadelphia

AFRICA, ASIA, AND
LATIN AMERICA

CLAES BRUNDENIUS and MATS LUNDAHL, eds., *Development Strategies and Basic Needs in Latin America: Challenges for the 1980s.* Pp. xii, 180. Boulder, CO: Westview Press, 1982. $17.50.

This volume is a collection of conference papers that represent an uneasy blend of advocacy and analysis. A primary objective of the editors is to convince the reader of the desirability of an approach to economic development that stresses the universal fulfillment of certain basic needs—for instance, minimum nutritional standards, standards of public health, and literacy—over maximizing the level of real per capita GNP. In a very general sense, advocates of the basic needs approach are making the perfectly valid point that broad statistical indices such as GNP are highly imperfect indicators of a society's overall level of well-being, so that an important supplement to such data is information on the extent to which an economic system has provided a minimum standard of living to its participants.

The specifics of this approach, however, can be questioned. A single-minded pursuit of basic needs fulfillment may very well lead to unwarranted neglect of the probable trade-offs between basic needs and other desirable objectives. A basic needs strategy will usually entail substantial redistribution of wealth or income, but many countries are simply too poor to meet all their citizens' basic needs. Paul Streeten grants that such countries must strive for growth, but refuses to consider the barrier to growth that a massive redistribution program is likely to present. Javier Iguíñiz E. points out that such a program is likely to induce an outflow of capital, but then is inexplicably led to argue for state ownership of manufacturing, commercial, and financial enterprises, without explaining how they will obtain sufficient financing from the remaining domestic sources. Claes Brundenius argues that the positive correlation between growth performance

and basic needs strategies shows that such strategies exact no cost in forgone growth, but Frances Stewart points out in her article that this is probably because greater per capita income simply enables a country to spend more on basic needs items. Streeten attempts to defend the basic needs approach against the challenge of paternalism, but with little success. Individual choice can prove inconvenient: Stewart notes that poor people will not infrequently "spend substantial sums on non-basic goods, even while suffering from serious undernourishment." While Brundenius and Lundahl infer from such evidence that Third World consumers are not competent to choose, it is at least as likely that they knowingly choose to give up some of life's basics for some of life's small pleasures, however tiny they might be.

The greater part of the volume is devoted to case studies of Haiti, the Dominican Republic, Peru, Brazil, and Cuba. The sample of countries is a good one, for those societies offer a wide variety of economic performance and development strategies. The poles of development strategies are represented by Brazil, which neglected redistribution to concentrate on growth, and Cuba, which has placed extraordinary emphasis on meeting basic needs. The case studies provide sufficient data to give the reader a feel for the material benefits and costs of those strategies, although nonmaterial considerations are neglected. The analysis of Cuba leaves unclear the quantitative significance of Soviet aid, so that the applicability of this experience to other countries is uncertain.

After reading this book I am convinced that it is a worthy goal to design, say, public-sector investment with greater attention to basic needs such as primary education and health, but unpersuaded that a basic needs approach should include the more drastic measures proposed by some of the contributors.

WILLIAM R. DOUGAN
Dartmouth College
Hanover
New Hampshire

RUTH BERINS COLLIER. *Regimes in Tropical Africa; Changing Forms of Supremacy, 1945-1975.* Pp. 221. Berkeley: University of California Press, 1982. $26.00.

Regimes in Tropical Africa is an analysis of political events in 26 countries of sub-Saharan Africa in the 1945-75 period. Collier explores "differences among countries in the initial experience with electoral politics and the implications of those differences for the emergence of different types of regimes and different patterns of regime change in the post-independence period." She defines regime as the "authority structure or the structure of formal, legitimate power. In this sense it may be thought of as the legitimating structure of the state." Collier asserts that the differences observed among the regimes can be related to the organization and unity of the political elites that grew out of the manner of transferring political institutions, and control thereof, from the colonial powers to the African colonies. Because of longer exposure to elections and the French colonial policy of direct rule, former French colonies were more likely to develop strong unified parties with the possibility, after independence, of using the electoral mechanism to mobilize and consolidate their power. Former British colonies, in contrast, suffered from the results of a decentralized colonial policy permitting the emergence of powerful ethnic and regional elites, which were not easily absorbed into the dominant political party. Thus elections exacerbated competition and conflict.

Throughout the study, computer analyses of the correlations among socioeconomic variables and political variables—such as voting, number of elections, various measures of party dominance, number of postindependence coups, and stability of the elite—are used to demonstrate the link between the degree of preindependence party dominance and the nature of the postindependence regime.

Collier's study is interesting and informative. She is thoroughly acquainted with the literature on party and regime in Africa, and with the debates of political scientists concerned with development and with the meaning and cause of various forms of preindependence and postindependence political behavior. Scholars in the development field will find her work worth studying. Neophyte students of African politics and general readers, however, will find her book of less interest, as it presumes a preexisting knowledge of events, without which the narrative may be found to be somewhat confusing.

Collier's conclusions in part reinforce the traditional interpretation of the importance of the differences between French and British colonial policy. Her emphasis on the importance of the developments in the internal power elites is a welcome contrast to scholars who consider only outside forces and/or economic variables as causative. One is tempted to complain, however, that the patterns proposed ignore too many other factors—factors that do not easily fit into a computer analysis. The geographic factor, mentioned by Collier as one to be explored; the presence or absence of a sizable settler population; other less easily measured variables, such as country size—Nigeria and Gambia, two of the four West African British cases, representing extremes; the characteristics of political leadership; these factors, to name only a few, explain as much of the difference among countries as the nature of the colonial regime and the length of exposure to electoral politics. Furthermore, contrasting British and French experience using systematic data analysis leads to a clear problem of sample size, given the small number of British cases with no substantial settler population. But this complaint is only a minor one. Collier presents her arguments well, and her computer analysis in general strengthens her analysis. This is a well-written and useful book.

LUCY CREEVEY
University of Pennsylvania
Philadelphia

H. E. MAUDE. *Slavers in Paradise: The Peruvian Slave Trade in Polynesia, 1862-1864*. Pp. xxii, 244. Stanford, CA: Stanford University Press, 1981. $22.50.

The Peruvian slave raids in Polynesia between 1862 and 1864 deprived many of the scattered island communities of Polynesia of two-thirds of their inhabitants. These raids were made, ostensibly, to fill the labor needs of the large Peruvian coastal plantations or *haciendas*. Since Negro slavery had been abolished in Peru in 1854, the large landowners or *haciendados* were constantly on the lookout for alternative sources of cheap labor to exploit. Even before slavery was abolished, land-owning interests pressured the Peruvian government centered in Lima to pass a liberal immigration law in 1849. This law permitted astute speculators to import hoards of cheap Chinese coolie laborers or "colonists" into Peru. These Chinese laborers, if they lived through the horrible passage to Peru, became the virtual slaves of the *haciendados*. Suffice it to say that the 1849 immigration law was suspended in 1856. However, by 1861 the Peruvian congress was once again persuaded by the politically powerful *haciendados,* who sought nothing less than the perpetuation of their slave labor system, to pass yet another immigration law to allow more "Asian colonists" into the country. In fact, this later law became the only legal basis for the so-called Polynesian labor trade. Significantly, the traffic of Chinese coolie laborers satisfied the greed of both the speculators in human cargo and the plantation owners until J. C. Byrne, an unscrupulous Irish adventurer, and B. D. Clark, an American hotelkeeper, pooled their resources to outfit a ship to recruit Polynesians, geographically much nearer than the Chinese, for the Peruvian labor market. So successful and profitable was Byrne's initial cache of 251 bewildered Tongarevan islanders—the men were sold for $200 each, women for $150 each, and boys for $100 apiece—that Peruvian entrepreneurs rushed pell-mell into the lucrative business of recruiting South Sea islanders for work on the mainland.

The enslavement of innocent Polynesians, most of whom were either duped or kidnapped for the Peruvian labor market, usually meant their early death through forced labor, melancholia, malnutrition, or disease. Many Polynesians died en route to the infamous Peruvian slave port of Callao in the dark, disease-ridden holds of the slave vessels. Those unlucky enough to survive the hellish passage to Peru were sold into bondage as house servants in Lima or for work on the *haciendas*. Most of the enslaved Polynesians sickened and died within six months of their arrival at Callao, principally because they had no immunity from the diseases peculiar to Peru—especially smallpox. Their early deaths, of course, "exasperated their employers," who had paid good money for them.

H. E. Maude's meticulously written book, *Slavers in Paradise,* based on over 20 years of research, graphically depicts the horrors of the Peruvian slave trade. Maude chronicles the permanently blighted lives of thousands of unsuspecting innocent South Sea islanders —those unfortunate enough to be kidnapped into slavery and almost certain death, and the loved ones left behind, whose grief must have been unbearable. Ironically, many of those enslaved Polynesians from exotic South Sea islands like Tongareva, Mangareva, the Marquesas, and Tuvalu had only recently been converted to Christianity before the raids commenced. The depopulation of most of the able-bodied men, women, and adolescents from the islands and the destruction of whole families naturally destroyed the existing social structure of the islands and seriously threatened with extinction their cultural ethos. It is significant to note that over 6000 Polynesians died as a direct or indirect result of the Peruvian slave trade. "For Polynesia," writes H. E. Maude in his concluding chapter, "the Peruvian slave trade thus constituted genocide of an order never seen before or since in her hisotyr; but this the islanders never knew themselves, for they were never told." That the islanders were never told about this important aspect of their history certainly seems a curious statement for Maude to make, but it is nonetheless a true irony of Pacific islands history that no comprehensive account of Peruvian slave trade in Polynesia has existed until now. Apart from piecemeal accounts of the period usually found in general histories of the islands, only oral traditions of the "terror and pathos of it all" survive. Unfortunately, most of the oral traditions are questionable, since they have lost much of their original content and reliability due to the rapid acculturation of the island communities following World War II. As Maude poignantly writes in his introduction, "The time has now arrived when the whole story can, and should, be told: not to exacerbate old wounds but because it is an essential link in the common historical heritage of the Polynesian peoples." Maude has written a scholarly yet enthralling historical narrative and one that may indeed stand the test of time.

FREDERICK J. STEFON
Pennsylvania State University
Wilkes-Barre

GAIL MINAULT. *The Khilafat Movement: Religious Symbolism and Political Mobilization in India.* Pp. x, 294. New York: Columbia University Press, 1982. $25.00.

Minault has produced a thorough and comprehensible account of the politics behind the Khilafat Movement as it developed among Indian Muslims after World War I. She has correctly drawn our attention to the Indianness of this movement, both in regard to the particular political and factional alignments within the Indian Muslim community, which gave shape to the movement, and in regard to the Indian Muslims' need for group solidarity, which made the Khilafat a kind of symbol for Indian Muslims which it could not be for Muslims elsewhere in the Islamic world.

There are some relatively minor problems in this book, some of which seem to stem from an assumption that the reader comes equipped with a good background in Islamic

and Indo-Islamic history. How else could the statement that "the emphasis at Firangi Mahal remained upon the *dars-e-nizamiya,* rather than on the Quran and *hadith* as at Deoband" be left with virtually no explanation of the critical significance of that seemingly small variation in academic orientation? Other problems seem to be needlessly introduced into the work by an inappropriate use of the phrase "the ulama" when "some ulama" or simply "ulama" would have been better. Thus, for example, it is stated that "the ulama tapped their own networks of influence and also reached consensus on a *fatwa* in favor of noncooperation addressed to all Muslims," implying that all Islamic religious scholars were active in the cause and in agreement on the issue, clearly an unwarranted implication.

Despite these problems the book does offer a wealth of information on the Khilafat Movement, and it presents the reader with a good analysis of its internal workings. The value of this must not be underestimated. This reader would, however, have appreciated some additional analysis of the broader ideological significance that this mass mobilization had for Indians generally, and for the Indian Muslims particularly. This movement was a watershed in India's Muslim politics, and it dramatically altered both the language and the stakes involved in political activity. Given Minault's considerable knowledge of this period, I look forward to additonal work, which might expand our understanding of its wider significance.

WARREN FUSFELD
University of Pennsylvania
Philadelphia

MILES L. WORTMAN. *Government and Society in Central America, 1680-1840.* Pp. xvii, 374. New York: Columbia University Press, 1982. $27.50.

In his "inquiry into the relation between society and government" in Central America, Miles Wortman emphasizes the region's long history of internal diversity and conflict. Following the destruction of the conquest Central America developed into a complex society outside the main centers of power in the Spanish American empire. While indigo dyes became an important export, the economy of Central America formed principally around the internal needs for food, livestock products, and craft manufactures. Society remained relatively free, in Wortman's view, from the domination of either foreign merchants or domestic urban elites. Buttressed by the Roman Catholic Church, the flexible governmental institutions of the Spanish Hapsburgs generated strong loyalty for the monarchy and wove a single social fabric from the multiple provinces and groups of Central America.

A deep crisis between 1680 and 1730 changed this pattern, Wortman finds. Silver discoveries in Honduras forced alterations in traditional social and economic ways, while natural disasters continually disrupted life through insect infestation, earthquake, drought, and disease. Simultaneously, the weakened Hapsburg dynasty expired. The new rulers of the empire, the Bourbons, began to introduce forms of government centralization into the region.

Ultimately the eighteenth century created a new Central America, one "dramatically different from its economically isolated Hapsburg predecessor, more integrated within its confines and within the European trade network." These changes benefited a new merchant elite in Guatemala, whose control of trade and credit allowed it to dominate farming, mining, and livestock operations throughout Central America.

The reformed governmental institutions of the Bourbons could not cope with the ramifications of international political and economic changes. As Spain collapsed before the French in Europe, Guatemalan merchants came to favor free trade and finally independence as the means of securing access to British and U.S. trade. Opponents of Guatemalan hegemony and cheap British textiles could no longer rely upon a weakened Spain to defend them. After independence, localism degenerated into constant civil war. By

1840 efforts at a regional federation had failed, leaving Central America divided into five independent states.

Based upon solid research in the Archivo General de Indias in Seville and the Archivo General de Guatemala, Wortman's work is a good complement to Murdo MacLeod's *Spanish Central America: A Socioeconomic History, 1520-1720.* Wortman's coverage of the colonial period is stronger than his treatment of the independence era. His discussion of Central American society in the late eighteenth and early nineteenth centuries would have benefited from a comparison with Mexico and the works of Romeo Flores Caballero, Doris Ladd, and Timothy Anna. *Government and Society in Central America* also very much needs a better map than the one provided. Despite these deficiencies, this study of Central American government and society should be read by anyone interested in attaining a deeper perspective on the region's contemporary civil wars.

ARTHUR SCHMIDT

Temple University
Philadelphia
Pennsylvania

EUROPE

PIERRE BIRNBAUM. *The Heights of Power: An Essay on the Power Elite in France.* Translated by Arthur Goldhammer. Pp. xii, 172. Chicago: University of Chicago Press, 1982. $17.00.

Pierre Birnbaum's *The Heights of Power* is an analytic essay that studies France's governing elite, both politicians and bureaucrats, in order to elucidate the nature of the French state. For, as he argues, the state's actions as an institution depend on the people who direct it. He stresses the heterogeneity of the "politico-administrative" elite and argues that relations between politicians and civil servants have alternated between hostility and unity. In France, an extremely centralized nation, the governmental bureaucracy has long organized all aspects of life, and yet the state has asserted its independence, its role as arbiter above the forces at work within society.

Birnbaum investigates the power structure and its changes from the July Monarchy to the Fifth Republic. That structure was most unified under the July Monarchy since administrators controlled political life. Yet the state lacked independence, since a homogeneous, powerful ruling class—the *grande bourgeoisie*—held not only economic but also political and administrative control. With the Third Republic, the unity of the power structure collapsed as an increasingly sharp break developed between politicians and administrators. To Birnbaum, universal suffrage separated the political sphere from the upper levels of the civil service, eliminated civil servants from parliament, and created a new group of professional politicians. These politicians, from middle-class backgrounds, came primarily from the liberal professions, especially law, medicine, and education, and they derived their strength from local roots. Government ministers generally came from similar backgrounds and emerged from parliament. Civil servants, however, were more economically affluent and socially prestigious. Considerable antagonism developed between politicians and civil servants, and it persisted through the Fourth Republic. This hostility impaired governmental functioning and precluded coherent policy formulation. The Fifth Republic has marked a distinct change in the roles of these two groups. Executive preeminence and relative parliamentary decline have fostered the decline of the professional politician. As government and parliament have grown further apart, the executive has relied on the bureaucracy. The professional backgrounds of deputies have altered, with heavier representation of civil servants and industrialists and less of disadvantaged social groups. Governmental ties to big business have also become closer. Under the Fifth Republic, the bureaucracy has exerted considerable influence over the executive; technocratic professionalism of the senior bureaucrats has taken precedence over the political professionalism of the deputies. Instead of emerging from parliamentary careers, ministers generally move from cabinet staff positions to ministerial rank. With the increased hold of civil servants on policy formation, governmental machinery has become estranged from parliamentary operations. The increased unity of government and bureaucracy has also been reflected in tighter control over economic life and the exclusion of parliament from economic decision making. Government bureaucrats have also begun to move into private business, especially banking and mass media. The Fifth Republic's integration of the various power centers has been achieved primarily through the mobility of the senior civil servants. Birnbaum briefly investigates the effects of the 1981 Socialist party victory on the pattern of Fifth Republic relations. Although the increasing gulf between politicians and civil servants is reminiscent of an earlier pattern, the dominance of the executive over the legislative branch has not been altered. He sees the socialist move toward a controlled decentralization as a policy at odds with the inherent logic of the state. The experiment is, however, too recent to allow a full evaluation.

Birnbaum's essay is a clearly written and persuasively presented analysis of the nature and development of the two groups—parliamentarians and civil servants—who have controlled political power in France over the past 150 years. It is thus an important contribution to understanding the upper levels of the French bureaucracy and the parliamentary elite, and a valuable addition to the literature of political science on this issue.

MARJORIE M. FARRAR
Chestnut Hill
Massachusetts

PATRICK DUNLEAVY. *The Politics of Mass Housing in Britain, 1945-1975: A Study of Corporate Power and Professional Influence in the Welfare State.* Pp. xvi, 447. Oxford: Clarendon Press, 1981. $39.50.

In the period discussed by this book, nearly 1.5 million people were rehoused in Britain, from inadequate or slum accommodations. The cities chosen by Dunleavy are Birmingham, Bristol, and Newham. This experience represents an important drive to move citizens into high-rise public housing. However, the program now is regarded as a major policy failure, the volume emphasizing this by charts, figures, and other data.

The new type of housing was not only unpopular; it was very expensive and had a bad effect on social life in inner urban areas, such as the three that Dunleavy examines. Today the disaster of high-rise policy has contributed to the lack of public support for commercial housing programs and for the planning system.

Patrick Dunleavy, lecturer in government at the London School of Economics, concentrates on mass-housing policies as a case study of a new kind of policy process in the welfare state. For high-rise housing and its concomitant problems he demonstrates how this configuration leads in the long term to massive distortion of public policy by private interests, namely, large construction corporations and the design professions.

Dunleavy raises a number of issues in social science, including contemporary theories of the state and alternative analyses of the dynamics of urban policy change. He also illuminates some of the most central issues in the recent history of the British welfare state and planning system.

To add to the problems, the Conservative government from May 1979 appears to be committed to reducing the size of the public sector altogether. "The construction industry has entered a profound and chronic slump in which there is no quick prospect of an upturn." The largest building firms and architectural practices have withdrawn "from the rump of the public housing program which remains, turning their attention since the early 1970s to overseas markets. Thus the policy system . . . and organizations with which this study is primarily concerned has substantially changed."

Dunleavy's analysis of the housing dilemma is divided into two parts: one examining the national political process on high-rise, "using some fairly extensive statistical analysis to characterize the overall trends in local authority decision-making"; with part two analyzing this directly by case studies of particular areas. The case studies are one of the most important aspects of the book. These are reinforced by adequate data of various kinds.

Dunleavy stresses that a balance sheet of the policy changes carried out in the 1970s has yet to be written. When it is, "the ideological effects may prove to have been some of the most significant legacies of the high-rise/mass housing era."

The author's notes are more than adequately prepared to sustain his viewpoint, and his bibliography and data obtained from students and others interviewed might well be the envy of anyone writing in the field of applied economics.

MARY E. MURPHY
California State University
at Los Angeles

WARREN B. MORRIS, Jr. *The Weimar Republic and Nazi Germany.* Pp. viii, 392. Chicago: Nelson-Hall, 1982. $25.95. Paperbound, $12.95.

Considering the plethora of studies on Germany between the two world wars, the publication of yet one more account needs justification. To be sure, its claims are modest enough, for it purports to be only a basic survey history. Morris is at his best when adopting a thematic approach: the first two background chapters, and then "The Youth of a Dictator," "Society and Culture in Weimar Germany," "The Nazi Dictatorship," and "Culture in the Third Reich." Unfortunately the other 14 chapters parade intriguing titles but come off as a potpourri.

Apparently Morris subscribes to the great-man theory of historiography, wherein the motivations and quirks of the *dramatis personae* upstage the socioeconomic and intellectual forces. Morris also seems strongly drawn to unraveling military campaigns, and while introducing no novel analyses devotes considerable space to strategy and tactics. In his judgment Project Ultra merited high praise for remarkable success in decoding intercepted Nazi messages and hastening Allied victory.

To his credit or discredit, depending on the reader, Morris generally does not shrink from taking a position on controversial issues. He accuses Ebert, Scheidemann, and other moderate Weimar socialists of running scared in confrontation with the radicals, and committing the egregious error of appealing to the military command for succor—thereby permanently dooming civilian leadership. He castigates two American presidents for their blundering moralism—Wilson in his endeavor to remake imperial Germany after his own image; Roosevelt in demanding unconditional surrender, thus cutting the ground from under the anti-Nazi movement. Morris never makes clear whether the anti-Hitler cabal represented more than eliminating a madman and restoring the tarnished honor of the officer corps. Regarding religious opposition to the regime, Morris maintains that "pronazi Catholics were only a minority," but that with the ascension of Pope Pius XII, "relations between the Third Reich and the Roman Catholic Church would improve."

At bottom, what this volume lacks is that theoretical penetration necessary for an adequate treatment of Weimar's collapse. Granted, it must be acknowledged that Morris does take up Germany's economic debacle during the post-World War I period: the crushing Reparations burden, the devastating inflation, the progressive radicalization of the people, and the tragedy of Allied indifference to the plight of German constitutional democracy. Yet the roles of both big business and the middle class in Hitler's rise to power are treated superficially. As for socialism in its various permutations, the reader is abandoned to his or her own ponderings. When examining German-Soviet relations, Morris fudges. After citing the alarm in Moscow following the 1934 nonaggression pact concluded between Berlin and Moscow, and mentioning the Russian initiative urging a popular front against fascism, Morris drops the matter without further comment. He also too readily accepts the at least contestable proposition that most Germans were "unaware of the horror of the concentration camps."

The dissatisfaction of this reviewer also stems from Morris's failure to identify a target readership, and from his structural vacillation between chronicling and attempting a conceptual framework. Organizational weakness discourages consideration of the book as a college text. Moreover, repeated forays into journalistic flashiness detract from the tone of scholarship preferred by most academicians. Yet a certain tedium resulting from excessive cluttering of the pages with disparate names and events mars the book's appeal to the general public. In sum, the most serviceable employment of this volume would be in a softbound edition, as a supplement to a standard history of Europe between the two world wars.

ELMER N. LEAR

Pennsylvania State University
Middletown

HENRY PACHTER. *Weimar Etudies.* Pp. xvii, 387. New York: Columbia University Press, 1982. $19.95.

Historians are generally more fascinated by brilliant failures than dismal successes. Germany between the two world wars has attracted more attention than contemporary France or Britain, which preserved the essence of democracy and decency, however shabbily. Tolstoy's preference for problem-ridden families over more normal ones seems to apply to historians as well.

Henry Pachter, late professor of political science at the City College of New York and professor of history and political science at the New School for Social Research, explores this problem in a collection of reminiscences and essays informed by personal experience. He examines a series of important and secondary figures who epitomized the era— Meinecke, Rathenau, Hesse, Heidegger, Musil, Mühsam, and others—and issues that affected the antecedents, development, and consequences of Weimar Germany. The work has the charm of the essayist who, while raising fundamental questions, feels no compulsion to cover all and can thus recreate the historical atmosphere with a leisurely, sometimes even conversational, intimacy in the manner of a diarist or novelist. This sense of place and time is the most salient of the book's appeals.

But beyond mood, the work raises a multitude of monumental issues. It presents Weimar as a contradictory congeries reminiscent of Dickens's evaluation of revolutionary France as the best and worst of times. It was at once "one of the freest states that ever existed," and yet restrictive and intolerant, and Pachter's attitude remained "ambivalent". Indeed "ultimately, there is no 'Weimar,' there is only the spirit that can be grasped from its contradictions." Precisely these contradictions, which rendered Weimar at once so frustrating and fascinating, were virtually ensured by its antecedents and nigh unavoidably led to the descent into Nazism.

Pachter's particular interest is Weimar culture's origin and character. He sees German culture between Bismarck and Weimar as an irrational, racist revolt against Western rationalism and a substitute for intellectuals' desire for some ill-defined revolution that had been frustrated by Bismarck's political success. The most able

and admirable of these intellectuals—such as Meinecke—sought unsuccessfully to reconcile pre-1870 German idealism with post-1870 German power.

Like many German intellectuals, Pachter is fascinated, almost obsessed, by the interplay between ideas and action. While stopping short of establishing a specific causal relationship between cultural causes and political results, he comes close to the view that the world wars, Weimar politics, and Hitler followed from the cultural milieu. At the same time, he sees cultural and artistic works as deeply shaped by historical circumstances. His observations on the intellectual in exile are at once poignant and revealing. He rejected the alternative of Israel in the belief that Jews should be the intellectual salt of the earth, but saw his choice of America as an admission of defeat for his radical political activities in Europe. Exile left him a stranger between these two worlds but with a special detachment encouraging objectivity about both. Though forthright about American drawbacks, Pachter is at once insightful and idyllic on American character. Above all, he reminds the historian and social scientist concerned with mass movements and long-range trends that history is constituted of individuals of whom Pachter is himself one of the most appealing.

L. L. FARRAR, Jr.

Princeton
New Jersey

SIMON WINCHESTER. *Their Noble Lordships: Class and Power in Modern Britain*. Pp. xix, 281. New York: Random House, 1982. $14.50.

Using a chatty, anecdotal style, Simon Winchester presents a series of verbal snapshots of the hereditary British nobility— royalty and life peers are excluded—as it exists today. The six classes of nobles, comprised of dukes, marquesses, earls, viscounts, barons, and Irish peers, really have few privileges left. Chief among these privileges are the right to sit in the House of Lords, virtual exemption from arrest for civil causes, exemption from jury service, and, theoretically, access to the sovereign. Right of trial by their peers, meaning "peers of the realm," was revoked in 1948; and in 1963, English and Scottish, but not Irish, peers were given the right to renounce their titles for their lifetime.

If so few privileges remain to the nobility, from where does their power emanate? The sources of the nobility's authority are tradition—a deference to the titled, along with a certain style that most possess—and land, lots of real estate. Fifteen hundred families own over one-third of Britain's land, much of it either prime urban property or agricultural estates and farms. This land provides substantial wealth and a great deal of influence and power.

After describing how the House of Lords operates, and how one accedes to the peerage, Winchester sketches portraits of various peers. Most of them seem to be sensible, likeable, if very private people, with a sense of history and responsibility both to their titles and to those connected with their estates. Admittedly, most are very conservative in their orientations, but there are some exceptions.

To Winchester, the nobility are an anachronism, both as an institution and as a social group. He admits that most of the peers are decent, well-meaning, and even conscientious people, but their very existence is incongruous in the days of worker democracy and the socialist state. Winchester feels that the somewhat feudal estates and property holding should be eliminated and the peerage abolished. In his view Japan benefited by abolishing its peerage after World War II, and Britain would reap similar benefits.

Possibly so, but Winchester fails to see the stabilizing role that the peerage still plays in Britain. Moreover he fails to demonstrate that abolition would produce the same benefits that he alleges it did in Japan. Abolition may not be necessary as titles increasingly become vacant; since 1965 no more hereditary peers have been created.

Their Noble Lordships is an informative and entertaining book, valuable for its insights into the rituals of the peerage and its membership in the late twentieth century. As a study of "Class and Power in Modern Britain" it is less an analysis than an assertion that the nobility is outmoded. Mr. Winchester informs without proving his assertion.

RANZ ESBENSHADE

Knoxville
Tennessee

UNITED STATES

NORMA BASCH. *In the Eyes of the Law: Women, Marriage, and Property In Nineteenth Century New York,* Pp. 255. Ithaca, NY: Cornell University Press. $19.50.

This splendid book comes close to being a paradigm of what legal historiography is all about. Well written, meticulously researched, and using the past to comprehend the problems of the present, its range comprehends a span stretching from the natalistic values of Blackstone to the nonnatalistic one of ERA. Basch's feminist sympathies are apparent, but her style is temperate and her analysis is acute.

Formally and materially, the story concerns two New York statutes—the Married Women's Property Act of 1848, and the Married Women's Earnings Act of 1860. In telling how these laws came to pass, the author's tribute to Mary Beard's pioneering *Women As A Force in History* in many ways holds a mirror up to her own—"provocative, imaginative, scholarly," to which one might add the label "panoramic," for Basch has an eye nicely cocked for the seemingly random social fact, and a deft touch for fitting it into her own tapestry.

The author's thesis is that enactment of the historic 1848 property statute was, contrary to the received tradition, neither silent nor revolutionary. Rather, she conveys a sense of inexorability of the transplanted common-law tradition yielding to a new environment, and doing so under aggressively managed efforts at change.

An interesting but regrettably underdeveloped aspect of the story concerns the liberating aspect of the contemporaneously emergent finance capitalism. Here developments in insurance—permitting the widow to receive insurance on her husband's life, free of the claims of his creditors; savings banking—where operational necessity permitted unilateral withdrawal of a married woman's deposit; and extended stock holdings paralleled institutional reform efforts to sap the inertial power of tradition and became especially formidable with the appearance of a female wage-earning class.

In a sense the book is behind its time, for it is precisely a grass-roots look at the interplay of jurisprudential ideals and social reality in the best tradition of the American legal realists. On the other hand, it is significantly current in providing a headnote to understanding the recent controversy on the value of housewifely contributions to Social Security. Somewhere in between is its obviously unintended reopening of the Shakespeare-Bacon dispute, with the assertion that the dower declamation in the *Taming of the Shrew*—whereby Petruchio expanded common-law dower but yielded Kate no real autonomy—shows Shakespeare's familiarity with personalized marriage contracts.

GERALD T. DUNNE
St. Louis University
St. Louis
Missouri

LARRY BERMAN. *Planning a Tragedy: The Americanization of the War in Vietnam.* Pp. xvi, 203. New York: Norton, 1982. $14.95.

Despite the vast literature on Vietnam, we are actually at an early point of serious scholarship on the war. Even with the early accessibility of documentation such as the *Pentagon Papers,* the material necessary for major academic research is not yet, or is just now becoming, available. The climate today is more conducive to dispassionate research than in previous decades. The questions asked today and the purpose of research are changing. Scholars are motivated less by defending or condemning the war than by attempting to understand fully why and how the crucial decisions were made. Among several fine recent studies on policy formation, Larry Berman's slim volume is one of the very best.

Berman focuses intensively on July 1965, the period when Lyndon Johnson opted to Americanize the war. Although his personal view of the war is evident, the author is interested more in the dynamics of the decision process than in its results. He documents the argument, earlier developed by Leslie Gelb and Raymond Betts's *The Irony of Vietnam: The System Worked* (1979), that the president was not misled or duped by his advisers, but was in fact well served. The advisory process functioned as it was constructed to perform. Johnson's advisers provided a range of cogent policy options, and they astutely projected the results that would most likely transpire from the pursuit of each alternative. The president's choices may not have been easy ones, but he was aware of the probable outcomes of each policy decision.

With all this information before him, Johnson deliberately chose options which the consensus of his advisers deemed to be the least promising for long-term success. The president did not disagree with their projections, but he branded the other options politically unacceptable. Honest and forthright escalation would disrupt his domestic programs and inspire national outcry against the costs of the war; extrication would damage his personal reputation. Thus Johnson staged a political debate among his advisers to demonstrate that his quest for peace knew no bounds, but he realized that a true searching evaluation of American policy could prove far too expensive. So he continued halfway measures that staved off immediate defeat, although he knew that these actions had little chance of achieving his stated objectives. Berman concludes that the result was a deep American overcommitment to a cause that had no hope of success.

The treatise, which is based upon recently released National Security Council records augmented with abundant oral interviews with participants, is well documented, and the argument is tightly constructed. Berman prefers to let the documents speak for themselves as much as possible; his lengthy reproductions of transcripts verify his contentions. In sum, this is one of the most important books on the war now in print. It is must reading for serious students of the Vietnam War or of recent American foreign policy formation.

JOE P. DUNN

Converse College
Spartanburg
South Carolina

JAMES BOLNER, ed. *Louisiana Politics: Festival in a Labyrinth.* Pp. xviii, 375. Baton Rouge: Louisiana State University Press, 1982. $35.00. Paperbound, $8.95.

James Bolner, professor of political science at Louisiana State University, has edited a series of 12 essays to explain Louisiana politics, which he holds is "clearly among the most exciting in the nation." He also stated in the Preface that he had toyed with numerous subtitles, such as "The Pelican's Maw," "Come to a Political Crawfish Boil," and "A Recipe for Political Jambalaya." He finally hit upon "Festival in a Labyrinth" to denote both the colorful quality and the complexity of the state's politics.

The first essay, "The Louisiana Political Culture," written by David M. Landry and Joseph B. Parker, explains the complex political milieu within which the political process takes place. It confirms the labyrinth thesis as well as providing the unifying theme for the remaining essays. Four basic factors underlie the states' politics, the first and most fundamental being the ethnic heterogeneity. The population has a unique mixture of Mediterranean (French, Hispanic, and Italian), Anglo-Saxon, and Afro-American, which creates diversity and divergent clienteles. This also divides the electorate into two religious camps, 40 percent Catholic and 60 percent Protestant. Another factor involves economic status. The lines are drawn between the liberal Populists—white farmers and workers plus blacks and Hispanics—versus the neo-Bourbons—businessmen and suburbanites. Since Huey Long, the state has provided a large number of services, and this has provoked an ongoing debate as to how extensive they should be and who will pay for them. Finally, a one-party system further compounds the complexity of the whole system by placing a premium upon political personalities rather than issues, since all the candidates are Democrats. Hence we end up with both a festival and a labyrinth.

Within this orientation, the following topics are discussed: "The Louisiana Constitution of 1974," by Mark T. Carleton; "The Legislature," by Patrick F. O'Connor; "The Governor," by Ed Renwick; "The Judiciary," by Charles Holbrook and Mark T. Carleton; "Parish [County] Government" and "Municipal Government," by Richard L. Engstrom; "International Relations," by Riley Baker; "Political Parties," by Paul Grosser; "Blacks in Louisiana Politics," by Jewel L. Prestage and Carolyn Sue Williams; and "Voting Behavior in Gubernatorial Elections," by John Wildhen.

The essayists are all political scientists who teach at institutions within the state of

Louisiana or in the South—Louisiana State University, University of New Orleans, University of Southern Louisiana, Nicholls State University, Southern University, and Loyola University of New Orleans.

Political scientists will particularly enjoy and appreciate these essays. Louisiana politics is indeed both complex and colorful.

FREDERICK H. SCHAPSMEIER
University of Wisconsin
Oshkosh

PHYLLIS F. FIELD. *The Politics of Race in New York: The Struggle for Black Suffrage in the Civil War Era.* Pp. 264. Ithaca, NY: Cornell University Press, 1982. $19.50.

The Politics of Race in New York is an important contribution to the historical literature on American race relations. Drawing extensively on manuscript collections, newspapers, and government documents, Phyllis F. Field carefully examines the response of ethnic groups and political parties to the movement for black voting in New York in the middle decades of the nineteenth century. Her skillful use of quantitative methods and evidence reveals much about public attitudes, party needs, and racial reform during this period.

Popular division over black rights in the 1840s broke down along ethnocultural lines. Closely analyzing local voting returns on an equal-suffrage proposition, Field shows that Catholic Irish and German towns were predominantly antisuffrage; support for black voting was confined to a few towns consisting mostly of New England-born migrants and immigrant Protestant groups. The 1850s saw greater affinity between cultural background and political affiliation. Proposals to abolish property qualifications for black voters got caught up in the controversy over the growing influence of immigrants, economic dislocations, and the sectional debate over

slavery extension; the result was a realignment in the popular sources of support for the major political parties in New York. Field details a party polarization in the state legislature over black rights. Democratic rejection of equal suffrage catered to the racial fears of Catholic immigrants The new Republican Party promoted black suffrage to win the backing of Yankees, black activists, and white abolitionists.

The Civil War and Reconstruction aggravated party differences over racial issues and centered attention on black voting rights. New York's electorate rejected a state constitutional amendment for equal suffrage in 1869. Field demonstrates convincingly that the significance of the suffrage referendum resided less in its reflection of Democratic racism and more in its expression of Republican liberalism; half of the state's 59 counties showed modest gains in prosuffrage support, and another 16 counties greatly increased their suffrage votes. This endorsement of black voting did not signify disapproval of other forms of racial inequality. Field shrewdly observes that New York's Republican organization "seemed not to have dispelled prejudice so much as to have organized support against a particular form of discrimination without necessarily trying to reduce prejudice." *The Politics of Race in New York* is an impressive example of judicious interpretation and deserves a place on the shelf of any scholar concerned with the interaction of ethnic loyalties, party politics, and racism in nineteenth-century America.

MARTIN J. SCHIESL
California State University
Los Angeles

J. DAVID GREENSTONE, ed. *Public Values and Private Power in American Politics.* Pp. xiv, 286. Chicago: University of Chicago Press, 1982. $20.00.

Grant McConnell's *Private Power and American Democracy* (Knopf, 1967) challenged the prevailing pluralist orthodoxy of postwar political science and influenced a generation of political science students. While others glorified interest-group liberalism, McConnell argued that the interests of the general public were ill served by a system that allowed groups to seize large chunks of public power to use in the pursuit of their own narrowly defined self-interest. He saw the fundamental cleavage of politics as the conflict between the welfare of the whole community and the interests of the groups and individuals that made up the community.

Public Values and Private Power in American Politics consists of eight essays written by former students of McConnell, seeking to expand upon themes in McConnell's work. The papers are divided equally among four categories: Perspectives on the Study of American Politics, the American Executive, Interest Groups, and Cities in the Federal System. While the papers are widely divergent in style, subject matter, and methodology, the common thread running through them is a concern about the distinction between private and public interests, which was so central to McConnell's work.

In the interest-group section, Ronald Kahn reviews federal highway policies since the 1950s to test McConnell's thesis that the president and the Senate, because of their broader constituencies, will be more public-regarding than the House. Examining votes on such issues as mass transit, truck-weight limitations, highway beautification, and relocation assistance, he finds general support for the thesis. The article's limited scope and assumptions of what constitutes a public-regarding position can be criticized, but its research does clearly illustrate that size of constituency, not ideology, was what

determined an official's responsiveness to lobbying pressures in highway policy.

Greenstone's article, "The Transient and the Permanent in American Politics," tries to identify criteria by which to measure the public interest. Greenstone argues that the concept of "public" has had two sets of criteria throughout American history: "an empiricist set concerned with inclusiveness and equity, and a set of substantive standards which has animated humanitarian reform." McConnell's work, Greenstone contends, was built around this bipolar concept of "public" and, when properly elaborated, provides "sufficiently clear criteria to have a central place in American political practice."

The most unusual article in the volume is Michael Paul Rogin's "The King's Two Bodies: Lincoln, Wilson, Nixon and Presidential Self-Sacrifice." Illustrated with paintings of Christ's crucifixion, stills from *Birth of a Nation,* and presidential photographs and cartoons, the article explores the tensions between the body natural and the body politic. McConnell had argued that the president, because of his national constituency, was the public's bulwark against private-regarding politics, but Rogin shows that a president's own private needs and wants can undermine his public-regarding leadership. Rogin sees the Lincoln, Wilson, and Nixon presidencies as "problematic just to the extent that the presidents' self-regarding ambitions were not informed by a legitimate public purpose."

In addition to these, there are articles by Mark Kesselman tracing the evolution of political science from "Apologetic Pluralism to Trilateralism and Marxism," Peri Arnold on Herbert Hoover, Karen Orren on organized labor, Matthew Crenson on urban politics, and Paul Peterson on federalism and distributive and redistributive politics. All the articles in *Public Values and Private Power in American Politics* are interesting individually, but they are so very different in both style and subject matter that the collection's overall appeal may be limited to those interested in examining the variety of ways the influence of a master teacher is reflected in the works of his students.

JAMES FAIRBANKS

University of Houston
Texas

DANIEL N. HOFFMAN. *Governmental Secrecy and the Founding Fathers: A Study in Constitutional Controls.* Pp. xii, 339. Westport, CT: Greenwood Press, 1981. $35.00.

Daniel N. Hoffman is a lawyer and scholar currently teaching political science in Vermont. His first two books, both in collaboration with Morton H. Halperin, appeared in 1977. *Top Secret: National Security and the Right to Know* sustains a legal-constitutional argument against what the authors felt was the excessive and often deplorable secrecy of the Nixon administration. *Freedom vs. National Security* is a massive compilation of statutes, judicial decisions, and commentaries relating to loyalty, security, espionage, and dissent. These are drawn chiefly from the modern era stretching between World War I and 1974. The preface to *Top Secret* holds "that the problem of secrecy cries out for and is susceptible to principled regulation," and concludes, "As the Founding Fathers well knew, a people will be only as free and as informed as they are determined to be."

Government Secrecy and the Founding Fathers tests that invocation of the Founding Fathers. It finds, much as Leonard Levy did when he scrutinized their behavior with respect to free speech, that the Founding Fathers were casual, inconsistent, and far below modern ideals in their practices. Hoffman finds the Constitutional Convention, itself meeting in secret, largely indifferent to the issues of secrecy and disclosure in our fundamental law. He further finds that the Senate met in secret and offered no record of its debates for its first five years. President Washington regularly consulted his cabinet on whether he should comply with requests for documents from the House and Senate, and he early held back materials he considered necessary to keep confidential. In an atmosphere of increasing crisis and partisanship, Washington became more secretive, in part because members of his cabinet, congressmen, and diplomats often leaked and published matters he wished to keep secret. While most of the book studies secrecy under Washington and Adams, Hoffman tell us enough about Jefferson and Madison to illustrate his view that their behavior was substantially like that of the Federalists.

Hoffman is no vulgar debunker. He respects the Founding Fathers and reports their deeds accurately if not always completely, but he deplores their inconsistency with regard to state secrets. Rather than providing a standard to which we might return, they prove to have introduced many of the practices that now appear so ominous. Hoffman must therefore invoke idealism rather than history for his conclusion:

The laws and judicial doctrines abridging political speech and publication should not be toughened but repealed or overruled. In the present situation, as in the founding era, their impact is not to protect the national interest but to maintain a rigid barrier between the rulers and the ruled, those with and those without a "need to know," those with and those without access to the private elite channels of influence and information [pp. 262-63].

ROBERT McCOLLEY

University of Illinois
Urbana-Champaign

WILBUR C. RICH. *The Politics of Urban Personnel Policy: Reformers, Politicians, and Bureaucrats.* Pp. ix, 178. Port Washington, NY: Kennikat Press, 1982. $18.50.

Imagine a soap opera. The cameras roll. The actors are politicians—sometimes machine oriented, sometimes genteel reformers, sometimes academic reformers—

union leaders, and members of the financial community. All play to the camera. And many times the actor who plays to the cameras or media best wins, regardless of the merits of his or her cause. Such is how Rich portrays urban personnel policy.

Rich's book is a history of municipal personnel policy in New York City. The situation is traced in a chronological fashion from the early 1800s to the present. The stated purpose of the book is to assess the impact of interest-group interaction on public employment. Rich classifies various time periods when various interest groups dominated the personnel policy. However, at no time did any group make public policy single-handedly. Rather, it was a resolution of forces, and at times some groups were stronger than others.

While the individual chapters are investigative in nature, it is the summary-and-recommendations chapter that analyzes the personnel situation as a game and as theatrical performances by the leaders to woo the audience, or public, to their point of view.

Machine politics, in general, attempted to expand the patronage system to create a loyal constituency. Reformers, whom Rich regards as being incredibly successful, attempted to isolate municipal jobs from politics by creating a civil service, attempting to recruit quality performers to municipal positions, and promoting on a merit rather than political basis.

Rich feels that our system of decentralized representative democracy precludes an absolutely efficient bureaucracy. Of course, the word "absolutely" is his, but no proof of such a statement is offered. Perhaps I follow from the line of academic reformers, but I believe that efficiency gains galore exist in the public sector, waiting to be implemented by the appropriate manager/administrator, or waiting to be discovered. While this may not be absolutely efficient, if the move is toward greater efficiency, it is a move in the appropriate direction.

Rich also feels that political party influence is now limited in urban personnel, the bureaucracy is poorer because of it, and as a result, "a serious flaw in our participatory democracy" has been opened. He never mentions why this flaw is and I, for one, cannot agree with the statements. Having served in government, I can see no merit in the patronage system of bureaucracy. It wastes time and people power. It makes for continuous reorganizations, not of merit but of personal preference.

In sum, the book is of moderate interest. But it falls significantly below what I would regard as its potential. The summary-and-recommendations chapter is not logically tied to the earlier chapters.

W. BRUCE ALLEN
University of Pennsylvania
Philadelphia

FRANK TARIELLO, Jr. *The Reconstruction of American Political Ideology, 1865-1917.* Pp. viii, 200. Charlottesville: University Press of Virginia, 1982. $20.00.

This small volume may raise hackles. Conventionally, historians have tended to view the Progressive movement with at least measured approval, as a necessary and reasonable adaptation of governmental functions to post-Civil War developments in American society. Today the Progressives' contention that political intervention was required to achieve fairness and freedom from tyranny in the economic and social, as well as political, facets of our national life is widely accepted. Indeed, most of what criticism has surfaced comes from revisionists deeming Progressives camouflaged conservatives or, at best, too timidly restrained in their reforms, leaving undemocratic capitalism still dominant.

Not so with this work. While this reviewer found the pleonastic, polysyllabic erudition difficult at times, possibly Tariello's style affords the impression of dispassion crucial to any palatability for his challenging thesis. Essentially, he says, Progressivism was no mere readjustment of America's traditional republican values; it represented revolt against the very principles of natural rights, individual liberties as conceived by the

Founding Fathers, and the idea of limited government itself.

The attack was an indirect one; Progressive reformers asserted that they were, at least in spirit, preserving or restoring the old ideals. Governmental action, they insisted, was necessary to bring any reality to freedom and equality in modern times. Actually, they saw society as a continually evolving organic entity, something more than the sum of its parts, whose interests dominated all other considerations. Thus free society—with an altruistic elite determining the general welfare in the broadest sense—came to supplant free government, and a democratic collectivism demolished the barriers erected by earlier patriotic statesmen.

Sociologists, not political theorists, were to determine the public good; any meaningful distinction between government and society had been eliminated. Assenting to pragmatists' argument that change was the essence of reality, Progressives held truth to be communal and subjective, making legalism and written constitutions outdated. While they publicly might have disclaimed the politician's cynical "If you've got the votes, you can do anything," that was actually the inevitable consequence of such relativism.

In his conclusion Tariello concedes— almost as an afterthought—that many of the Progressives' complaints against the social and economic abuses of their day were quite justified, but he perceives their establishment of an unlimited social interest as the supreme touchstone and criterion to be worse than the evils they sought to remedy. His thesis, if the reader chooses to accept it, goes far to explain much of today's social, political, and intellectual perplexity.

DONALD H. STEWART
State University of New York
Cortland

G. EDWARD WHITE. *Earl Warren: A Public Life*. Pp. x, 429. New York: Oxford University Press, 1982. $25.00.

G. Edward White's *Earl Warren: A Public Life* is not very successful as an analytical

biography of the late chief justice. Attempting to explain contradictions in Warren's public stances and to flesh out a sparse impersonal record left by the intentionally private Warren, White insists that Warren must be viewed as a man of his times. Asserting that the key to Warren's life is his formative years, he perceives Warren as a man raised in a rough-and-tumble early twentieth-century California, where racist sentiment toward Asians was a measure of patriotism and where individuals struggled against the stranglehold of big business, especially the railroad. From this background emerged Earl Warren, who, as governor of California during World War II, interned Japanese-Americans in detention camps, but as an avowed Republican appointed by Eisenhower, surprised everyone with his staunch support of individual rights. White concludes that Warren's tenure on the court was less a vanguard of liberalism and more a harking back to the values of those relatively simple California days, with the anti-Asian sentiment finally giving way to the belief in individual rights and a broader definition of patriotism. White may be right, but his presentation of this thesis is neither persuasive nor carefully substantiated. In the end, it is not the most interesting part of the book.

Although the attempt to present a coherent thesis about Warren's life may not be successful, in the process White reveals fascinating information about Warren. Earl Warren was an influential justice who led the court to mandate reform and create social upheaval. All this from a man who was not considered an intellectual; in a letter, Learned Hand once stated that Warren had "relatively a small capacity for verbal analysis." All this from a man who had never been a judge and who had not practiced law for 12 years before he joined the Supreme Court. All the criminal reform cases like *Miranda* from a man who, as Alameda County district attorney, was considered "very aggressive" and "crusading." Earl Warren was a complex man, and White's description of the myriad strands of his personality and politics makes for interesting reading.

White is best when he analyzes the decisions of the Warren court. Looking at Warren's style and analysis of the law, White concludes that Warren's jurisprudence was result oriented; he asserts that Warren would find the solution to a controversy by searching through his private code of ethics and then, having decided the best course, would manipulate precedent to support it. According to White, Warren's was a freewheeling approach to law, less afraid of exceeding the court's powers than of allowing an injustice to continue. While admiring this fearlessness in Warren's approach, White also recognizes that this personal use of the law may not have left a strong jurisprudential legacy. In the end, White seems to conclude that Warren was a successful justice because he was a highly ethical man rather than a great legal thinker.

ELIZABETH RENAUD

Philadelphia
Pennsylvania

J. ALLEN WHITT. *Urban Elites and Mass Transportation: The Dialectics of Power.* Pp. viii, 231. Princeton, NJ: Princeton University Press, 1982. $20.00. Paperbound, $6.95.

The paradox in the relationship between businessmen and politics is an old one. It can even be seen in *The Shame of the Cities,* where Lincoln Steffens castigates all businessmen while he himself practices speculation in securities and real estate. "The typical businessman is a bad citizen," he tells us in the introduction to his book. Now J. Allen Whitt repeats the charge and adds that businessmen are not only bad citizens, but they also act in an organized, informed, and class-conscious manner to protect the business class from an incursion by nonbusiness classes. Whitt does not use journalism, nor does he present his thoughts as a political manifesto. He uses scholarship and carefully presented research methods to stress the point that what follows are simply the

findings of a research effort, the results of a test. However, when the statistics are not convincing enough, the researcher calls in reinforcements in terms of a historical background, which, he maintains, will help to shed special color on the findings, to explain them better, but which are based on a socioeconomic framework of a scale different from the research under scrutiny. The result is a classic Marxist handling of a sociopolitical issue, which produces only one obvious explanation of the events discussed: a fully developed class conflict in action in the field of urban transportation.

Whitt examines five major issues in mass transportation in California: the 1962 bond vote for the San Francisco BART; the 1968 vote in Los Angeles on Proposition A for a similar metro transit system; the 1970 California vote for opening up the California highway trust fund; and the 1974 second vote in Los Angeles for a BART metro transit system in this region. In the process, the author examines the pluralist model of continuously evolving and competing power centers among interacting multiple and overlapping interest groups, as presented by Robert Dahl, Arnold Rose, and Nelson Polsby, and finds the model wanting. He also examines the elitist model of social interaction along a pyramidical social structure where the elites at the top exercise major power—influence—on all major social issues as discussed by C. Wright Mills, Floyd Hunter, and Thomas Dye; he finds that theory too falling far short of providing a sufficient explanation of what happened in the five cases examined. He then proceeds to extend the elitist model into a class-based model in which dialectic interactions ensue.

What Whitt proposes as an improvement is the use of comprehensive planning that will be able to withstand any pressure from powerful classes, such as the business class. Yet time and again he castigates city planners and their plans as being little more than manifestations of the preferences of the powerful business class. Obviously the call for total, comprehensive planning includes much more than it says. It is in essence a call for all-encompassing planning exercised by an all-powerful governmental machinery that can eliminate all pressures from the business class, or, in its generic form, from the capitalist class. Planners with experience in urban transportation in several regions in this country and abroad—including socialist countries—would most probably find the explanation offered by Dr. Whitt bordering on the naive, and its generalizations bordering on the simplistic. Scholars, however, may appreciate his research approach and its systematized and well-ordered examination of data. As a scholar Dr. Whitt gains my appreciation. It is, however, where he, hard pressed by the missing evidence, provides supplementary support from ideological sources that we part company, and disbelief wins over the previous hard-won concurrence. In spite of all this, the book deserves both to be read by active urban scholars, and to stay on the bookshelf of social scientists involved with urban problems.

ANTHONY R. TOMAZINIS
University of Pennsylvania
Philadelphia

SOCIOLOGY

JOHN A. ARMSTRONG. *Nations before Nationalism*. Pp. xxxvi, 411. Chapel Hill, NC: University of North Carolina Press, 1982. $30.00.

Armstrong sets out in this ambitious work to trace the rise of the attachment to nations which we find today, beginning in the ancient Near East. Out of the ancient Near East come ethnic myths, creating the nomadic culture of Islam and the sedentary world of Christianity. Each great Near Eastern religion had its "mythomoteurs."

Armstrong, whose previous books have been on the politics of the Soviet Union and on the European administrative elite, attempts to address questions that obviously arise from his primary field of concern and to trace them to their roots. He is not alone in his concerns. Among recent works covering some of this terrain are the monograph by the well-known peace researcher Johan Galtung, *Cosmology and Western Civilization* (Oslo, 1979), which stresses the "essentially western propensity for centralism"; and *Class and Nation: Historically and in the Present Crisis* (1980), an anarchist view of nations from a Marxist viewpoint by Samir Amin, who also begins in the ancient Near East.

Professor Armstrong's results are a complicated series of typologies based on the idea of the dichotomy. Many of his empirical sources are drawn from the orientalist repertoire; his theoretical sources include works by Fredrik Barth, Levi-Strauss, Ernst Cassirer, and Karl Deutsch—many of which induce this dichotomous type of thinking. The results for areas in which I am competent do not impress me.

In a chapter called "Ethnicity and Way of Life," which is subsumed under the heading of "Sedentary versus Nomad," Armstrong chances on the Maronites, a Christian community among several found in Lebanon and Syria. One might already be put off by the notion of Islam as nomadic, or of the state emerging in isolation from the nomad, or of the nomad incapable of thinking in terms of states and ethnicities—which is the matter at hand—or even of a nomad; but what are the results?

After speaking of Arabized Berbers, who construct houses like their neighbors to seclude their women, showing thereby the totality of mutation from the nomadic free life to the settled, Armstrong proceeds to speak of the Maronites of Lebanon as Arab in language and lineage myths, but lacking the intense Muslim concern for sequestering women. Such are the advantages of dichotomies, that one can project an entire landscape or mirror-world onto less powerful—here Muslim—peoples, thereby making one's own reality come clear! This, by the way, is the point of Edward Said's *Orientalism*. The

Berbers who are and were Muslim did not sequester their women until they were forcibly made sedentary in an insecure urban life, which they share with all the people around the Mediterranean, with its great stress on the protection of the family. Armstrong, meanwhile, is arguing that sexual exploitation comes from the nomadic origins of Islam! The Maronites, long regarded as a conservative Christian group by other Christians as well as Muslims, were favored in the colonial period. A part of the Maronite community developed an international bourgeois lifestyle for both men and women. Another and larger part of the same community continues to live with much the same value system as their Lebanese neighbors of different persuasions, sharing the class values of workers, peasants, and so on—which sometimes involves sequestering.

The discussion of the Maronites and the Berbers highlights the problem of taking shifting ideological currents and attempting to work with them as stable national characteristics over time. Armstrong recognizes this at several points. Even in his own specialty, his polarities approach yields disappointing results. The Islamic world, he claims, failed to utilize imperial administrations, preferring segmented elites, whereas the West repeatedly tried and failed at imperial strategies. Yet it is not unconventional to refer to some Islamic states, including the Ottomans, as prebendial; that is, they exacted tribute through agents from an imperial center. Others, meanwhile, were more like the feudal West; that is, the lord in Lebanon had to live on the land. The West certainly succeeded in imperial strategies in India.

Perhaps it seems unfair to choose details as a way of discussing or sampling a book that covers millennia. The justification in this case is that the book has no real argument and no real documentation. The reader is expected to believe that ancient and premodern national sentiments exist and need to be considered as linear antecedents to those of modern history. History simply moves ahead without ruptures. History is a collection of static essences that can be decoded, thereby clarifying the nationalisms of occidents and orients. History thus explains our problems in the Middle East. I simply wish to observe how romantic this is.

PETER GRAN

Temple University
Philadelphia
Pennsylvania

H. M. BLALOCK. *Conceptualization and Measurement in the Social Sciences.* Pp. 285. Beverly Hills, CA: Sage, 1982. $19.95.

This book attempts to address "the problem of generalizability and comparability of one's measurements across diverse settings . . . [and] the implications of indirect measurement of important variables . . . and how these most necessary expedients affect our ability to generalize across settings."

A brief introductory chapter is followed by four chapters dealing with issues of measurement, scaling, and dimensionality; comparability of measures; the problems of conceptualization and comparability of categorical variables; and the implications of omitting variables from causal explanations. Following these rather abstract chapters are two more chapters that are somewhat more concrete, dealing with confounding variables, oversimplification of interpretations, and measurement errors introduced by aggregation of data. Parts of these last two chapters are revisions of previously published work.

While each chapter is more or less independent of the others, there are common threads that hold them together. The first of these threads is the emphasis on the need for proper conceptualization of variables, since the task of explanation is not possible until our concepts are clearly and sharply defined. A second thread is the emphasis on the need to measure carefully in such a way that findings are generalizable from one setting to another.

Probably the most important thing that ties the book together is the emphasis on the necessity of stating auxiliary theories of measurement that link unmeasured variables to their indicators. Blalock claims that without an explicit and sometimes complicated auxiliary theory, none of the problems discussed in the chapters is soluble.

However, it is perhaps a little less than useful when, in discussing a reduced form of a model linking two exogenous variables (Zs) to an endogenous variable, it is concluded that "it is always possible to obtain the reduced form if we are given the structural parameters. . . . And if we have (perfect) measures of Z_1, Z_2 and Z_3 we may also estimate the reduced form parameters . . . from the data." If we knew the values of the structural parameters and could measure perfectly, we would not need an auxiliary theory in the first place. There are several places in the book where the auxiliary theory is useful if variables can be measured without error, but when measurement error is included the theory is indeterminate.

Auxiliary measurement theory aside, the book points out a number of pitfalls in conceptualization and measurement in the social sciences in general and sociology in particular. This volume is another example of Blalock's thoughtful and valuable criticism of social science. The almost inescapable conclusion is that although social sciences may not be impossible, they certainly are not very feasible.

JERRY L.L. MILLER

University of Arizona
Tucson

DAVID ELKIND. *The Hurried Child: Growing Up Too Fast Too Soon.* Pp. vii, 210. Reading, MA: Addison-Wesley, 1981. $5.95.

There has been a spate of recent works whose focus is children. The theme of many of these books is, What is wrong with or happening to our children? David Elkind's *The Hurried Child* is one of these.

Children in premodern Europe after maturing beyond the age of total dependency were treated like miniature adults. Childhood, according to the social critic Ivan Illich in *Deschooling Society* (1972), "developed only recently." To Illich we need to disestablish it as a modern aberration. Elkind too briefly discusses the rise of the modern childhood. In contrast, he argues that "in the end, a childhood is the most basic human right of (all) children."

To Elkind the contemporary American child is rushed into achieving, succeeding, and becoming the obviously "superior person she/he is." Elkind emphasizes the pathological nature of this developmental rush by examining the dynamics of hurrying: parents, schools, and the media. Also there is some discussion of Piagetian developmental periods, the symptoms and responses of stressed children, and the ways of helping these children. *The Hurried Child* can be seen as a clinical sociology work, that is, the impact of differential social structure on child personality and pathology. For example, a real strength of the book, though role-reciprocity is far from an original idea, is an analysis of several parent-child contracts. These fractured contracts, including freedom-responsibility, achievement-support, and loyalty-commitment, lie at the heart of the rushed-child problem.

The book has flaws. There are a number of declarations without documentation. Personal anecdotes are occasionally used to validate generalizations, rather than as illustrations. Assertions are too often categorical, rather than problematic. Further, Elkind takes a quite conservative stance on maturational ages. "Keep 'em young" seems to be the guiding premise. Oddly, in one anecdote he talks of his 15-year-old son as a senior in high school. Was he hurried? And delayed maturation, which seems relevant to *The Hurried Child,* goes undiscussed. What about those children who are not challenged or pushed, but need to be? Finally, documentation supporting the central claim that stress—and stressors—produces hurried children is largely missing. Why then do some children apparently adjust well to severe family stress and even pathology? Elkind claims that these "invulnerables" would be prodigies in different families. Perhaps so, but this is speculative and not substantiated.

Nonetheless, essentially Elkind is on solid ground. We know children are hurried in this society, and society abets this rush. Intuitively the case is clear. The book is persuasive, well written, and quite thought provoking. It is meant for the general but educated reader who will grasp the situations and accept many of the ideas readily. *The Hurried Child,* therefore, should add to our collective understanding of what makes Johnny tick, tick, tick, tick.

WILLIAM M. BRIDGELAND
Michigan State University
East Lansing

JOHN FINNIS. *Natural Law and Natural Rights.* Pp. xv, 425. Oxford: Clarendon Press, 1980. £9.00.

This is the most excellent comprehensive and sensitive work in legal theory to come out of the tradition of analytical jurisprudence. The book is fundamentally a comprehensive restatement of classical natural law; Plato, Aristotle, and Aquinas are the philosophers from whom Finnis borrows liberally. But his style is not to use their authority alone to settle disputes as those who speak to the converted tend to do. On the contrary, Finnis reinterprets, elaborates, and adds many arguments to the classical theories on which he relies.

The book is divided into three parts. The first part illustrates the radical misrepresentations and apprehensions to which natural law ideas have been subject by modern opponents like H.L.A. Hart, J. Raz, and Hans Kelsen. Finnis attributes some of the contemporary misunderstandings of Thomistic natural law to the late scholasticism of men like Vazquez and Suarez, whose theories "differed radically" from Aquinas's. For them, reason's decisive act in discerning the content of natural law was to grasp the difference between morally good and evil acts. This view is open to the objections of Hume and the whole Enlightenment and post-Enlightenment—namely, what motive does anyone have for regulating his actions according to reason's apprehension of moral good and evil? Finnis elaborates the Thomistic theory that is not vulnerable to such objections.

In the second part of the book, Finnis develops a theory of practical reason grounded in the self-evident apprehension of basic goods. He identifies life, play, aesthetic experience, friendship, practical reasonableness, and religion as exhaustive and equally fundamental. Unless we recognize these goods, we cannot make sense of human flourishing. The recognition of these basic goods enables us to distinguish between good and bad desires. And practical reason enables us to attain or, more accurately, to participate in those goods. More than one way will be open to us, and the one we choose will depend on our taste, abilities, circumstances, and opportunities. The fact that no one choice is reasonable does not mean that no choices are reasonable, as Weber and Sartre imagined. Sartre's famous example of the young man contemplating whether to join the resistance against Nazi occupation or to care for his aging mother does not show that there is no rational foundation for choice. Both choices would be rational; what would be irrational would be to shoot his mother, join the occupying forces, commit suicide, or drink himself into stupefaction.

Because we live in community, we must answer the questions about the good life not only on an individual, but on social and political levels. We must use practical reason to direct us toward the common good. The latter is nothing other than the flourishing or opportunity for flourishing of every individual in society. Societies, like individuals, must make rational choices to direct them to the common good. We must keep in mind that the means to the common good are not only instrumental and external but often constitutive and internal to that good because of the good's nature. Human flourishing has to do with what kinds of beings we become and not just with the attainment of particular states of affairs. Because Finnis maintains that certain goods are truly and self-evidently so, he avoids the shallow understanding of the common good as maximum satisfaction of desire. It is the common good that is the object of justice, law, authority, and rights.

The third part of the book addresses religious issues. Can natural law be defended independent of a belief in God? The answer is obviously "yes." However, the recognition of the basic goods of human flourishing independent of human volition or decree points to the existence of a divine order of things. In following the order of reason, we implicitly recognize that God and not man is the measure of all things. Nor is it surprising to find a continuity between the proper human order and cosmic order. Human nature is a microcosm of the universe since it incorporates the inorganic, the organic, and the mental.

This is a most rewarding book.

SHADIA B. DRURY
University of Calgary
Alberta
Canada

WILLIAM H. FRIEDLAND et al. *Revolutionary Theory.* Pp. xiv, 249. Totowa, NJ: Allanheld, Osmun, 1982. $21.50.

William H. Friedland, a professor of community studies and sociology at the University of California, Santa Cruz, believes that a truly socialist future is genuinely democratic, permits fuller expression of individual interests and concerns, and reduces the horrors of exploitation. This book reveals that

revolutionary theory to date leaves much vagueness in dealing with these aspirations, both in theory and in possible applications to "the work of revolutionaries in advanced capitalist societies." Not that the author is really impartial: insightful, systematic criticism of communist and socialist theory is barely scratched; permissive compassion and empathy are the trademarks of his dealing with Marxist hesitations, that is, unresolved prescriptions for societal rearrangement; pivotal in-group struggles and crossed loyalties are portrayed as ad hoc and episodic only, for example, black versus women's-liberation issues in the United States; meager and fledgling attempts to theorize, especially in the United States, appear to have been produced by analytical giants; and everything good and appealing, to Friedland, such as Thoreau, Gandhi, communes, and so on, seems to be intimately related to mainstreams of revolutionary thought.

These incomplete and often invalid linkages are possibly drawn first from the works selected for analysis, which are all in English or in English translations. Russian, German, French, and other theoreticians, not all of a lesser status within the revolutionary school, are not utilized. Indeed even several important American analysts are also missing, even in key areas that the book highlights. Thus William Kornhauser's contributions to stages of development in mass society, Rose Cantor's living cooperatives and theory, or William Gamson's conceptualization of mobilization are barely mentioned in this study.

A second reason for the book's limited perspective is its choice of the American scene, the history of the communist movement, especially in the USSR, and continuities in the theorizing of Marx, Trotsky, and Mao as focal points in a comprehensive review. Clearly conditions in capitalist society, intricacies in differing interpretations of how to revolutionize it, and the classic theoretical works are all presented in neat, well-orchestrated summaries. But in the absence of real evidence that socialist regimes develop classless societies or that communist mobilization can contribute substantially to a healthy, nonviolent democratic process, the major message of the book is the irrelevance of revolutionary theory to modern man. The naked king is badly in need of a tailor.

In all fairness, a beginning student of theory will benefit from reading this book. Several key intellectual questions are actually answered. Capturing well the shifts in foci in communist theory, the book deals with who must be the driving force; how to generate organization and how to push for mobilizational options in virtually any and all of the revolutionary theaters is recounted in a detailed discussion rich in historical materials that illustrate successful and unsuccessful mobilization. Military underground warfare and future revolutionary theory are less skillfully reviewed. Here and there the reader may find excellent summaries of theoretical constructs that are succinct and yet inclusive: such are the summaries of factory committees à la Trotsky, Mao's exemplary action, unionism in the United States, and a revolutionary analysis of nationalization. The reader who wants a comprehensive analysis of revolutionary theory—including systemic treatment of and in third world countries—will have to wait or to learn, first, a foreign language.

JOSEPH D. BEN-DAK
University of Haifa
Israel

HOWARD JONES. *Crime, Race and Culture: A Study in a Developing Country.* Pp. xv, 184. Chichester, NY: John Wiley, 1981. $30.50.

This book is a major contribution to comparative studies, methodology, and the study of crime in pluralistic Third World countries. The focus is on the ex-British colony of Guyana. The comparisons are of two kinds. One is with other ex-British colonies, especially Barbados, Jamaica, and Trinidad-Tobago, and with England and Wales—all with very similar reporting systems and police organization. The second set of comparisons is internal, focusing on the differences between the Negro and East Indian communities.

The two major communities differ markedly in origins and culture. The Negro community, about one-third of the population, is decended from Negro slaves—mainly plantation workers. Their culture is primarily an adaptation of British culture transmuted by the plantation experience. The East Indians are a mixture of Hindu, Moslem, and perhaps other religious groups brought in as indentured workers on plantations after the abolition of slavery. As a group they cling to traditional Indian values and culture. Contrasts between the two groups abound. Negroes are primarily urban, they are heavily involved in wage labor—and hence the problems of unemployment—and they have a loose family structure in which single-parent families with female heads are common. Life conditions of slavery have left a legacy of short-range hedonism, and respect for authority is low. East Indians are primarily rural small farmers, possess a strongly knit extended family structure, tend to have long-range goals, and respect authority. Although Negroes are the smaller group, they hold most of the political power.

The study of crime, always difficult, is compounded by statistical inadequacies. The black figure of unreported crime is probably higher than in most countries, a problem compounded by the settlement of many minor crimes in the East Indian community through such mechanisms as the Panchayat. Such problems as the definition of crime, inadequate record keeping, and differential arrest and sentencing rates are perhaps exaggerated, more through inexperience than design. All these difficulties are given due weight by Jones, and his constant reminders seem to suggest that his findings are more tentative than is justified. The official records are augmented by a lengthy interview program among prison inmates. A fairly elaborate schedule was completed for each interview, although the method of interviewing was informal and essentially open ended. The interview material is from a carefully drawn sample and provides interesting and important additional data, although some of the numbers in Jones's classifications seem too small to warrant the statistical analysis.

Jones makes a good case for differential criminal behavior arising from differences in locality, opportunity, structural factors in the differing societies, and a long list of further demographic, historical, and cultural factors in which race and racism play little if any part. His analysis of dependency and relations between the underdeveloped and developed nations is cogent and fairly convincing, although at times it seems to rest on philosophically based opinions and assumptions rather than upon research.

In summary, this is a readable and often surprising book that makes a real contribution to the understanding of differential criminal behavior.

RALPH L. BEALS

University of California
Los Angeles

LANCE LEIBMAN, ed. *Ethnic Relations in America.* Pp. vii, 179. Englewood Cliffs, NJ: Prentice-Hall, 1982. $13.95. Paperbound, $5.95.

This volume is the product of papers presented by an array of individuals from government, academia, business, law, and ethnic organizations, who met at Arden House under the sponsorship of the American Assembly in the Fall of 1981. The volume purports to examine several issues revolving around ethnicity: immigration policies and their domestic social impact, bilingualism, the assimilation aspects of government policies, and institutional roles. Each contributor focuses on the area of his interest and expertise, and perhaps it would

be useful to summarize the six papers included in the volume.

Possessing excellent credentials, especially with the publication of the major reference work, *Harvard Encyclopedia of American Ethnic Groups,* Stephan Thernstrom's article is entitled "Ethnic Groups in American History." It is a capsule survey of ethnic immigrant history, which demonstrates a metamorphosis from a society that believed in the capacity to absorb strangers, into one that sought to protect itself against those coming from the wrong areas of Europe. Suprisingly, Thernstrom regards ethnic interest as a fad. Thus, by reference to five criteria—linguistic, occupational and educational assimilation, as well as residential dispersion and intermarriage—he traces the assimilation of the Old Immigrants. Likewise, New Immigrant peoples will keep their identity for a time and likewise come to feel secure in their Americanism.

Charles B. Keely, an expert on population movements and labor impact, wrote "Immigrants and the American Future," in which he considers the problems of continued group pluralism through an examination of recent United States immigration policy. Overall he sees American policy as ambivalent. On the one hand it demonstrates a need for labor, while on the other hand it raises concern over the country's capacity to absorb newcomers. His article touches on not only American immigration laws, but also the sensitive topic of illegal aliens. In analyzing the latter subject, he concludes that "in the aggregate, the United States economy probably does not suffer from illegal immigration."

Robert Weaver, the first black to serve in a presidential cabinet, offers an article entitled "The Impact of Ethnicity Upon Urban America," which stresses the differences between the typical European immigrant of the nineteenth century and the nonwhite newcomers to urban America. Averring that the difference is more than a matter of degree, he maintains that it is a difference in kind, which in due course has accommodated European immigrants but has resisted the acceptance of nonwhites. He therefore emphasizes the importance of the governmental role in enabling blacks to enter into structural dimensions of urban life. In the process he is critical of European ethnics because of their alleged resistance to black advancement.

"The Language Question: The Dilemma of Bi-Lingual Education for Hispanics," is the subject of an essay by Pastora San Juan Cafferty. He emphasizes the importance of this clearly vital topic to Hispanics, whose numbers are increasing every year. Cafferty, moreover, contrasts the migration of Spanish-speaking immigrants with earlier waves of predominantly European immigrants and reviews the story of the importance of linguistic assimilation, which has produced a virtually monolingual society. This English-speaking preference notwithstanding, he cites a history of bilingualism as Europeans, especially German-Americans, sought to retain native language and culture. But for the Spanish-speaking of today, bilingual education is even more imperative because of the greater necessity to be literate in English in today's labor market. Lags in educational skills preclude economic and social assimilation into the majority American society.

The noted sociologist Nathan Glazer wrote "Politics of a Multiethnic Society," an examination of ethnic-racial interactions through two basic paradigms. One is the southern strategy, which acknowledged the existence of two separate cultures within its midst. These groups were affirmed by local legal codes until recently, when the victimized group became the beneficiary of special legal protection. The northern model, which was a mixture of many groups competing and existing side by side, was the second historic paradigm. Glazer suggests the possibility of still a third contemporary paradigm—the western model, which encompasses the benefited and nonbenefited. He maintains that pure and simple assimilation is not in the cards in the immediate future,

although the goal of assimilation is still held out as desirable.

The final article is "Ethnic Groups and the Legal System," authored by Lance Liebman, which explores the role of the courts in dealing with ethnic group problems. He notes that courts are at the center of political and social developments and that insofar as legal actions such as lawsuits are a branch of politics, they may be expected to reflect the many interests that exist in the political world. Thus it is natural for there to be interest groups in the judiciary system, just as there are interest groups in our political system.

Although much of what is contained in this volume is not new, it nevertheless succinctly synthesizes many important points and provides useful and even provocative ideas for further thinking on the nature of our pluralistic society. As such, it makes a worthwhile contribution to the examination of contemporary ethnic/immigration questions.

SALVATORE J. LaGUMINA
Nassau Community College
Garden City
New York

DOROTHY MILLER et al. *Runaways—Illegal Aliens in Their Own Land: Implications for Service*. Pp. iii, 220. New York: Praeger. $22.95.

Perhaps as many as 1.5 million young people run away from home each year, according to the Runaway Youth Division of the Administration of Children, Youth and Families. Locating these young people, assuring their health and safety, and reuniting them with their families complicates greatly the old-fashioned act of running away from home. So, in 1974, Congress legislated the Runaway Youth Act (PL 93-415), which required a variety of public officials to report the location of runaway youths as a first step in assuring their health and safety. The law itself caused controversy among child rights advocates, who claimed the reporting violated children's rights to choose their own way of life. As an underfunded and controversial law, it had little impact on the runaway youth problem, and it has since become part of President Reagan's block grant program. But the law did attract public attention and social study of the runaway youth problem. The book by Miller and three colleagues is one study.

Without such an introduction to *Runaways* a reader would be completely befuddled by this book. The authors are members of the Scientific Analysis Corporation of San Francisco. They are reporting on a two-year study of runaways in two "metropolitan West Coast Communities," a study designed to "(1) develop a useful runaway typology and (2) determine the needs of runaways." From this simple statement follow 200 pages of poorly organized findings and unconvincing conclusions. The problems with the research stem from a rejection of previous research to guide the study, confusion over testable hypotheses, and awkward handling of research methodologies.

The authors interviewed 215 runaway youths, in two communities. We deduce from the discussion that these 215 were the total number of runaways the interviewers could locate who were not previously known as runaways to organizations or families. Miller and her colleagues engage in a form of content analysis of the interviews, which they call "vocabulary of motives," and from this they construct six categories of runaways from the motives the interviewees give for running away: victim, exile, rebel, fugitive, refugee, and immigrant. There is less than one full page devoted to defining these categories, and there is no listing of the language or the motives identified in the content analysis in determining which youths would be assigned to which category.

Appendix I describes the research methodology. Runaways were identified and interviewed at congregation sites, paid, then asked to bring other runaways in for interviewing—a technique they call "snowball

sampling." As a result, there is no way of telling how representative this sample may be of the runaway population. There are no statistical methods used to test the interaction of the variables, such as the categories, with race, sex, parental attitude or knowledge, and use of social service resources by the runaways. As a result, the study fails to present any reliable profile of the runaway population, let alone legitimize the categories Miller et al. construct.

Once the categories are established, Miller et al. examine each category to describe the racial, sexual, and socioeconomic characteristics of each category. The whole group of runaways is then compared with another sample of young people from a local school—some of whom ran away and others who did not. Finally the information about the runaways is compared with information gleaned from interviews with 38 parents of the 215 runaways in the study. The motivations for running away are compared to the categories of runaways. For example, 72 percent of the exiles got along poorly with their mothers according to the parents' statements. Since the category exile was defined from the content analysis as a child who left home because of parental rejection, one wonders why the other 28 percent did get along with their mothers. Most of the conclusions are presented with similar authority.

A glaring irony of this study is that Miller et al. deliberately discard previous analysis of the runaway, developed under more rigorous study conditions, such as the well-known study by Clifford English in 1973. "Based upon the clinical experiences of a few researchers with a few runaways, they fail to do justice to the phenomenon." But these same authors point with pride to the power of their typologies developed from interviews with 215 runaway youths.

The book does offer a "runaway resource guide" from San Francisco and Los Angeles, California, but this guide is somewhat selective of the agencies and programs included. Since so little is known about runaway youth and since funds for research are shrinking, it is unfortunate to undertake poorly designed and implemented research projects. It is also unfair to the professional public when such research is published by respectable publishers. While runaway youths continue to present problems for a variety of social agencies, it seems doubtful this book will be of much help in providing better services to this often neglected group of young persons.

ANDREW W. DOBELSTEIN
University of North Carolina
Chapel Hill

BHIKHU C. PAREKH. *Marx's Theory of Ideology*. Pp. 247. Baltimore: Johns Hopkins University Press, 1982. $24.50.

A short review can hardly do justice to the complexities of the issues raised in this book. To this reviewer's mind, even the purpose of the book is in question. Although labeled *Marx's Theory of Ideology,* the book is really concerned with presenting Parekh's views on the relationship between consciousness and society, and the problem of truth. Marxism certainly supplies most of the content of the book, but Parekh is mainly interested in showing that when Marx is correctly interpreted, his theories lead to the very position that the author upholds in these areas. By the same token, Parekh must show that Marx has been misinterpreted by even his most sophisticated followers, such as Lukacs or Gramsci.

It is in pursuit of this aim that Parekh offers an analysis of Marx's views of the nature and basis of ideology. For some, particularly sociologists of knowledge, this may be the most valuable part of the book. Parekh certainly provides a clear, logical, and exhaustive exposition of this area and along the way manages to clear up many obscurities in Marx's thought. Briefly, for Marx ideology is a special form of consciousness but by no means the totality of human consciousness. In general, the pervasiveness of an ideology is a function of the power of the class that has evolved or adopted that ideology. Thus the ruling ideas of society are the ideas of its ruling classes.

But even when dealing with ideological consciousness, an important distinction must be drawn between vulgar ideologists who are prepared to lie and distort on behalf of a given class, and those whose work, while containing ideological elements, is oriented to the discovery of truth. Malthus is an example of the former; Ricardo and Adam Smith, and many other classical economists, of the latter. These latter writers are undoubtedly bound and limited by the perspective of a given class; but they also pursue knowledge, and in pursuing knowledge they are guided not be any class interest but by the *telos* of truth.

The limitation of this latter type of thought rests on the limitations imposed by the classes to which the thinkers are bound. In what may be called the classical interpretation of Marx, valid knowledge can be achieved only by a class whose deepest interests, even to the physical survival of its members, are in total opposition to the society. Today there is only one class in this position—the proletariat.

From within this perspective, truth can be achieved in two interrelated ways. On one hand, a given theory must be shown to be consonant with the perspective of the proletariat; on the other, it must be shown to be capable of providing guides to the proper type of *praxis* for the proletariat. But in the latter case, this too means grasping the nature and development of the society, of its people, and of the historical process.

It is this classical interpretation that Parekh fundamentally disputes. He denies that Marx's thought is proletarian thought, that it is merely a sophisticated articulation of the proletarian perspective, either contemplative or active. There can be no doubt that Marx borrowed many of his ideas from the proletarian perspective; but he also borrowed many ideas from the bourgeois perspective. At all times, however, Marx's selections and borrowings of ideas were governed neither by their supposed consonance with the proletarian perspective nor by their fruitfulness in guiding *praxis,* but by the criteria by which truth is established anywhere—that is, by subjecting theory to the criteria of logic and by constant and repeated empirical verification of hypotheses drawn from the theory.

Obviously Parekh departs strongly from the usual interpretation of Marx's notions of the sources of consciousness. Not all consciousness is formed immediately by society; some ideological thought is independent of social influence, and whole realms of thought are completely free of it. The human mind, whatever its ultimate sources, is capable of independent, value-free, creative expression. It can and occasionally does transcend class and society.

Thus we have here an antideterminist argument, yet one that seeks to enlist in its cause what has generally been considered one of the most quintessentially determinist of theories. Those with a taste for these high-level abstractions will find this latter argument absorbing. Others will find the elucidation of Marx's theory of ideology more valuable.

EUGENE V. SCHNEIDER
Bryn Mawr College
Bryn Mawr
Pennsylvania

THOMAS A. SPRAGENS, Jr. *The Irony of Liberal Reason.* Pp. xii, 443. Chicago: University of Chicago Press, 1982. $23.00.

The irony of liberal reason, Thomas Spragens tells us, is that it no longer supports the humane values of its old ally, political liberalism. The skepticism of liberal reason, which philosophers of the Enllightenment employed so effectively against Scholasticism, has turned destructively upon the humane political convictions of the Enlightenment. We no longer recognize the so-called self-evident truths of political liberalism. Instead liberal reason leads us to conclude that either (1) we cannot ascertain that liberal political or moral principles are better than any others—value-noncognitivism; or (2) we can ascertain the worth of political or moral principles only under the tutelage of rational authorities who possess the appropriate scientific bona fides—technocracy. In either case, the classic ideals of human liberalism cannot rely on liberal reason for support.

Spragens characterizes liberal reason as a paradigm of human cognition that arose from common elements in the rationalism of Descartes and the empiricism of Locke. The paradigm asserts that all genuine knowledge is scientifically verifiable and that such knowledge is accessible to all persons with normal faculties of reason. Each person begins the search for knowledge with a clean slate. Knowledge is then based on the self-evident foundation of simple, unambiguous ideas or perceptions. These ideas or perceptions are used to discover absolute truths in accordance with explicit logical modes of inquiry. In the end, therefore, the entire body of human knowledge is unified, both in method and in substance.

The paradigm creates an epistemological manicheanism, a division of questions into intelligible ones—those involving genuine knowledge—and unintelligible ones—those involving opinions, judgments, and other metaphysical uncertainties. It soon becomes apparent that the moral precepts of political liberalism which relate to questions of freedom and justice, fail to meet the criteria of genuine knowledge. Such questions cannot be discussed scientifically, for they are matters of judgment and taste. Indeed, twentieth-century positivists like Russell and Wittgenstein conclude that they cannot be discussed meaningfully at all.

Nevertheless the paradigm of liberal reason holds that genuine knowledge is genuinely good. Knowledge of the universe gives humankind power over the environment. It is the basis for all human progress. It follows, then, that those with the most genuine knowledge are the most virtuous, and, for the sake of human progress, they ought to enlighten their less knowledgeable compatriots. In this manner, liberal reason is used to justify the imposition of technocratic political programs to produce a properly ordered polity. Before long the humane liberalism of Locke or Jefferson gives way to the technocratic orders of Helvetius, St. Simeon, Bentham, Lenin, or B. F. Skinner.

Can we restore intelligibility to the classic ideals of political liberalism? Yes, Spragens answers, but only if we abandon liberal reason. We must recognize the impossibility of satisfying its demand for certain knowledge of clear and simple truths. Instead we ought to organize rational enterprises that seek more modest warranted beliefs. Such beliefs are by no means subjective or arbitrary, but they remain open to revision, as, in fact, do the findings of modern science. "In a final ironic twist, then, the human core of the liberal tradition may be salvaged most effectively precisely by abandoning the epistemological conceptions that were originally thought to guarantee its success."

Spragens spends most of the book explicating the philosophical development and destruction of the paradigm of liberal reason. The discussion is thorough, and the writing often is elegant. But the book is too long. In his enthusiasm for his subject, Spragens tries to communicate to both a professional and a general audience. He recognizes the dilemma this presents, but he does not succeed in resolving it. Instead he ends up splitting hairs for the professional and repeating himself for the layperson. At 400 pages this is a good book. At 200 pages it would be a better one.

MICHAEL MARGOLIS
University of Pittsburgh
Pennsylvania

JENNY TEICHMAN. *Illegitimacy. An Examination of Bastardy.* Pp. 200. Ithaca, NY: Cornell University Press, 1982. $18.50.

Do not think that behind the title of this book lies another poorly planned research effort on a topic that continues to rankle the sense of British propriety. In *Illegitimacy* a philosopher illuminates one of the most complex social issues, succeeding where volumes of standard social-science literature fail. Teichman, a fellow and director of studies in philosophy at New Hall, Cambridge, cautiously warns us, "No philosopher has attempted analysis of the idea of illegitimacy. I have here . . . partly because it is a misunderstood idea and partly because it is an idea of undeniable human importance." Teichman's effort returns concern for the human condition to the analysis of illegitimacy, which provides greater understanding of the subject.

"Illegitimacy," says Teichman, "is not a natural attribute. Rather, it is a status, like poverty or bankruptcy." Around this theme of social status, Teichman constructs a convincing argument in which she concludes that the state has a right and consequently a responsibility to limit reproduction through law, marriage, social status and, in this case, an assignment to the socially disabling status of illegitimacy. Certainly those efforts to eradicate illegitimacy, argues Teichman—infanticide, stricter civil laws, and certain child-maintenance policies—are much more harsh and mischievous than the status of illegitimacy, and given the overwhelming attention to illegitimacy in literature and religion, one is forced to conclude, on the basis of this evidence, that illegitimacy is much too valuable to the social order to think it is a social problem that can or should be solved.

In fact Teichman artfully dismisses most social-science research attributing both social and personal causes to illegitimacy, including the important early work of sociologist Kingsley Davis (1940) and the later studies of Clark E. Vincent (1963). "All research which explains illegitimacy proves in the end that its causes are multitudinous. . . . [T]o show that a phenomenon can not be explained by reference to a cause or covering law may be as useful and as significant as to show that it can." While this may leave many social scientists gasping for breath, Teichman argues that existing civil laws of property, custody, marriage, and divorce provide no better explanation for the causes of illegitimacy. For Teichman it is the idea of illegitimacy, from which the endless measurable social-science research variables are generated, which must be better understood.

The linchpin of her polemic centers on marriage, which she identifies as the logical connection between the ideas of kinship, descent, lineage, legitimacy, and illegitimacy. Teichman concludes that marriage is neither a necessary condition for legitimacy nor a sufficient one. In other words, illegitimacy does not take definition from marital status. Since marriage is the legal and social institution that creates the family, the relationship between illegitimacy and the family is equally spurious. In a style that would please Gilbert Steiner, Teichman concludes,

When politicians and religious leaders anywhere speak about a need to defend and protect the family and family life they are generally inspired, first, by a wish to protect and strengthen the institution of marriage ... and second, by a wish to protect and strengthen parents' rights and powers to control the education and general lifestyle of their own children (p. 86).

Lurking behind these motivations is a larger social purpose: the need to regulate reproduction.

Public-policy analysts will find Teichman's discussion of financial support for the illegitimate child particularly enlightening. Marriage and the family do provide some assurances for child support, both in law and, to a great extent, in practice. No such protection is assumed for the illegitimate child. Earlier English *filius nullius* common law meant that no person has a legal obligation to support an illegitimate child. Yet in practice the burden for support usually fell to the mother. As these practices matured, great financial burdens on mothers and children have been transferred to the state in one form or another. Elimination of economically disabling characteristics of illegitimacy without serious adverse social consequences has become one objective of American welfare policy. The present efforts to develop a successful child support enforcement program in this country is one step that proposes mitigation of financial disabilities of illegitimacy without transferring the burden to the state.

Illegitimacy is straightforward, stripped of most of the rhetoric that usually accompanies a discussion of this subject, and insightful about the larger issues that have made illegitimacy a puzzling topic for the social scientist. It is a discussion about the ideas behind illegitimacy, not a discussion explored in a problem-solution framework, which is the foundation for contemporary social research. As such, some may find Teichman abrasive. Yet here is a humanist treatment, which neither pities nor extols the subjects. It is refreshingly clear of British paternalistic homilies, thus offering insights to the American reader who wants them. With so much useless material available on illegitimacy, Teichman's work will surely fill an important place on personal bookshelves. the book jacket predicts that reviewers will find good things to say about this book. Teichman lives up to these expectations.

ANDREW W. DOBELSTEIN
University of North Carolina
Chapel Hill

ROBERT BRENT TOPLIN. *Freedom and Prejudice: The Legacy of Slavery in the United States and Brazil.* Pp. xxvi, 134. Contributions in Afro-American and African Studies No. 56. Westport, CT: Greenwood Press, 1981. $23.95.

Robert Brent Toplin describes his latest book as "a study of the tensions that arose out of the quest for emancipation in the nineteenth century and the struggle for racial equality in the twentieth." In fact, however, the book is a collection of seven separate articles, most originally published in the early 1970s and hardly any incorporating more recent studies. Thus the slim volume is much more an anthology than a monograph; the absence of a conclusion pulling the arguments together confirms this impression.

Toplin begins by summarizing the older scholarly contributions to comparative race relations, from Frank Tannenbaum through Carl Degler and Harmannus Hoetink. He points to three primary patterns affecting attitudes toward race: demographic ratios, such as the relative numbers of whites and African slaves and of bachelors and families; political traditions, understood with Pierre L. Van den Berghe as either democratic and competitive or hierarchical and paternalistic; and the history of slavery and abolition. The book then examines more closely the third pattern: two chapters deal with the United States, three with Brazil, and two make explicit comparisons.

Toplin makes essentially one major point: the experiences with slavery, abolition, and race relations in the two countries have been much more similar than is usually recognized A traditional opinion saw these two societies as sharply contrasting. In the United States, laws governing slaves were supposed to be more rigorous and inhuman; the tense work relation and the bitterness culminating in the Civil War and Reconstruction polarized society into blacks and whites; and this polarization encouraged segregation and exacerbated race prejudice. In Brazil, on the other hand, miscegenation and easier manumissions supposedly leavened the treatment of slaves, abolition came gradually and peacefully, and the multiplicity of admitted racial types inhibited the development of segregation and prejudice. Class prejudice, not race prejudice, hinders the social mobility of Afro-Brazilians today.

Throughout the chapters, Toplin introduces interesting revisions by himself and others of the traditional view. In Brazil, as Carl Degler has emphasized, but also in the United States, miscegenation produced increasing numbers of mulattoes, who, as the masters' descendants and as bearers of a somatic type closer to that of the dominating whites, enjoyed privileges and opportunities not available to black slaves. While slaves revolted more often and more successfully in Brazil, Toplin believes that the fear of slave revolt was as prevalent in nineteenth-century America as in Brazil, and that Brazil's final abolition campaign, marked by considerable upheaval and violence, suggests that U.S. slaveholders' fears were justified. In the aftermath of abolition, whites in both countries generally scorned the freedman's capacity as workers, thereby strengthening racial prejudices, at the same time as both whites and blacks continued preferring lighter-colored marriage partners. Even today, considerable race prejudice still exists in both the United States and Brazil.

Toplin sees one important difference between the two societies. In the United States racial polarization and vigorous repression provoked a strong political solidarity among blacks and an effective twentieth-century movement to abolish segregation laws and fight prejudice. In Brazil, the recognized hetereogeneity of the nonwhite population weakened black solidarity and efforts to combat informal segregation and prejudice. But Toplin cannot resist the temptation to speculate that in the United States, if race prejudice is receding, class prejudice may be increasing, a situation once again reminiscent of Brazil.

Toplin writes clearly and incisively. Upon completing this book, the reader feels excitement and curiosity about the many parallels in the history of the two largest slaveholding societies in the Americas. He also wonders where are the monographs, in demographic, political, and economic history, that would put Toplin's hypotheses to the test.

PETER L. EISENBERG
Universidade Estadual de Campinas
Sao Paulo
Brazil

YI-FU TUAN. *Segmented Worlds and Self: A Study of Group Life and Individual Consciousness*. Pp. 222. Minneapolis: University of Minnesota Press, 1982. $19.50. Paperbound, $8.95.

A static universal for historic human nature is no longer an acceptable assumption. Subjective experience in stable settings and times tends to construe a Nature legitimated as objective and as reality. Turbulent and transitional times produce paradigm crises, announce the relativity of perspectives and points of view, discover the relevance of contexts, and affirm that change is the only certainty. We stand at such a place in such a time when older categories of the nature of things, and the conventions and presuppositions that ordered stable and customary worlds, no longer seem tenable.

Segmented Worlds and Self is a study of the historical development of individual consciousness, and of the shift from a public aggregate world anchored upon an external armature to the differentiation of human consciousness and its habitat. Yi-Fu Tuan traces the ways in which the individual and his or her setting have become increasingly differentiated and segmented into discrete entities. Exploring changes in household spaces and furnishings, in food and its etiquette, changes in the architecture and public relations within the theater, he traces these developments as steps in the internalization of experience, the elaboration of a sense of subjectivity, and the invention of the individual and his ethos. He also remarks upon the associated consequences of such developments of individuation as isolation, alienation, and the loss of community membership.

The author, a professor of geography at the University of Minnesota, uses the resources of the social sciences and the humanities to assess human ecological relationships. In a thoughtful, clearly written, and well-documented survey he explores the fragmentation of earlier cohesive relationships and their support systems, the shifting balances between public and private life, and the ways in which such activities are institutionalized. He examines changing behaviors and environments in family and village, in churches and theaters, as over the last 300 years shifting

sensory experience in increasingly segmented habitats has altered consciousness and the growing sense of self, its isolation, and its loss of membership.

This thoughtful, stimulating study of consciousness over the last 300 years joins such works as Sennett's *Rise and Fall of Public Man,* Norbert Elias's *The Civilizing Process* and *The History of Manners,* and Walter J. Ong's studies of the shift from speech to written language. Like these studies, *Segmented Worlds and Self* examines the ways in which consciousness is historically restructured and the tension between the personal and the communal, a shifting ratio, is resolved in different ways at varying times.

NATHAN ADLER

California School of
  Professional Psychology
Berkeley

MARVIN E. WOLFGANG and NEIL ALAN WEINER, eds. *Criminal Violence.* Pp. 350. Beverly Hills, CA: Sage Publications, 1982. $27.00. Paperbound, $12.95.

This compilation of seven articles on criminal violence was produced by Law Enforcement Assistance Administration funding through the Center for Studies in Criminology and Criminal Law at the University of Pennsylvania. The senior editor, Marvin Wolfgang, is director of the Center, while the junior editor was project director for the grant that commissioned the papers. The two editors commissioned literature reviews in seven important areas of criminal violence and chose as authors those persons who are most prominent in each of the topical areas. Each chapter represents a successful attempt to synthesize the literature in a given area so that future research might be directed to fill the gaps. The volume is easily the best currently available on criminal violence and would be an excellent text for any advanced course in criminology or violence. Though one might quarrel with the choice of topics—for example, such factors as criminal careers, alcohol, race, subculture, urbanization, and self-image are mentioned only in passing—those that are addressed are synthesized by the leading authorities. The bibliographies alone are worth the price of the book.

The first area addressed is that of biology and violence, and the authors, Mednick et al., provide an exhaustive review of the research on biological correlates of violence. the authors conclude that there is a general relationship between biological factors and violence but caution against misinterpretations of that relationship. They conclude that biological factors will not replace social variables as explanations but may explain violence in those cases not explained by social variables or interact with social variables.

The second chapter is on psychological correlates and determinants of criminal violence. Megargee, the author, summarizes the wide range of theoretical and empirical literature on the psychology of violence and aggression and presents a general formulation of the psychology of violence involving five major components. Farrington's chapter on longitudinal analyses of criminal violence surveys the major longitudinal studies conducted worldwide on criminal violence and demonstrates the utility of this type of research. Domestic violence is the fourth topical area presented in this volume, and Gelles presents an historical review of the work in this area.

In perhaps the finest chapter in the volume, Cook discusses several issues related to firearms and violent crimes. He critiques prior research and suggests where the knowledge gaps are. He includes an excellent critique of evaluations of gun control laws and projects the consequences of any successful effort to reduce the availability of firearms.

The sixth chapter addresses situational approaches to understanding and predicting criminal violence. Monahan and Klassen attempt to define this topical area and suggest a means by which an understanding of this aspect of violence can be useful in prevention. The final chapter by Greenwood evaluates the deterrent, rehabilitative, and incapicative goals of the criminal justice system and surveys research that examines the determinants of decisions on violent offenders at various stages of the system.

WILLIAM WILBANKS
Florida International University
Miami

MURRAY WOLFSON. *Marx: Economist, Philosopher, Jew. Steps in the Development of a Doctrine.* Pp. xx, 279. New York: St. Martin's Press, 1982. $25.00

With but a single reference to Althusser's controversial depiction of an irreconcilable humanistic and scientific Marx, Wolfson argues that Marx marched through three distinct and contradictory intellectual phases.

Up to 1843, Marx's intellectual journey was characterized by a rejection of the deductive epistemology of Hegel, in favor of an inductive, empiricist epistemology in which individuals in civil society "reason from concrete particulars to general universals." From a utilitarian starting point, Marx defended the extension of democratic political rights over against Hegel's Absolute State.

Around 1844, Marx backs into a secular Hegelianism, propounding an essential human nature of creative, expressive persons thwarted, in their inherent inclination to be in harmony with nature, by the alienation of private property and the market, which reduce people from subjects to predicates. To restore the human species/being to its proper status, a science of society is needed to expose and change the class nature of society. The proletariat, as the increasingly impoverished universal class, will come to express their fundamental essence in the revolutionary establishment of communism.

By 1845, Marx finds the error of his 1844 humanistic interim to be his ahistorical reversions to Hegelian essences, albeit in a form purged by Feuerbach's atheism. Returning quietly to aspects of utilitarianism, history progresses as ever-increasing human needs go unfulfilled due to the fetters of the current social relations of production. However, Marx runs aground in the contradictory dual assertion of (1) the primacy of forces of production in the endogenous transformation of modes of production and ideological consciousness, and (2) the independent role of voluntaristic action directed by scientific analysis to bring about the transition to communism.

Wolfson's argument, however, is not without its troubles—in both its content and its mode of exposition. In search of a dynamic behind Marx's changing views, Wolfson offers not a sociology of knowledge but a psychohistory of Marx. Marx's first, individualist period is born not out of critical response to the social circumstances of the bureaucratic, elitist Prussian state; rather it derives from Marx's own "overweening pride compensating for shame [of his Jewish heritage], a bemusement with his own words, and a compulsion to effect a triumph of his own ideas. Marx's tortuous relation to his pragmatically converted Christian father, Heinrich, is counted—in amount of words and emphasis—more significant than Marx's rational assessment of his day. Heinrich and Karl, Heinrich and Karl—the first the representative of Jewish shame, the latter engaged in a "catarsis of self-hate." Psychohistory, with a heavy hand. Wolfson writes that in view of "the reality of his [Heinrich Marx's] sychophancy, . . . one has to feel compassion for his driven, compulsive son, attempting to escape from the web of shame." Since Marx identifies the market with "dirty Jewish" behavior, he "felt compelled," "is driven" in his second, humanistic phase to reject Smith's confidence in the invisible hand. It is not that Marx has moved to France where bourgeois freedoms and industrial capitalism exposed their inability to ensure liberty for the masses; it was not that his new intellectual colleagues raised different challenges. When the third Marx falters in reconciling deterministic structural tendencies in history with his position that agents also must remake themselves, Wolfson suggests that Marx, no longer rebelling against his heritage, reached back into the recesses of his Jewish tradition to argue by personal analogy that the human agent retains a role in the unfolding of inevitable social logic just as the Hebrew prophets "from Amos to Marx" served in conjunction with the deterministic will of God. While dozens of scholars have waded their way more or less conclusively through the dilemma of structure and free will, Wolfson ignores their work, content to have caught the dark professor in a subtle argument by metaphor.

In the end, the book remains useful in its attention to the epistemological underpinnings of Marx's analyses. But with the exception of the preface and a few later chapters, the argument is not built coherently, transitions are hard to follow, topic sentences are almost nonexistent, and unattractive snideness are too frequent. Wolfson quotes Marx's doctoral dissertation to the effect that "We see Democritus wandering through half the world in order to acquire experiences, knowledge, and observations." While the main line of Wolfson's argument is fairly straightforward, regretably the author himself tends to wander half the world to formulate what turns out to be a too obscure exposition of what otherwise might have been a reasonable though controversial argument.

PAUL G. SCHERVISH
Boston College
Chestnut Hill
Massachusetts

ECONOMICS

FRANCOIS CROUZET. *The Victorian Economy*. Translated by A. S. Forster. Pp. xiii, 430. New York: Columbia University Press, 1982. $32.50. Paperbound, $16.00.

If this book had existed 15 years ago my life as a graduate student would have been a

little easier. It is a well-written and- translated, beautifully organized, and perceptive
synthesis of the most important research in
nineteenth-century British economic history.
The footnotes, placed at the bottom of the
page, help one follow the numerous historiographical developments that Crouzet tracks.
Although the title suggests that the book is
limited to a study of the Victorian economy,
it covers more than this. Crouzet picks up
strands of economic development beginning
with the Industrial Revolution and follows
them up to World War I, although the bulk
of the work is restricted to the period from
1830-1900. He synthesizes developments
during these 70 years in a way found in no
other work on the subject. Consequently *The
Victorian Economy* occupies a significant
evolutionary niche in British economic history writing.

Crouzet organizes his work around one
overriding theme but approaches it from two
distinct directions. The theme is the rise,
persistence, and decline (?) of British economic dominance during the Victorian era.
In the first third of the book Crouzet
approaches his theme from the macroec-
onomic perspective of economic growth. He
discusses in turn the demographic boom, the
measurements of economic growth, the
periodization of growth, the resulting
changes in economic structure, and the problems associated with the growth. In the
remainder of the work, except for an epilogue, Crouzet analyzes specific nineteenth-
century economic activities: agriculture, textiles, iron, steel, coal, transportation, banking credit, foreign trade, and investment. In
the last chapter, the epilogue, he surveys the
Victorian economy in decline. The author
intersperses 68 tables, charts, and graphs
throughout the book. They allow one to
follow more easily the complicated quantitative data that are central to his interpretation.

In writing this book Crouzet aimed it at
upper-division French university students,

but emphatically it is not a textbook treatment. In masterful style he moves from
elementary to sophisticated information and
conceptual material. He is particularly interested in historiographical issues and admittedly relishes the free-wheeling nature of
British historians' debates with one another.
Nor does he avoid the combat himself. He
summarizes the major facets of historiographical debates, assesses the relative
merits of the contenders' interpretations,
and then gives his own views. One will not
always agree with him but must admire his
dauntless spirit.

As suggested above, this work may not
provide much that is new for specialists, but
they will find it a wonderful source for
lecture material or, failing this, a place to
send students for an authoritative commentary.

NEAL A. FERGUSON
University of Nevada
Reno

DANIEL M. HAUSMAN *Capital, Profits and
Prices: An Essay in the Philosophy of
Economics.* Pp. x, 253. New York:
Columbia University Press, 1981. $24.00

Alone among the social sciences, economics has no systematic interest in the
philosophical underpinnings of what it does.
Most graduate-level theory courses refer in
the first week to one or two methodological
articles, but they get short shrift and no
further attention. This is a great pity, for as
Daniel Hausman shows, the standard microeconomic general-equilibrium theories are,
philosophically speaking, very odd objects
indeed.

Hausman adopts a view of theories derived from the work of Sneed and Steg-
muller. Roughly, a theory is defined by
abstract Suppes set theory as a predicate—
"is a perfectly competitive market," for
example; and anything satisfying the predi-

cate is an applied model—"the wheat market is a perfectly competitive market"—of which one may ask traditional philosophical questions, such as explanatory adequacy. But from this formulation questions immediately arise. First, it seems that no real-world economic entity fully satisfies the microeconomic predicates. Is microeconomics, then, a vacuous theory? Hausman suggests that it should rather be considered as a set of simplified or idealized laws, but this conception is in need of philosophical justification. Hausman analyzes a simplification as legitimate only if it is necessary in order to derive confirmed testable consequences of the theory; if its role in explanation is clear; if, when the simplification is relaxed, one obtains either more explanations, or explanations with smaller margins of error; and if it is possible to determine when a particular simplification is a closer approximation to the world, and when it is, either more or closer predictions are obtained.

Second, even if simplifications are legitimate, it is rare that one is able to explain exactly. Economists generally assert that their laws are true under *ceteris paribus* conditions, but again philosophical justification is required. Too ready a use of the *ceteris paribus* qualification will result in trivial laws. Again, Hausman provides such an analysis. Inexact laws of this type are properly considered as scientific laws only if they are lawlike; reliable—in some domains, disconfirmations are rare; refinable—as explicit qualifications are added, reliability increases; and excusable—with rare exceptions, interferences resulting in failure of the unqualified law can be identified. It seems to me that both these analyses produce a fruitful step forward in the philosophy of social science.

It is then possible to provide a philosophical assessment of microeconomic general-equilibrium and intertemporal-equilibrium theories. Hausman finds that the laws of these theories do not satisfy the excusability condition; economists, says Hausman, do not attempt to identify interferences that result in failure of lawlike statements. Moreover, even if such statements are taken to be simplifications, they do not, according to Hausman, result in confirmed testable consequences. This does not necessarily mean that such theories have no value. As these comments indicate, it is economic practice that Hausman finds wanting. Current equilibrium theories may eventually result in explanations but, claims Hausman, do not now do so. In fact, at present he regards Sraffa's theory, although "at best a limiting case of a scientific theory," as "the best account of exchange values economists have."

Such a conclusion is bound to be controversial, and the controversy is unlikely to be lessened by the sometimes puzzling opacity of the discussion. The crucial conclusion on the excusability of equilibrium theories occupies no more than a couple of lines; and the analyses of inexact laws and of simplification, for all their initial plausibility, are not so much justified as merely stated. The book contains some lengthy economic expositions; it seems to me that it would have been useful to abbreviate these while expanding the philosophy, but perhaps philosophers would feel otherwise. In addition it seems to me that Hausman ignores the investigations of applied economists. For we do in fact know a good deal about market failure and unworkable competition at the industry level, and this knowledge surely constitutes a basis for excusing general-equilibrium models. But despite these qualms, Hausman's book can be recommended as a valuable and thought-provoking initial analysis of a class of topics too long slighted by economists.

PHILIP A. VITON
University of Pennsylvania
Philadelphia

THE ANNALS OF THE AMERICAN ACADEMY

YUJIRO HAYAMI and MASAO KIKUCHI. *Asian Village Economy at the Crossroads: An Economic Approach to Institutional Change.* Pp. xx, 275. Baltimore, MD: Johns Hopkins University Press, 1982. $25.00

Village communities in many Asian countries have been undergoing significant changes that are likely to affect the rates of their economic growth and the future of their social and political institutions. Many fundamental factors, such as population growth and improved agricultural technology, including better irrigation systems, improved varieties of grain, use of fertilizers, and better land tenures, influence such changes. In this book, Professors Hayami and Kikuchi focus their attention on the implications of such changes for traditional rural institutions based on mutual help, moral codes, and income sharing. The study revolves around the question whether the changes will polarize a peasant community into capitalist landlords and a mass of landless proletariat, or into peasant stratification ranging from landless laborers to poor peasants to wealthy landlords, all claiming a portion of the output of land. The answer depends largely on the rate of growth of agricultural productivity.

The book consists of four major parts. Part I (chapters 2 and 3) develops the authors' analytical framework, identifies the institutional characteristics of Asian village communities in a historical framework, and examines the general features of the modernization process at work in such communities. The peasant, accroding to Hayami and Kikuchi, is motivated essentially by his own interests. Therefore, he may conform to the traditional norms and institutions of the village community only so long as the costs of such conformity are not in excess of its benefits. However, as factors such as population growth and improved agricultural technology exert pressure on the

relative economic benefits of traditional institutions and social systems, conformity to traditions becomes costly. The result is gradual but cumulative adjustments in the social and insitutional arrangements that contribute to the formation of new socioeconomic structures. The basic analytical framework of the study, thus, is developed in terms of competition among varius socioeconomic groups to gain a more efficient allocation of resources and to establish claims for a larger share of economic gains. In examining the major economic factors that are pressing changes on Asian village communities, the authors find that the decrease in the relative returns to labor due to increasing population pressure is not offset by improvements in technology, and that the rapid growth of the rural labor force may make it difficult to reverse this trend anytime soon. As a result, the agrarian structure in peasant communities may move in the direction of greater polarization between a landed oligarchy and an increasing mass of landless proletariat, or a continuous spectrum of peasant stratification with intense class differentiation. In the former case, impersonal market forces will become stronger and replace the economic relations based on tradition and moral principles.

Part II of the book attempts to test this hypothesis by analyzing the process of institutional changes in Philippine village communities. An analysis of such factors as the evolution of the land tenure and labor contract institutions in the central plain of Luzon, the impact of increasing population pressure, and the introduction of institutional innovations like subtenancy and the gama system—where only those who contributed free labor for weeding are employed for harvesting and receive the output share— leads to the general conclusion that the peasant community is moving in the direction of stratification. Although this is a likely trend, a close look at two village communities undergoing social and institutional changes leading to stratification and polarization, respectively, reveals the importance of prevailing social environment in influencing the trend toward stratification or polarization. In Part III, the focus of analysis shifts to Indonesia. Here, the authors identify the broad trends in the transformation of village community institutions in Java. An empirical analysis of the effects of modern technology on both rural community institutions and income distribution in two villages in West Java leads them to conclude that a relatively stagnant technology results in greater poverty and income inequality. The final part of the book contains a summary of the major findings of village studies and the inferences on the course of rural change in Asia.

Hayami and Kikuchi's conclusion that substantial improvements in agricultural technology result in greater equality in the distribution of rural income contradicts the radical economists' contention that technological improvements such as better varieties of grains, benefit only richer farmers, thus widening the disparities in the distribution of income and wealth. In fact, the study finds the real wages of landless laborers substantially higher where modern technology is employed. Also, the authors find peasant stratification the dominant form of agrarian change in Southeast Asia. "To that extent, social interactions in peasant communities bound by traditional moral principles have been effective in blocking the route to polarization." However, it is quite possible that, sooner or later, increasing population pressure, relatively stagnant technology, and greater penetration of impersonal market environment may change peasant stratification into a polarization process. Rural reforms based only on ideology and not on economic realities may promote such a change.

I found the book analytically sound and intellectually stimulating. Although the writing style is occasionally tedious, for serious students and practitioners of rural development it offers a challenging analytical framework and interesting policy insights.

P. I. MATHEW

U.S. Coast Guard Academy
New London
Connecticut

BURTON I. KAUFMAN. *Trade and Aid: Eisenhower's Foreign Policy, 1953-1961.* Pp. xiv, 279. Baltimore, MD: Johns Hopkins University Press, 1982. $25.00.

Politics and economics are inseparably linked, although the relationship between the two is not as yet fully understood. Despite this, Kaufman does a laudable job in documenting the interrelationship between these two disciplines by carefully outlining the transformation of Eisenhower's foreign economic trade policy during his presidency. The main theme concerns the transition of foreign economic policy from one of "trade *not* aid," in which a free and liberalized world trade and foreign investment policy was encouraged as the means of assuring world economic growth and prosperity, to one of "trade *and* aid," whereby it was the free trade policy which was perceived as neither adequately addressing the problems of the Third World nor alleviating the growth of communism. As a by-product Eisenhower's leadership qualities as well as the success of his economic programs are considered.

The book contains 12 chapters. Chapter 1, the introduction, serves as an excellent summary of the general themes. The remaining chapters supply the detail, with the last chpater providing a cogent summary.

The themes of the book, although not new in spirit, are novel because of the way Kaufman so adeptly portrays the conflicting incentives facing a policymaker. Free trade, building a free Third World, preventing the spread of communism, and protecting our own industries are all aspects of the politico-drama involved in presidential policy-making. As it turns out, Eisenhower fares fairly well in his main objectives. He is not, as some have portrayed him, the "bumbling ineffectual president who preferred a game of golf to the duties in his office." Nor is he the brilliant statesman, as others have characterized him. Instead, Kaufman depicts Eisenhower as a pragmatist who assiduously attempts to balance the wishes of various constituencies, while at the same time trying to fulfill his own visions concerning the necessity of countering the communist menace and the spread of Soviet domination.

Trade and Aid is well researched, and the research well docomented. Kaufman has apparently spent much time in the Eisenhower library and elsewhere, sifting through reams of information, and putting the facts together in a meaningful and consistent manner.

While the book is strong on detail, it is weak on theory. This is no fault of the author, since a grandiose theory linking economics to both domestic and international politics does not exist. Nevertheless, without such a theory it is difficult to put into perspective Eisenhower's behavior versus the potential behavior of any other president facing similar circumstances. Put differently, without a standard for judging optimal behavior, it is difficult to assess existing behavior. Despite this almost unavoidable shortcoming, I found the book an insightful, carefully written depiction of the change in U.S. economic and foreign policy during the Eisenhower years.

SOLOMON WILLIAM POLACHEK

University of North Carolina
Chapel Hill

OTHER BOOKS

ACHENBAUM, W. ANDREW. *Shades of Gray: Old Age, American Values, and Federal Policies since 1920.* Pp. xi, 216. Boston: Little, Brown and Co., 1982. Paperbound, no price.

BRESSAND, ALBERT. *Ramses 1982: The State of the World Economy.* Pp. xxx, 351. Cambridge, MA: Ballinger, 1982. $29.00.

BUEVA, L. P. *Man: His Behavior and Social Relations.* Pp. 254. Moscow: Progress, 1982. Distributed by Imported Publications, Chicago, IL. Paperbound, $4.00.

CALDERON de la BARCA, FRANCES. *Life in Mexico.* Pp. 548. Berkeley, CA: University of California Press, 1982. $25.00. Paperbound, $6.95.

CHRISTOL, CARL Q. *The Modern International Law of Outer Space.* Pp. xiii, 932. New York: Pergamon Press, 1982. $85.00.

DAVIS, GEORGE and GLEGG WATSON. *Black Life in Corporate America: Swimming in the Mainstream.* Pp. 204. New York: Doubleday, $14.95.

DiCLERICO, ROBERT E. *The American President.* 2nd ed. Pp. xiv, 400. Englewood Cliffs, NJ: Prentice-Hall, 1983. Paperbound, no price.

EDWARDS, WARD and J. ROBERT NEWMAN. *Multiattribute Evaluation.* Pp. 96. Beverly Hills, CA: Sage Publications, 1982. Paperbound, $4.50.

FREUND, JOHN E. and FRANK J. WILLIAMS, *Elementary Business Statistics: The Modern Approach.* 4th ed. Pp. xvi, 606. Englewood Cliffs, NJ: Prentice-Hall, 1983. $19.95.

GIBBS, JACK P., ed. *Social Control: Views from the Social Sciences.* Pp. 288. Beverly Hills, CA: Sage Publications, 1982. $25.00. Paperbound, $12.50.

HESS, BETH B., ELIZABETH W. MARKSON, and PETER J. STEIN. *Sociology.* Pp. xvi, 653. New York: Macmillan, 1982. No price.

HOKENSTAD, MERL C.,Jr. and ROGER A. RITVO, eds. *Linking Health Care and Social Services.* Vol. 5. Pp. 304. Beverly Hills, CA: Sage Publications, 1982. $25.00. Paperbound, $12.50.

JAMES, LAWRENCE R., STANLEY A. MULAIK, and JEANNE M. BRETT. *Causal Analysis: Assumptions, Models, and Data.* SOIM, vol. 1. Pp. 175. Beverly Hills, CA: Sage Publications, 1982. $17.95. Paperbound, $7.95.

KINDERMANN, GOTTFRIED-KARL, ed. *Sun Yat-sen: Founder and Symbol of China's Revolutionary Nation-Building.* Vol. 1, Band 1. Pp. 332. Muenchen-Wien: Guenter Olzog Verlag, 1982. Paperbound, DM 48.

LANE, FREDERICK S., ed. *Current Issues in Public Administration.* 2nd ed. Pp.xi, 526. New York: St. Martin's Press, 1982. $18.95. Paperbound, $11.95.

MARSHALL, GORDON. *In Search of the Spirit of Capitalism.* Pp. 236. New York: Columbia University Press, 1982. $22.50. Paperbound, $10.00.

PAINE, WHITON STEWART, ed. *Job Stress and Burnout: Research, Theory, and Intervention Perspectives.* Pp. 296. Beverly Hills, CA: Sage Publications, 1982. $25.00. Paperbound, $12.50.

POPE, RONALD R., ed. *Soviet Views on the Cuban Missile Crisis: Myth and Reality in Foreign Policy Analysis.* Pp. xi, 285. Washington, DC: University Press of America, 1982. $20.75. Paperbound, $11.25.

RUNDLE, R. N. *International Affairs, 1939-79.* Pp. 208. New York: Holmes & Meier, 1982. Paperbound, $14.50.

SLAVIN, SARAH. *The Equal Rights Amendment: The Politics and Process of Ratification of the 27th Amendment to the U.S. Constitution.* Pp. 163. New York: Haworth Press, 1982. Paperbound, $15.00

TEICH, ALBERT H. and RAY THORNTON, eds. *Science, Technology, and the Issues of the Eighties.* Pp. xv, 290. Boulder, CO: Westview Press, 1982.

$25.00. Paperbound, $12.00.

VUCINICH, WAYNE S., ed. *The First Serbian Uprising, 1804-1813*. Pp. ix, 389. New York: Columbia University Press, 1982. $27.50.

WEINSTEIN, MARTIN E., ed. *Northeast Asian Security After Vietnam*. Pp. xii, 182. Champaign, IL: University of Illinois Press, 1982. $17.50.

ZAGORIA, DONALD S., ed. *Soviet Policy in East Asia*. Pp. xiii, 360. New Haven, CT: Yale University Press, 1982. $25.00.

INDEX

FOREIGN POLICY USA/USSR

edited by **CHARLES W. KEGLEY, Jr.**, *Dept. of Government
and International Studies, University of South Carolina*
& PAT McGOWAN, *Dept. of Political Science,
Arizona State University*

No global issue has greater potential—and actual—effects on
our lives than the far-ranging competition between the two
superpowers. **Foreign Policy: USA/USSR** provides the first
systematic comparison of American and Soviet foreign policies, and their impacts on current international politics. Distinguished scholars explore settings for American and Soviet
foreign policies since World War II, the impact of conflicting
ideologies on foreign policy behaviors, and the superpowers'
foreign policy responses to mutual international challenges.
Their original essays address such timely issues as arms control, alliance politics, and interactions with other world
powers—and illuminate future prospects for U.S.A.-U.S.S.R.
relations. Policymakers, diplomats, scholars, and students
will welcome these authoritative, exceptionally lucid investigations of this central strategic problem of our times.

Sage International Yearbook of Foreign Policy Studies, Volume 7
1982 / 320 pages / $28.00 (h) / $14.00 (p)

SAGE PUBLICATIONS
The Publishers of Professional Social Science
275 South Beverly Drive, Beverly Hills, California 90212

*Now in its 2nd edition, a classic work
of strategic analysis . . .*

DETERRENCE
A Conceptual Analysis

by **PATRICK M. MORGAN,** *Washington State University*

Morgan clearly analyzes the concepts of immediate and general deterrence, focusing on their utility for understanding contemporary world affairs. **Deterrence,** 1st edition, provoked widespread interest among policymakers, political scientists, academics, and students. This updated and revised edition adds a completely new preface and concluding chapter. Integrating the events and studies of the past five years, it reflects the growing worldwide restlessness with conventional wisdom about deterrence policies, and increasing awareness of how much rides on the success or failure of national strategic assumptions.

Praise for the 1st Edition . . .

"An important contribution to the growing debate over the role and conduct of deterrence in international politics... . The book as a whole is extremely perceptive, imaginative, bold, and provocative. This book will shake the confidence of those comfortable with present deterrence policy, will arouse controversy among strategists of bargaining, and will encourage theorists to be more sensitive to the complexities of the human condition."
    —*The American Political Science Review*

"This is a fine book. There is material here for the beginning graduate student who will appreciate the excellent review of both the deterrence and decision-making literature. The development of the model of 'sensible decision-making' deserves to be seriously considered by scholars."
    —*Perspective*

Sage Library of Social Research, Volume 40
1983 (April) / 240 pages / $28.00 (h) / $14.00 (p)

SAGE PUBLICATIONS
The Publishers of Professional Social Science
275 South Beverly Drive, Beverly Hills, California 90212